Who Should Read T

We've all heard the scenario: the family on vacation stops at a road-side "dig your own" gem mine. Junior finds a sapphire the size of a peach and ends up on national television telling the world how he will spend his fortune.

T This book is for those who have read these stories and want their chance to find their own fortune. It is also a book for those who would enjoy the adventure of finding a few gems, getting them cut or polished, and making their own jewelry. It is a book for those people who want to plan a gem hunting vacation with their family. It is a book for those who study the metaphysical properties of gems and minerals and would like to add to their personal collections.

T This book is for those who would like to keep the art of rock-hounding alive and pass it on to their children. It is a book on where to find your own gems and minerals and on how to begin what for many is a lifelong hobby.

T This is a book for those who aren't interested in the "hidden treasure map through mosquito-infested no-man's-land" approach to treasure hunting but do want to find gems and minerals. It is for those who want to get out the pick and shovel and get a little dirty. (Although at some mines they bring the buckets of pre-dug dirt to you at an environmentally temperature-controlled sluicing area.)

Many an unsuspecting tourist has stopped at a mine to try his or her luck and become a rockhound for life. Watch out! Your collection may end up taking the place of your car in your garage.

Good hunting!

This volume is one in a four-volume series.

VOLUME 1: **Northwest States**
Alaska
Idaho
Iowa
Minnesota
Montana
Nebraska
North Dakota
Oregon
South Dakota
Washington
Wyoming

VOLUME 2: **Southwest States**
Arizona
California
Colorado
Hawaii
Kansas
Nevada
New Mexico
Oklahoma
Texas
Utah

VOLUME 3: **Southeast States**
Alabama
Arkansas
Florida
Georgia
Kentucky
Louisiana
Mississippi
Missouri
North Carolina
South Carolina
Tennessee
Virginia
West Virginia

VOLUME 4: **Northeast States**
Connecticut
Delaware
District of Columbia
Illinois
Indiana
Maine
Maryland
Massachusetts
Michigan
New Hampshire
New Jersey
New York
Ohio
Pennsylvania
Rhode Island
Vermont
Wisconsin

VOLUME 1

VOLUME 4

VOLUME 2

VOLUME 3

The Treasure Hunter's

GEM & MINERAL GUIDES TO THE U.S.A.

6TH EDITION

Where & How to Dig, Pan, and Mine Your Own Gems & Minerals

VOLUME 3: SOUTHEAST STATES

by KATHY J. RYGLE AND STEPHEN F. PEDERSEN
Preface by Antoinette Matlins, PG, FGA,
author of *Gem Identification Made Easy*

GEMSTONE PRESS

The Treasure Hunter's Gem & Mineral Guides to the U.S.A., 6th Edition:
Where & How to Dig, Pan, and Mine Your Own Gems & Minerals
Volume 3: Southeast States

2016 Sixth Edition

© 2016 by Kathy J. Rygle and Stephen F. Pedersen

Preface © 2008 by Antoinette Matlins

ISBNs for sixth edition:

Volume 1 (NW): 978-0-9904152-8-2 (pbk.), 978-0-9970145-8-7 (eBook)
Volume 2 (SW): 978-0-9904152-9-9 (pbk.), 978-0-9970145-9-4 (eBook)
Volume 3 (SE): 978-0-9970145-1-8 (pbk.), 978-0-9970145-7-0 (eBook),
          978-1-68336-556-3 (hc)
Volume 4 (NE): 978-0-9970145-0-1 (pbk.), 978-0-9970145-6-3 (eBook)

Cover design by Bronwen Battaglia
Text design by Chelsea Dippel

Manufactured in the United States of America

Published by GemStone Press
An Imprint of Turner Publishing Company
4507 Charlotte Avenue, Suite 100
Nashville, TN 37209
Tel: (615) 255-2665
www.gemstonepress.com

Dedications, with love, to our parents and children:

To my parents, Joe and Helen Rygle, who taught me the love of nature; my earliest remembrances of "rockhounding" are hikes with my dad in the fields, forests, and streams near our home. I also remember weekend trips with my mother to a shop that sold specimens of minerals from around the world. To my daughter, Anastasia (Annie) Rygle, who shares with me the wonders of nature. I love you, Annie, and am proud of your own literary accomplishments.   —K. J. R.

To my parents, Cliff and Leone Pedersen, who taught me to value nature and to not quit. To my daughters Kristi and Debbie, who challenge me to keep growing.   —S. F. P.

To our combined families, including son-in-law Brian Wagner (Debbie's husband) and grandsons Jennings and Creighton, and to family no longer with us.

To Blossom, for her support throughout the sixth edition updates.

With special thanks:

To all the owners of fee dig mines and guide services, curators and staff of public and private museums, mine owners, miners, and fellow lapidarists. Our thanks to all those individuals both past and present who share the wonders of the earth with us.

To our agent, Barb Doyen, and her childhood rock collection.

To our publisher, Stuart M. Matlins; editors Emily Wichland, Rachel Shields, and Catherine Woodard; production members Tim Holtz and Thor Goodrich; and all the staff at GemStone Press for their guidance, assistance, patience, and attention to detail in this enormous project.

To Mrs. Betty Jackson for, in her own way, telling Kathy to write the books.

To God and the wonders He has given us.

And finally, to each other, with love and the perseverance to keep on trying.

Volume 3—Southeast States

CONTENTS

All-American Gems

by Antoinette Matlins, PG, FGA

When Americans think of costly and fabled gems, they associate them with exotic origins—Asia, South Africa, or Brazil. They envision violent jungle quests or secret cellars of a sultanate, perhaps scenes from a Jorge Amado novel or from *A Thousand and One Nights*, a voluptuous Indian princess whose sari is adorned with the plentiful rubies and sapphires of her land, or a Chinese emperor sitting atop a throne flanked by dragons carved from exquisitely polished jade.

Asked what gems are mined in the United States, most Americans would probably draw a blank. We know our country is paved with one of the finest highway systems in the world, but we don't know that just below the surface, and sometimes on top of it, is a glittering pavement of gemstones that would color Old Glory. The red rubies of North Carolina, the white diamonds of Arkansas, the blue sapphires of Montana—America teems with treasures that its citizens imagine come from foreign lands. These include turquoise, tourmaline, amethyst, pearls, opals, jade, sapphires, emeralds, rubies, and even gem-quality diamonds.

Not only does America have quantity, it has quality. American gems compare very favorably with gems from other countries. In fact, fine gemstones found in the U.S. can rival specimens from anywhere else in the world. Some gems, like the luxurious emerald-green hiddenite and steely blue benitoite, are found only in America. Others, like the tourmalines of Maine and California, rival specimens found in better-known locations such as Brazil and Zambia.

The discovery of gemstones in U.S. terrain has been called a lost chapter in American history. It continues to be a saga of fashion and fable that, like the stones themselves, are a deep part of our national heritage. Appreciation of our land's generous yield of sparkling colored stones reached a zenith at the end of the nineteenth century with the art nouveau movement and its utilization of them. When the Boer Wars ended, South Africa's diamonds and platinum eclipsed many of our own then so-called semiprecious stones. Not until the 1930s, and again starting with the 1960s, did economics and the yen for color make gems more desirable again.

In the late 1800s, the nation sought out and cherished anything that was unique to the land. The search for gemstones in America coincided with the exploration of the West, and nineteenth-century mineralogists, some bonafide and others self-proclaimed, fulfilled that first call for "Made in America." Their discoveries created sensations not only throughout America but in the capitals of Europe and as far away as China. The Europeans, in fact, caught on before the Americans, exhibiting some of America's finest specimens in many of Europe's great halls.

But the search for gemstones in this country goes back even further than the nineteenth century. In 1541, the Spanish explorer Francisco Coronado trekked north from Mexico in the footsteps of Cortés and Pizarro, searching not only for gold but also for turquoise, amethyst and emeralds. In the early 1600s, when English settlers reached Virginia, they had been instructed "to searche for gold and such jewels as ye may find."

But what eluded the Spanish explorers and early settlers was unearthed by their descendants. Benitoite, which may be our nation's most uniquely attractive gem, was discovered in 1907 in California's San Benito River headwaters. A beautiful, rare gem with the color of fine sapphire and the fire of a diamond, benitoite is currently found in gem quality only in San Benito, California.

Like many of America's finest stones discovered during the "Gem Rush" of the nineteenth century, benitoite was held in higher regard throughout the rest of the world than it was on its native U.S. soil.

The gem occurs most commonly in various shades of blue. A fine-quality blue benitoite can resemble fine blue sapphire, but it is even more brilliant. It has one weakness, however: in comparison to sapphire, it is relatively soft. It is therefore best used in pendants, brooches and earrings, or in rings with a protective setting.

While benitoite is among the rarest of our gems, our riches hardly stop there. America is the source of other unusual gems, including three even more uniquely American stones, each named after an American: kunzite, hiddenite and morganite.

The story of all-American kunzite is inseparable from the achievements of two men: Charles Lewis Tiffany, founder of Tiffany & Co., and Dr. George Frederick Kunz, world-renowned gemologist. By seeking, collecting and promoting gems found in America, these two did more for the development of native stones than anyone else during, or since, their time.

While working for Tiffany in the late 1800s, Dr. Kunz received a package in the mail containing a stone that the sender believed to be an unusual tourmaline. The stone came from an abandoned mine at Pala Mountain, California, where collectors had found traces of spodumene—a gemstone prized by the ancients but which no one had been able to find for many years. Dr. Kunz was ecstatic to find before him a specimen of "extinct spodumene of a gloriously lilac color." A fellow gemologist, Dr. Charles Baskerville, named the find "kunzite" in his honor.

Kunzite has become a favorite of such designers as Paloma Picasso, not only because of its distinctive shades—lilac, pink, and yellow-green orchid—but because it is one of a diminishing number of gems available in very large sizes at affordable prices. It is a perfect choice for the centerpiece around which to create a very bold, dramatic piece of jewelry. Designer Picasso's creations include a magnificent necklace using a 400-carat kunzite. Although it is a moderately hard stone, kunzite is easily fractured, and care must be taken to avoid any sharp blows.

Kunzite's sister gem, hiddenite, is also a truly "all-American" stone. In 1879, William Earl Hidden, an engraver and mineralogist, was sent to North Carolina on behalf of the great American inventor and prospector Thomas Alva Edison to search for platinum. Hidden found none of the precious white metal but in his pursuit unearthed a new green gemstone, which was named "hiddenite" in his honor.

Less well known than kunzite, hiddenite is an exquisite, brilliant emerald-green variety of spodumene not found anyplace else in the world. While light green and yellow-green shades have been called hiddenite, the Gemological Institute of America—this country's leading authority on gemstones—considers only the emerald-green shade of spodumene, found exclusively in the Blue Ridge Mountains of Mitchell County, North Carolina, to be true hiddenite.

The foothills of the Blue Ridge Mountains also possess America's most significant emerald deposits. While output is minimal compared to Colombia, Zambia or Pakistan, the Rist Mine in Hiddenite, North Carolina, has produced some very fine emeralds, comparable to Colombian stones. The discovery was first made by a farmer plowing his field who found them lying loose on the soil. The country folk, not knowing what they had come across, called the stones "green bolts."

In August 1970, a 26-year-old "rock hound" named Wayne Anthony found a glowing 59-carat "green bolt" at the Rist Mine only two feet from the surface. It was cut into a 13.14-carat emerald of very fine color. Tiffany & Co. later purchased the stone and called it the Carolina Emerald. "The gem is superb," said Paul E. Desautels, then the curator of mineralogy at the Smithsonian Institution. "It can stand on its own merits as a fine and lovely gem of emerald from anywhere, including Colombia." In 1973, the emerald became the official state stone of North Carolina.

A California prize, the warm peach- or pink-shaded morganite, was named by Dr. Kunz for financier John Pierpont Morgan, who purchased the Bement gem collection for donation to the American Museum of Natural History in New York, where it can be viewed today. Morganite is a member of the beryl family, which gives us aquamarine (the clear blue variety of beryl) and emerald (the deep green variety of beryl). However, morganite is available in much larger sizes than its mineralogical cousins and is much more affordable.

Many consider the core of our national treasure chest to be gems like the tourmalines of Maine and California and the sapphires of Montana, gems that are mined in commercial quantities and have earned worldwide reputations. One day in the fall of 1820, two young boys, Ezekiel Holmes and Elijah Hamlin, were rock hunting on Mount Mica in Oxford County, Maine. On the way home, one of the boys saw a flash of green light coming from underneath an uprooted tree. The find was later identified as tourmaline, and Mount Mica became the site of the first commercial gem mine in the United States. The mine was initially worked by Elijah Hamlin and his brother Hannibal, who later became Abraham Lincoln's vice president.

The colors of the rainbow meld delicately in the tourmalines of Maine, producing some of the finest specimens in the world, rivaling in Quality even those from Brazil. A 150-mile strip in central Maine provides shades of apple green, burgundy red and salmon pink, to mention just a few. Some stones are bi-colored.

Miners are kept busy in the Pala district of San Diego County, California, as well. California, in fact, is North America's largest producer of gem-quality tourmaline.

The hot-pink tourmalines, for which California is famous, began to come into greater demand in 1985, as pastel-colored stones became more and more coveted by chic women around the globe. Curiously enough, over one hundred years ago the Chinese rejoiced in the fabulous colors of this fashionable stone. The Empress Dowager of the Last Chinese Imperial Dynasty sent emissaries to California in search of pink tourmalines. She garnished her robes with carved tourmaline buttons and toggles, and started a fad which overtook China. Much of the empress's collection of fine carvings was lost or stolen when the dynasty fell around 1912, but artifacts made from California's pink tourmaline can be seen today in a Beijing museum. China's fascination with pink tourmalines lasted long after the empress. In 1985, a contingent of the Chinese Geological Survey came to California with two requests: to see Disneyland and the Himalaya Mine, original site of California pink tourmaline.

While the Chinese are mesmerized by our tourmalines, Americans have always been attracted to China's jade. But perhaps we ought to take stock of our own. Wyoming, in fact, is the most important producer of the stone in the Western Hemisphere. The state produces large quantities of good-quality green nephrite jade—the type most commonly used in jewelry and carvings. California also boasts some jade, as does Alaska. Chinese immigrants panning for gold in California in the late 1800s found large boulders of nephrite and sent them back to China, where the jade was carved and sold within China and around the world.

The U.S. is also one of the largest producers of turquoise. Americans mostly associate this stone with American Indian jewelry, but its use by mainstream designers has regularly come in and out of fashion.

Some of the most prized gems of America are the stunning sapphires from Yogo Gulch, Montana. These sapphires emit a particularly pleasing shade of pale blue, and are known for their clarity and brilliance.

The Montana mine was originally owned by a gold-mining partnership. In 1895, an entire summer's work netted a total of only $700 in gold plus a cigar box full of heavy blue stones. The stones were sent to Tiffany & Co. to be identified. Tiffany then sent back a check for $3,750 for the entire box of obviously valuable stones.

Once one can conceive of gem-quality sapphires in America, it takes only a small stretch of the mind to picture the wonderful diamonds found here. A 40.23-carat white gem found in Murfreesboro, Arkansas, was cut into a 14.42-carat emerald-cut diamond named Uncle Sam. Other large diamonds include a 23.75-carat diamond found in the mid-nineteenth century in Manchester, Virginia, and a greenish 34.46-carat diamond named the Punch Jones, which was claimed to have been found in Peterstown, West Virginia.

Each year, thousands of people visit Crater of Diamonds State Park in Arkansas, where, for a fee, they can mine America's only proven location of gem-quality diamonds. Among them is a group known as "regulars" who visit the park looking for their "retirement stone."

In 1983, one of the regulars, 82-year-old Raymond Shaw, came across a 6.7-carat rough diamond. He sold it for $15,000 uncut. According to Mark Myers, assistant superintendent of the state park, the stone was cut into an exceptionally fine, 2.88-carat gem (graded E/Flawless by the Gemological Institute of America). Myers says the cut stone, later called the Shaw Diamond, was offered for sale for $58,000.

Diamonds have also been found along the shores of the Great Lakes, in many localities in California, in the Appalachian Mountains, in Illinois, Indiana, Ohio, Kentucky, New York, Idaho and Texas. Exploration for diamonds continues in Michigan, Wisconsin, Colorado and Wyoming, according to the U.S. Bureau of Mines. The discovery of gem-quality diamonds in Alaska in 1986 initiated a comprehensive search there for man's most valued gem.

Many questions concerning this country's store of gems remain unanswered. "Numerous domestic deposits of semiprecious gem stones are known and have been mined for many years," wrote the Bureau of Mines in a 1985 report. "However, no systematic evaluations of the magnitude of these deposits have been made and no positive statements can be made about them." Even as the United States continues to offer up its kaleidoscopic range of gems, our American soil may hold a still greater variety and quantity of gems yet to be unearthed.

And here, with the help of these down-to-earth (in the best possible way!)

guides, you can experience America's gem and mineral riches for yourself. In these pages rockhounds, gemologists, vacationers, and families alike will find a hands-on introduction to the fascinating world of gems and minerals … and a treasure map to a sparkling side of America. Happy digging!

T

Antoinette Matlins, PG, FGA, is the most widely read author in the world on the subject of jewelry and gems (*Jewelry & Gems: The Buying Guide* alone has over 400,000 copies in print). Her books are published in nine languages and are widely used throughout the world by consumers and professionals in the gem and jewelry fields. An internationally respected gem and jewelry expert and a popular media guest, she is frequently quoted as an expert source in print media and is seen on ABC, CBS, NBC, and CNN, educating the public about gems and jewelry and exposing fraud. Ms. Matlins has gained wide recognition as a dedicated consumer advocate, and continues to spearhead the Accredited Gemologists Association's nationwide campaign against gemstone investment telemarketing scams and other types of consumer misrepresentation. In addition, Matlins is active in the gem trade. Her books include *Jewelry & Gems: The Buying Guide*; *Jewelry & Gems at Auction: The Definitive Guide to Buying & Selling at the Auction House & on Internet Auction Sites*; *Colored Gemstones: The Antoinette Matlins Buying Guide—How to Select, Buy, Care for & Enjoy Sapphires, Emeralds, Rubies and Other Colored Gems with Confidence and Knowledge*; *Diamonds: The Antoinette Matlins Buying Guide—How to Select, Buy, Care for & Enjoy Diamonds with Confidence and Knowledge*; *Engagement & Wedding Rings: The Definitive Buying Guide for People in Love*; *The Pearl Book: The Definitive Buying Guide*; and *Gem Identification Made Easy: A Hands-On Guide to More Confident Buying & Selling* (all GemStone Press).

Introduction

This is a guide to commercially operated gem and mineral mines (fee dig mines) within the United States that offer would-be treasure hunters the chance to "dig their own," from diamonds to thundereggs.

For simplicity, the term *fee dig site* is used to represent all types of fee-based mines or collection sites. However, for liability reasons, many mines no longer let collectors dig their own dirt, but rather dig it for them and provide it in buckets or bags. Some fee-based sites involve surface collection.

This book got its start when the authors, both environmental scientists, decided to make their own wedding rings. Having heard stories about digging your own gems, they decided to dig their own stones for their rings. So off to Idaho and Montana they went, taking their three children, ages 8, 13, and 15 at the time, in search of opals and garnets, their birthstones. They got a little vague information before and during the trip on where to find gem mines and in the process got lost in some of those "mosquito-infested lands." But when they did find actual "dig your own" mines (the kind outlined in this book), they found opals, garnets, and even sapphires. They have since made other trips to fee dig mines and each time have come home with treasures and some incredible memories.

Upon making their second collecting trip out west, the authors purchased some lapidary equipment, i.e., rock saw and rock polisher. They first used them to cut thundereggs collected from a mine in Oregon.

Types of Sites

The purpose of this book is principally to guide the reader to fee dig mine sites. These are gem or mineral mines where you hunt for the gem or mineral in ore at or from the mine. At fee dig sites where you are actually permitted to go into the field and dig for yourself, you will normally be shown what the gem or mineral you are seeking looks like in its natural state (much different from the polished or cut stone). Often someone is available to go out in the field with you and show you where to dig. At sites where you purchase gem- or mineral-bearing ore (either native or enriched) for washing in a flume, the process is the same: there will usually be examples of rough stones for comparison, and help in identifying your finds.

Also included are a few areas that are not fee dig sites but that are well-defined collecting sites, usually parks or beaches.

Guided field trips are a little different. Here the guide may or may not have examples of what you are looking for, but he or she will be with you in the field to help in identifying finds.

For the more experienced collector, there are field collecting areas where you are on your own in identifying what you have found. Several fee areas and guided field trips appropriate for the experienced collector are available. Check out the listings for Ruggles Mine (Grafton, NH, volume 4); Harding Mine (Dixon, NM, volume 2); Poland Mining Camps (Poland, ME, volume 4); and Perham's (West Paris, ME, volume 4).

Knowing What You're Looking For

Before you go out into the field, it is a good idea to know what you are looking for. Most of the fee dig mines listed in this guide will show you specimens before you set out to find your own. If you are using a guide service, you have the added bonus of having a knowledgeable person with you while you search to help you find the best place to look and help you identify your finds.

Included in this guide is a listing of museums that contain rock and gem exhibits. A visit to these museums will help prepare you for your search. You may find examples of gems in the rough and examples of mineral specimens similar to the ones you will be looking for. Museums will most likely have displays of gems or minerals native to the local area. Some of the gems and minerals listed in this guide are of significant interest, and specimens of them can be found in museums around the country. Displays accompanying the exhibits might tell you how the gems and minerals were found, and their place in our nation's history. Many museums also hold collecting field trips or geology programs, or may be able to put you in touch with local rock and lapidary clubs.

For more information on learning how to identify your finds yourself—and even how to put together a basic portable "lab" to use at the sites—the book *Gem Identification Made Easy* by Antoinette Matlins and A. C. Bonanno (GemStone Press) is a good resource.

Rock shops are another excellent place to view gem and mineral specimens before going out to dig your own. A listing of rock shops would be too extensive to include in a book such as this. A good place to get information on rock shops in the area you plan to visit is to contact the chamber of commerce for that area. Rock shops may be able to provide information not only on rockhounding field trips but also on local rock clubs that sponsor trips. There are numerous listings on the Internet of rock and mineral clubs. Among these are the American Federation of Mineralogical Societies (www.amfed.org), which lists member clubs, and Bob's Rock Shop (www.rockhounds.com), which has a U.S. club directory (supplied information).

Through mine tours you can see how minerals and gems were and are taken from the earth. On these tours, visitors learn what miners go through to remove the ores from the earth. This will give you a better appreciation for those sparkly gems you see in the showroom windows, and for many of the items we all take for granted in daily use.

You will meet other rockhounds at the mine. Attending one of the yearly events listed in the guide will also give you the chance to meet people who share your interest in gems and minerals and exchange ideas, stories, and knowledge of the hobby.

How to Use This Guide

To use this book, you can pick a state and determine what mining is available there, or pick a gem or mineral and determine where to go to "mine" it.

In this guide are indexes that will make the guide simple to use. If you are interested in finding a particular gem or mineral, go to the Index by Gem or Mineral in the back of the book. In this index, gems and minerals are listed in alphabetical order with the states and cities where fee dig sites for that gem or mineral may be found.

If you are interested in learning of sites near where you live, or in the area where you are planning a vacation, or if you simply want to know whether there are gems and minerals in a particular location, go to the Index by

State, located in the back of the guide. The state index entries are broken down into three categories: Fee Dig Sites/Guide Services, Museums and Mine Tours, and Special Events and Tourist Information. Please note that the information provided in each individual listing is subject to availability.

There are also several special indexes for use in finding your birthstone, anniversary stone, or zodiac stone.

Site Listings

The first section of each chapter lists fee dig sites and guide services that are available in each state. Included with the location of each site (if available) is a description of the site, directions to find it, what equipment is provided, and what you must supply. Costs are listed, along with specific policies of the site. Also included are other services available at the site and information on camping, lodging, etc. at the site. Included in the section with fee dig sites are guide services for collecting gems and minerals.

In the second section of each chapter, museums of special interest to the gem/mineral collector and mine tours available to the public are listed. Besides being wonderful ways to learn about earth science, geology, and mining history (many museums and tours also offer child-friendly exhibits), museums are particularly useful for viewing gems and minerals in their rough or natural states before going out in the field to search for them.

The third section of each chapter lists special events involving gems and minerals, and resources for general tourist information.

A sample of the listings for fee dig mines and guide services (Section 1 in the guides) is on the next page.

Tips for mining:

1. Learn what gems or minerals can be found at the mine you are going to visit.
2. Know what the gem or mineral that you're hunting looks like in the rough before you begin mining. Visiting local rock shops and museums will help in this effort.
3. When in doubt, save any stone that you are unsure about. Have an expert at the mine or at a local rock shop help you identify your find.

Sample Fee Dig Site Listing

TOWN in which the site is located / *Native or enriched[1]* • *Easy, moderate, difficult[2]*

Dig your own *T*

The following gems may be found:
- List of gems and minerals found at the mine

Mine name
Owner or contact (where available)
Address
Phone number
E-mail address
Website address

Open: months, hours, days
Info: Descriptive text regarding the site, including whether equipment is provided

Admission: Fee to dig; costs for predug dirt
Other services available
Other area attractions (at times)
Information on lodging or campground facilities (where available)
Directions

Map (where available)

Notes:

1. Native or enriched. *Native* refers to gems or minerals found in the ground at the site, put there by nature. *Enriched* means that gems and minerals from an outside source have been brought in and added to the soil. Enriching is also called "salting"—it is a guaranteed return. Whatever is added in a salted mine is generally the product of some commercial mine elsewhere. Thus, it is an opportunity to "find" gemstones from around the world the easy way, instead of traveling to jungles and climbing mountains in remote areas of the globe. Salted mines are particularly nice for giving children the opportunity to find a wide variety of gems and become involved in gem identification. The authors have tried to indicate if a mine is enriched, but to be sure, ask at the mine beforehand. If the status could not be determined, this designation was left out.

2. Sites are designated as easy, moderate, or difficult. This was done to

give you a feel for what a site may be like. You should contact the site and make a determination for yourself if you have any doubts.

Easy: This might be a site where the gem hunter simply purchases bags or buckets of predug dirt, washes the ore in a flume or screens the gem-bearing gravel to concentrate the gems, and flips the screen. The gems or minerals are then picked out of the material remaining in the screen. A mine which has set aside a pile of mine material for people to pick through would be another type of site designated as "Easy."

Moderate: Mining at a "Moderate" site might mean digging with a shovel, then loading the dirt into buckets, followed by sifting and sluicing. Depending on your knowledge of mineral identification, work at a "Moderate" site might include searching the surface of the ground at an unsupervised area for a gem or mineral you are not familiar with (this could also be considered difficult).

Difficult: This might be a site requiring tools such as picks and shovels, or sledgehammers and chisels. The site may be out of the way and/or difficult to get to. Mining might involve heavy digging with the pick and shovel or breaking gems or minerals out of base rock using a sledge or chisel.

Maps

Maps are included to help you locate the sites in the guide. At the beginning of each state, there is a state map showing the general location of towns where sites are located.

Local maps are included in a listing when the information was available. *These maps are not drawn to scale!* These maps provide information to help you get to the site but are not intended to be a substitute for a road map. Please check directly with the site you are interested in for more detailed directions.

Special Note:

Although most museums and many fee dig sites are handicapped accessible, please check with the listing directly.

Fees

Fees listed in these guides were obtained when the book was updated, and may have changed. They are included to give you at least a general idea of the costs you will be dealing with. Please contact the site directly to confirm charges.

Many museums have discounts for members and for groups, as well as special programs for school groups. Please check directly with the institution for information. Many smaller and/or private institutions have no fee, but do appreciate donations to help meet the costs of staying open.

Many sites accept credit cards; some may not. Please check ahead for payment options if this is important.

Requesting Information by Mail

When requesting information by mail, it is always appreciated if you send a SASE (self-addressed stamped envelope) along with your request. Doing this will often speed up the return of information.

Equipment and Safety Precautions

Equipment

The individual sites listed in these guides often provide equipment at the mine. Please note that some fee dig sites place limitations on the equipment you can use at their site. Those limitations will be noted where the information was available. Always abide by the limitations; remember that you are a guest at the site.

On the following pages are figures showing equipment for rockhounding. Figures A and B identify some of the equipment you may be told you need at a site. Figure C shows material needed to collect, package, transport, and record your findings. Figure D illustrates typical safety equipment.

Always use safety glasses with side shields or goggles when you are hammering or chiseling. Chips of rock or metal from your tools can fly off at great speed in any direction when hammering. Use gloves to protect your hands as well.

Other useful tools not shown include an ultraviolet hand lamp, and a hand magnifier.

Not pictured, but something you don't want to forget, is a device (camera, phone, etc.) for photos or video of your adventures and "big" find, no matter what it might be.

Not pictured, but to be considered: knee pads and seat cushions.

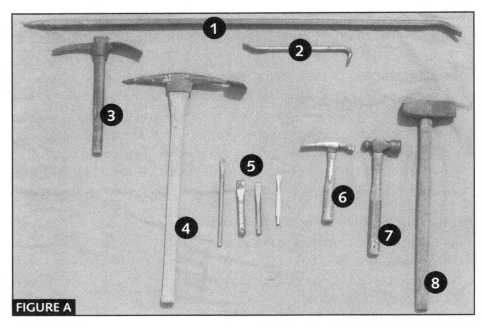

1. Crowbar
2. Pry bar
3. Smaller pick
4. Rock pick
5. Various-sized chisels (*Note:* When working with a hammer and chisel, you may want to use a chisel holder, not shown, for protecting your hand if you miss. Always use eye protection with side shields and gloves!)
6. Rock hammer (*Note:* Always use eye protection.)
7. 3-pound hammer (*Note:* Always use eye protection.)
8. Sledgehammer (*Note:* When working with a sledgehammer, wear hard-toed boots along with eye protection.)

Other Safety Precautions

- Never go into the field or on an unsupervised site alone. With protective clothing, reasonable care, proper use of equipment, and common sense, accidents should be avoided, but in the event of an illness or accident, you always want to have someone with you who can administer first aid and seek help.
- Always keep children under your supervision.
- Never enter old abandoned mines or underground diggings!
- Never break or hammer rocks close to another person!

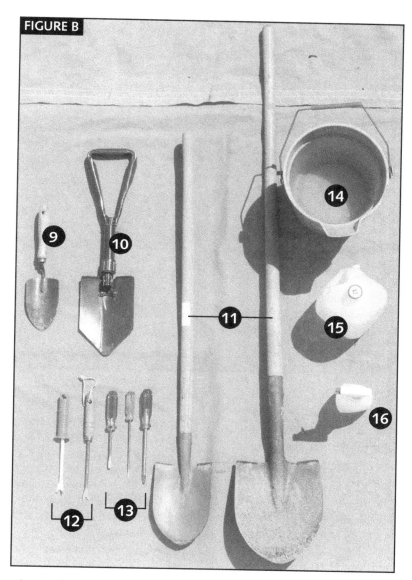

FIGURE B

9. Garden trowel
10. Camp shovel
11. Long-handled shovels
12. Garden cultivators
13. Screwdrivers

14. Bucket of water
15. (Plastic) jug of water
16. Squirt bottle of water; comes in handy at many of the mines to wash off rocks so you can see if they are or contain gem material

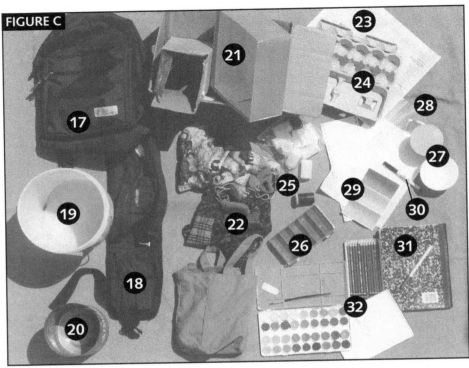

FIGURE C

17. Backpack
18. Waist pack to hold specimens
19. Bucket to hold specimens
20. Coffee can to hold specimens
21. Boxes to pack, transport, and ship specimens
22. Bags—various sized bags to carry collected specimens in the field
23. Newspaper to wrap specimens for transport
24. Egg cartons to transport delicate specimens
25. Empty film canisters to hold small specimens
26. Plastic box with dividers to hold small specimens
27. Margarine containers to hold small specimens

28. Reclosable plastic bags to hold small specimens
29. Gummed labels to label specimens (Whether you are at a fee dig site or with a guide, usually there will be someone to help you identify your find. It is a good idea to label the find when it is identified so that when you reach home, you won't have boxes of unknown rocks.)
30. Waterproof marker for labeling
31. Field log book to make notes on where specimens were found
32. Sketching pencils, sketchbook (waterproof notebooks are available), paint to record your finds and the surrounding scenery

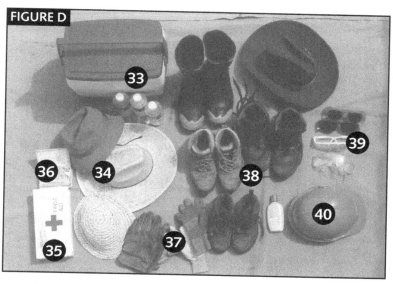

FIGURE D

33. Food and water—always carry plenty of drinking water. (*Note:* many sites tell you in advance if they have food and water available or if you should bring some; however, it is always a good idea to bring extra drinking water. Remember—if you bring it in, pack it back out.)

34. Hats. Many of the sites are in the open, and the summer sun can be hot and dangerous to unprotected skin. Check with the site to see if they have any recommendations for protective clothing. Also, don't forget sunscreen.

35. First aid/safety kit

36. Snakebite kit. If the area is known to have snakes, be alert and take appropriate safety measures, such as boots and long pants. (*Note:* while planning our first gem-hunting trip, we read that the first aid kit should contain a snakebite kit. Just like rockhounds, snakes seem to love rocky areas!) In most cases, if you visit sites in the book, you will be either at a flume provided by the facility, or with an experienced guide. At the first, you will most likely never see a snake; at the second, your guide will fill you in on precautions. For listings where you will be searching on a ranch or state park, ask about special safety concerns such as snakes and insects when you pay your fee. These sites may not be for everyone.

37. Gloves to protect your hands when you are working with sharp rock or using a hammer or chisel

38. Boots—particularly important at sites where you will be doing a lot of walking, or walking on rocks

39. Safety glasses with side shields, or goggles. Particularly important at hard rock sites or any site where you or others may be hitting rocks. Safety glasses are available with tinted lenses for protection from the sun.

40. Hard hats—may be mandatory if you are visiting an active quarry or mine; suggested near cliffs

Mining Techniques

How to Sluice for Gems

This is the most common technique used at fee dig mines where you buy a bucket of gem ore (gem dirt) and wash it at a flume.

1. Place a quantity of the gem ore in the screen box, and place the screen box in the water. Use enough gem ore to fill the box about a third.

2. Place the box in the water, and shake it back and forth, raising one side, then the other, so that the material in the box moves back and forth. What you are doing is making the stones move around in the screen box, while washing dirt and sand out of the mixture.

3. After a minute or two of washing, take the screen box out of the flume, and let it drain. Look through the stones remaining in the screen box for your treasure. If you're not sure about something, ask one of the attendants.

4. When you can't find anything more, put the box back in the flume and wash it some more, then take it out and search again.

Clockwise from top: Gold pan; screen box used for sluicing; screen box used for screening.

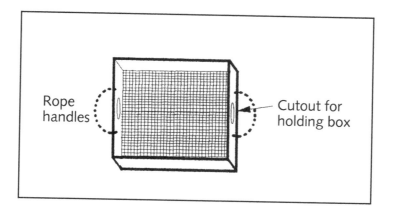

Rope handles

Cutout for holding box

How to Build a Screen Box

1. A screen box that is easy to handle is generally built from 1" x 4" lumber and window screening.

2. Decide on the dimensions of the screen box you want, and cut the wood accordingly. Dimensions generally run from 12" x 12" up to 18" x 18". Remember that the end pieces will overlap the side pieces, so cut the end pieces 1½" longer.

3. There are two alternative methods of construction. In one, drill pilot holes in the end pieces, and use wood screws to fasten the end pieces to the side pieces. In the other, use angle irons and screws to attach the ends and sides.

4. Cut the screening to be ¼" smaller than the outside dimensions of the screen box, and use staples to attach the screen to the bottom of the box. Use metal screening rather than plastic if possible. For a stronger box, cut ¼" or ⅜" hardware cloth to the same dimensions as the screening, and staple the hardware cloth over the screening. The hardware cloth will provide support for the screening.

5. Cut ¼" wood trim to fit, and attach it to the bottom of the box to cover the edges of the screening and hardware cloth and staples.

6. If you like, add rope handles or cut handholds in the side pieces for easier handling.

5. If possible, move your screen box into bright light while you are searching, since the gems and minerals often show up better in bright light.

How to Screen for Gems

This is another common technique used at fee dig mines where you buy a bucket of gem ore and screen it for gems. (The authors used this technique for garnets and sapphires in Montana.)

1. Place a quantity of the gem ore in the screen box, and place the screen box in the water. Use enough gem dirt to fill the box about a third.

2. Place the box in the water, and begin tipping it back and forth, raising one side, then the other, so that the material in the box moves back and forth. What you are doing is making the gemstones, which are heavier than the rock and dirt, move into the bottom center of the screen box while at the same time washing dirt and sand out of the mixture.

3. After a minute or two, change the direction of movement to front and back.

4. Repeat these two movements (Steps 2 and 3) three or four times.

5. Take the box out of the water and let it drain, then place a board on top and carefully flip the box over onto the sorting table. It may be helpful to put a foam pad in the box, then put the board over it. This helps keep the stones in place when you flip the box. If you have done it right, the gemstones will be found in the center of the rocks dumped onto the board. Use tweezers to pick the rough gemstones out of the rocks, and place them in a small container.

How to Pan for Gold

The technique for panning for gold is based on the fact that gold is much heavier than rock or soil. Gently washing and swirling the gold-bearing soil in a pan causes the gold to settle to the bottom of the pan. A gold pan has

a flat bottom and gently slanting sides. Some modern pans also have small ridges or rings around the inside of the pan on these slanting sides. As the soil is washed out of the pan, the gold will slide down the sides, or be caught on the ridges and stay in the pan. Here's how:

1. Begin by filling the pan with ore, about ⅔ to ¾ full.

2. Put your pan in the water, let it gently fill with water, then put the pan under the water surface. Leave the pan in the water, and mix the dirt around in the pan, cleaning and removing any large rocks.

3. Lift the pan out of the water, then gently shake the pan from side to side while swirling it at the same time. Do this for 20–30 seconds to get the gold settled to the bottom of the pan.

4. Still holding the pan out of the water, continue these motions while tilting the pan so that the dirt begins to wash out. Keep the angle of the pan so that the crease (where the bottom and sides meet) is the lowest point.

5. When there is only about a tablespoon of material left in the pan, put about ½ inch of water in the pan, and swirl the water over the remaining material. As the top material is moved off, you should see gold underneath.

6. No luck? Try again at a different spot.

Notes on Gem Faceting, Cabbing, and Mounting Your Finds

Many of the fee dig sites offer services to cut and mount your finds. Quality and costs vary. Trade journals such as *Lapidary Journal Jewelry Artist* and *Rock & Gem* (available at most large bookstores or by subscription) list suppliers of these services, both in the United States and overseas. Again, quality and cost vary. Local rock and gem shops in your area may offer these services, or it may be possible to work with a local jeweler. Your local rock club may be able to provide these services or make recommendations.

After their first gem-hunting trip, the authors had some of their finds faceted and cabochoned. They then designed rings and had them made using these stones, as shown in the photos below.

After saying for years that they would like to learn to cabochon and facet (and in the process learn how better to collect "usable" material), the authors were fortunate enough to meet a local gemologist at a gem and mineral show who taught classes in the lapidary arts. They have since cut

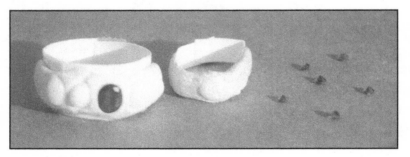

The authors sent their rough gems away for faceting. Using the faceted gems, they made crude mock-ups and sketches of the rings they wanted; then they sent the mock-ups, sketches, and gems to be made into rings.

The finished rings.

their own cabochons and faceted gemstones, getting a true appreciation for the art and knowledge of what to look for when field collecting.

Cutting your own finds can be a very rewarding hobby, and this hobby works two ways. You can cabochon, facet, and carve your special finds to your specifications, then make or have them made into jewelry. A cabochon is a highly polished convex-cut, but unfaceted gem. Facets are flat faces on geometric shapes which are cut into a rough gemstone in order to improve their appearance. The angles used for each facet affect the appearance of the gemstone. In learning the lapidary procedures, you also gain knowledge of what is a good find. You can look at a stone in the field and see if it is facetable, or if the pattern would make a spectacular cabochon.

Understanding what beautiful pieces you can make from your discoveries will amaze you, be they dug from a native mine, sluiced at a salted site, purchased from a local rock shop, or traded at a club meeting.

The first step to learning the lapidary arts is to do some research to see if it is for you. Search out books and articles on the topic and contact local clubs or rock shops to see if there are any classes near you.

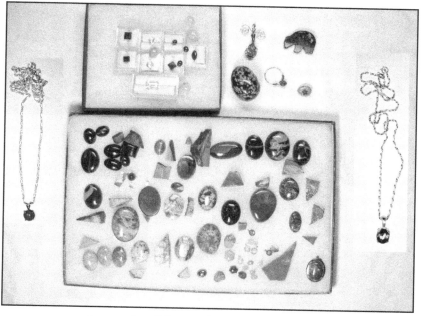

A sample of the authors' lapidary work.

Authors and daughters on their first adventure to fee-dig mines, taking sifted gravel to the jig at a sapphire mine in Helena, Montana. Pictured from left to right: Steve, Kathy, Anastasia (Annie) Rygle, Debra Pedersen, Kristin Pedersen.

ALABAMA

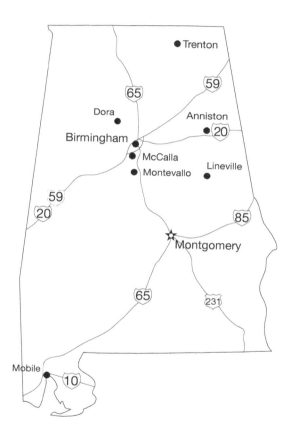

State Gemstone: Star Blue Quartz (1990)
State Mineral: Hematite (1967)
State Stone/Rock: Marble (1969)

Dates refer to when stones and minerals were adopted by the state legislature.

LINEVILLE / *Native n Easy to Moderate*

Pan or Prospect for Gold *T*

The following gems or minerals can be found:

- Gold; also garnets and citrine

Alabama Gold Camp
1398 County Road 5
Lineville, AL 36266
Phone: (256) 396-0389
E-mail: gold@alabamagoldcamp.com
www.alabamagoldcamp.com

Open: December, January, and February: 8:00 A.M.–5:00 P.M. daily; 7:00 A.M.–6:00 P.M. Saturday; rest of the year: 8:00 A.M.–5:00 P.M. daily; 7:00 A.M.–6:00 P.M. Saturday.

Info: The camp is located in the heart of the Alabama gold belt, with miles of creek to pan, sluice, dredge, high-bank, and metal detect.

Rates: Equipment is available to rent for additional fees. If you bring your own equipment, the prices are as follows: pan, sluice, or metal detector, $5.00/day per person; 11 and under, free with adult; dredges range from $15.00/day for a 2" dredge to $60.00/day for a 6" dredge; high-bankers range from $15.00–$25.00/day. You must sign a disclaimer before entering the prospecting areas.

Note: Cash/check only. Credit cards not accepted at this time.

Other services available: Primitive camping, $5.00/night per person over 17; full hook-ups, $25.00/night (30-AMP site) or $30.00/night (50-AMP site); prospecting shacks, $65.00/night for two adults, additional people $10.00 each, 17 and under free with adult. General store on-site sells all kinds of supplies. Washer/dryer and Wi-Fi available.

Directions: Call or check the website for detailed directions.

Note: Do not use GPS to find Alabama Gold Camp. GPS will put you on impassable dirt roads.

TRENTON / *Native ▪ Moderate*

Collecting Trip for Agate *T*

The following gems or minerals can be found:

- Paint rock agate

Dixie Euhedrals
Rodney Moore
E-mail: rodney@digforcrystals.com
www.digforcrystals.com

Open: Collecting occurs on specific dates; reservations required. Contact Rodney by e-mail.

Info: Paint rock agate is usually red and yellow, but can be other colors. On occasion, agate nodules are found with hollow places that may have quartz crystals. Paint rock agate is very good for making cabochons or other lapidary processing.

Collecting involves looking for pieces of agate and breaking them open with a hammer to look for color inside. In some cases, a piece may be partially exposed and must be pried from the ground. Getting to the site and collecting involves hiking on a mountain slope; a backpack and good hiking shoes are a must. At least four 12-ounce bottles of water or Gatorade, bug spray, rock hammer, pick or small mattock, and safety glasses are required. Children are not normally allowed on this collecting site.

Rates: $35.00/person; children, if approved, $10.00.

Directions: Meet at a local meeting point in Hollytree, Alabama, on the morning of the dig.

SECTION 2: Museums and Mine Tours

ALDRICH

Museum 🏛

Aldrich Coal Mine Museum
137 County Road 203
Montevallo, AL 35115
Phone: (205) 665-2886;
  (205) 999-0689 (cell)

Open: 10:00 A.M.–4:00 P.M. Thursday–Saturday, 1:00 P.M.–4:00 P.M. Sunday, or by appointment. In winter, call ahead to be sure they are open.

Info: Learn about the local coal mining history and history of the area. The museum is housed in the old Montevallo Coal Company company store, and includes a simulated coal mine.

Admission: Adults $5.00, children $3.00.

Directions: Take County Road 10 West in Montevallo to Aldrich, cross the railroad tracks, and turn left on County Road 203 and look for the museum.

ANNISTON

Museum 🏛

Anniston Museum of Natural History
P.O. Box 1587
800 Museum Drive
Anniston, AL 36202
Phone: (256) 237-6766
E-mail: info@annistonmuseum.org
www.annistonmuseum.org

Open: Winter hours: 10:00 A.M.–5:00 P.M. Tuesday–Saturday; 1:00 P.M.–5:00 P.M. Sunday. Summer: Also open 10:00 A.M.–5:00 P.M. Monday. Call or check website for hours, as opening times change when the museum is having special exhibitions. The museum is closed New Year's Day, Easter, Thanksgiving Day, Christmas Eve, and Christmas Day.

Info: The Dynamic Earth exhibit details the processes and products of the formation of the earth as it traces the history of our ever-changing planet. A mineral

exhibit is included. Explore a cave and get a shake from an earthquake in the Native Space exhibit (closes at 4:00 P.M. daily).

Admission: Adults $6.00, seniors (60+) $5.50, children (4–17) $5.00, ages 3 and under free. Children under 16 must be accompanied by an adult at all times.

Directions: Anniston, in Calhoun County, is 60 miles northeast of Birmingham and 80 miles west of Atlanta, GA. Located in Lagarde Park, Anniston, AL, at the junction of Highways 431 and 21. From Interstate 20, exit 185, 7 miles north on Highway 21. Allow 1½ hours driving time from Birmingham or Atlanta.

DORA

Museum

Alabama Mining Museum
120 E. Street
Dora, AL 35062
Phone: (205) 648-2442

Open: All year, 8:30 A.M.–1:00 P.M. Tuesday–Friday, 10:00 A.M.–12:00 P.M. Saturday. Call ahead for changes.

Info: The museum has been designated by the Alabama Legislature as the official State Coal Mining Museum, and has a focus on coal mining between 1890 and 1940.

Admission: Free.

Directions: Call for directions.

McCALLA

Museum

Tannehill Ironworks Historical
    State Park
Iron and Steel Museum of Alabama
12632 Confederate Parkway
McCalla, AL 35111
Phone: (205) 477-5711
E-mail: tannehillsp@bellsouth.net
www.tannehill.org

Open: Visitors' center: 8:30 A.M.–4:30 P.M. Tuesday–Friday; 9:30 A.M.–4:30 P.M. Saturday; 12:30 P.M.–3:00 P.M. Sunday. Park open seven days a week, sunrise to sunset.

Info: Exhibits include geology, iron furnace fuels, and the Birmingham cast iron pipe industry. The museum focuses on the Roupes Valley Ironworks at Tannehill, which operated nearby and which gave birth to the Birmingham iron and steel district. Museum exhibits graphically demonstrate how iron was made during the Civil War when thirteen different iron companies and six rolling mills made Alabama the arsenal of the Confederacy. Civil War weaponry actually used in battle is exhibited. A timeline traces growth of the iron trade from ancient Egypt to the modern steel industry.

Admission: Adults $2.00, seniors (62+) and children (6–11) $1.00, children 5 and under free.

SECTION 3: Special Events and Tourist Information

TOURIST INFORMATION

State Tourist Agency
Alabama Bureau of Tourism and Travel
Phone: (800) 252-2262
www.touralabama.org

Gold was discovered in the 1830s in the Piedmont Upland area of Alabama. When the California Gold Rush occurred the prospectors left and the Alabama gold fields were forgotten.

ARKANSAS

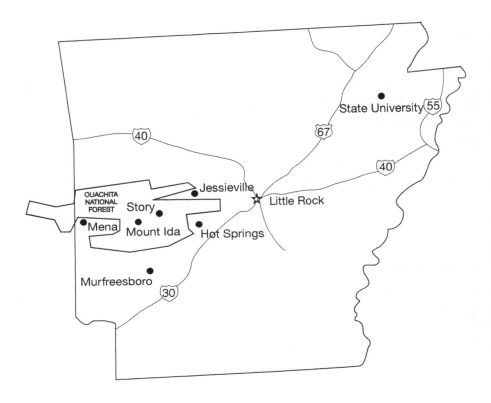

State Gemstone: Diamond (1967)
State Mineral: Quartz Crystal (1967)
State Stone/Rock: Bauxite (1967)

Dates refer to when stones and minerals were adopted by the state legislature.

Quartz Crystals

Although quartz makes up nearly 25% of the earth's surface, only three known places have enough high-quality crystal to warrant commercial mining. These are Brazil, Madagascar, and the Ouachita Mountain range of Arkansas. Quartz is the leading mineral mined in the Ouachita Mountains, which rank among the oldest mountain ranges in the U.S. Quartz is found in open crystal pockets formed in the sandstone, shale, and other rocks of the region. Crystals were once dug by Native Americans, who may have used and traded the crystals for religious and medicinal purposes.

Quartz crystals formed of silicon and oxygen are hexagonal structures that have the unique property of piezoelectricity, which means that they respond in a direct vibratory pattern when stimulated electrically or by pressure. Because of its piezoelectric qualities, quartz crystal can be used to amplify, transform, focus, and transfer energy. During World War II, quartz from Fisher Mountain was used by the U.S. Government for oscillators in radios.

There are several types of crystals, including single and double terminated, small to large clusters, and tabulars. Although a crystal can shatter, it is hard enough to cut glass (on the Mohs hardness scale a crystal is rated 7; a diamond 10). It is considered a semiprecious stone and is valuable to those who invest in and collect minerals.

Crystals are used in several fields, including industry, jewelry, and electronics. The piezoelectricity property makes quartz crystals indispensable to the international electronics industry for use in everything from radios and watches to Silicon Valley microcomputer chips, and thousands of products in between.

The use of quartz crystals in the metaphysical field to amplify, transform, focus, and transfer energy has led to a growing interest in them by groups and individuals who use the clear crystals for purposes generally described as healing. Quartz crystals are said to be healers that balance all elements needed to make a person whole. Quartz is claimed to be a purifier, which creates harmony and balance.

You can dig these quartz crystals in several mines located in the Mount Ida area.

JESSIEVILLE / *Native* ▪ *Moderate*

Dig Your Own Quartz Crystals *T*

The following gems or minerals may be found:

▪ **Quartz crystals**

Ron Coleman Mining, Inc.
211 Crystal Ridge Lane
Jessieville, AR 71949
Phone: (800) 291-4484
E-mail: colemanquartz@gmail.com
www.colemanquartz.com

Open: Year round, 7 days/week, 8:00 A.M.–4:30 P.M. Gift shop stays open a half-hour after mine closes.

Info: This is a working mine. Crystal digging is in 40 acres of mine tailings (material left over during mining operations) with fresh material routinely excavated, weather permitting. Keep all you find. Equipment is provided, including crystal washing stations. Leashed pets are welcome.

Rates: Adults $20.00, seniors $15.00, students (7–16) $5.00, children under 7 free. Guaranteed findings or trade in for your pick from the "back porch."

Other services available: Retail shop, wholesale showroom for dealers, gift shop, open 8:00 A.M.–5:00 P.M. daily. *Mine tour:* Take an Army truck ride down through the mine to see the crystal veins and water source, then on to the processing area.

Campground: Crystal Ridge RV Park (located on the grounds of Ron Coleman Mining, Inc.) has 24 quiet, shady sites (and one pull through) on a paved circle. Services offered: modern restrooms, clean hot showers, wash station, dump station, water and electric hookups; $12.50 + tax/night. Call for info.

Directions: Call for directions.

JESSIEVILLE / *Native* ▪ *Moderate*

Dig Your Own Quartz Crystals *T*

The following gems or minerals may be found:

▪ **Quartz crystals (clear and white, some with adularia and calcite)**

Jim Coleman's Rock Shop & Crystal Mines
5837 North Highway 7
Jessieville, AR 71949
Phone: (501) 984-5328
E-mail: jimcoleman@
    jimcolemancrystals.com
www.jimcolemancrystals.com

Open: 8:00 A.M.–dusk, daily, closed Christmas Day. Caretaker on site 24 hours/day.

Info: This is a working mine. Simply dig in the piles brought up daily by the mine workers. Mine personnel will show you

Digging Quartz

Bring a suitable digging tool such as a rock hammer, screwdriver, shovel, trowel, or anything to scratch around with. Wear old clothes, since the red clay stains anything it comes in contact with. On sunny days, a hat and sunscreen are suggested, along with drinking water. Hand tools are recommended to preserve the crystallography of the specimens.

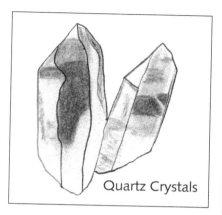

Quartz Crystals

Cleaning Quartz

One process for cleaning quartz is to soak the crystals in a mild solution of oxalic acid. Use 1 pound of oxalic acid to 2½ gallons water. The cleaning procedure should be carried out only by an adult. Dissolve the oxalic acid in warm water in any container except aluminum. Soak crystals 4 to 5 days. Keep the solution properly labeled and in a secure place covered from the sun when in use or not. The solution can be reused up to three times. Be sure to follow the safety instructions when working with oxalic acid.

(Information provided by Sonny Stanley's Mine)

where to find crystals. Stay away from flagged areas and from machinery. Coleman's sells digging tools for cost that guests can then take home with them. They also have drinks, water, and snacks, and sell cleaning material with instructions for the correct way to clean crystals that you find. Restrooms available.

Rates: Adults $10.00, children under 10 free. Pets on leash allowed. You will get directions to the mine when you pay your fee.

Directions: The Rock Shop is located on Highway 7, approximately 16 miles north of Hot Springs.

MENA / *Native · Moderate*

Dig Your Own Crystals *T*

The following gems or minerals may be found:

- **Quartz crystals**

Board Camp Campground and
 Crystal Mine
110 Hickory Ridge Road
Mena, AR 71953
Phone: (479) 243-0771
www.boardcampcampground.com

Open: Crystal digging is by prior reservation only. Mine and rock shop open March–October, 8:00 A.M.–7:00 P.M. or dusk daily. Plan to arrive at least 3 hours before closing.

Rates: Adults (16 and older) $10.00, plus mandatory mining bucket rental of $10.00/bucket.

Info: This is a relatively new crystal surface mine (opened to the public in 2012), located in the Ouachita National Forest. Bring containers, buckets, or bags to take your crystals home, as well as water, food, bug spray, sunscreen, allergy medications, and chairs or old rugs to sit on. People-friendly dogs are allowed on short leashes; bring water, pick up after them, and keep them away from other guests.

Other services available: Rock shop, public restroom at the shop, day use campground. Crystal Music Festival every July.

Directions: The mine is located about 10 miles east of Mena. Check the website or contact the camp for specific directions.

MOUNT IDA / *Native or Enriched · Easy to Moderate*

Dig Your Own Crystals *T*

The following gems or minerals may be found:

- **Quartz crystals, wavelite**

The Crystal Seen Trading Co.
Dennis & Julie Kincaid
2568 Highway 270 E
Mount Ida, AR 71957
Phone: (870) 867-4072;
 (870) 490-1026 (cell)
E-mail: ravenhawk@cebridge.net
www.digyourowncrystals.com

Open: Year-round. Mount Ida shop open 9:00 A.M.–6:00 P.M. Thursday–Sunday; later in the summer. If no one is at the shop, keys are also available at the Royal Oak Inn in Mount Ida. Mine open until dark, 7 days/week. New crystal and jewelry store and gallery in Hot Springs open 10:00 A.M.–6:00 P.M. Tuesday–Thursday; 10:00 A.M.–7:00 P.M. Friday–Saturday.

Info and Rates: The Crystal Seen Trading Co. offers four different packages for rockhounding visitors.

Package 1: Day's dig in the mine. Collect natural crystals and seeded material; a fun, treasure-hunting adventure for kids of all ages. Adults (12+) $22.00, children (7–11) $11.00, and children 6 and under are free with a paying adult.

Package 2: Four-hour crystal workshop (8:00 A.M.–12:00 P.M. Wednesday–Sunday). This workshop will be "preseeded" to approximate digging in an actual crystal pocket. You will be taught about the geology of the area, what to look for, and how to dig and identify these crystals. You will learn about the different crystal formations and some of their metaphysical properties. You will receive printed material with the course, and you will learn how to clean the crystals. Cost is $150.00 for the first person and $95.00 for each additional adult. You will have the rest of the day to dig in the mine. Package by appointment only.

Package 3: Workshop geared toward families who come to dig in the mine with children from 7–15. Introductory discussion at the shop, collection, and discussion of assorted minerals and fossils. Dig at the mine, and at the end of the day receive a certificate naming participants as honorary miners. The cost is $32.00 for children 7–11 and $42.00 for those 12 and up. By appointment only. (Girl and Boy Scout requirements for badges can be met with this program).

Package 4: Dig in over 100 yards of tailings at the shop. $12.00/hour/person for adults (12+). Children (7–11) are half-price and children 6 and under are free with a paying adult (use of tools free).

Other services available: Jewelry and gift shop; crystal workshops; jewelry design and repair.

Directions: On Highway 270, 4 miles east of Mount Ida. Call for specific directions.

MOUNT IDA / *Native • Moderate*

Dig Your Own *T* Quartz Crystals

The following gems or minerals may be found:

- **Quartz crystals**

Fiddler's Ridge Rock Shop &
 Bear Mt. Crystal Mine
Jim and Kathy Fecho
3752 U.S. Highway 270 E
Mount Ida, AR 71957
Phone: (870) 867-2127
E-mail: fecho@ipa.net
www.fiddlersridgecrystals.com

Open: Year round, 9:00 A.M.–5:00 P.M., 6 days/week; closed Sunday.

Rates: Adults $20.00/day, children (7–11) $10.00, children under 6 free.

Other services available: Gift shop. Get permit and instructions at gift shop. Supply your own tools, or small tools and gloves are sold at shop. Wear sturdy shoes. No sandals.

Info: The Bear Mt. Mine is located within a 20-minute driving distance from the rock shop. The area is primitive. There is a restroom on-site. Collect your own crystals. There are designated areas for you to collect in that are safe, and certain rules apply. You are not permitted in the pit area.

Directions: Located 7 miles east of Mount Ida on U.S. 270 E , and 28 miles west of Hot Springs. You will receive a map to the mine at the shop.

MOUNT IDA / *Native · Easy*

Collect Quartz Crystals 𝒯

The following gems or minerals may be found:

- Quartz crystals

Ouachita National Forest
Crystal Vista Crystal Collecting Site
Caddo/Womble Ranger District Office
1523 Highway 270 E
Mount Ida, AR 71957
Phone: (870) 867-2101
www.fs.usda.gov/ouachita (Recreation
  > Rocks and Minerals > Rockhounding
  > Crystal/Vista)

Open: All year, weather permitting.

Info: This is a former quartz crystal mine located at the end of a steep, mile-long hiking trail on top of Gardner Mountain in the Womble Ranger District in central Arkansas. No digging is allowed at the site; collect only the crystals lying on the ground surface. The Forest Service advises that the site is well picked over.

Note: This is a primitive site. You must bring water and food with you, and take all trash out.

Rates: Free.

Directions: South on Highway 27, 3.8 miles from Mount Ida, then turn left (east) on Owley Road (County Road 2237). The trailhead is 4.1 miles on Owley Road.

MOUNT IDA / *Native · Moderate*

Dig Your Own 𝒯
Quartz Crystals

The following gems or minerals may be found:

- Quartz crystals

Judy's Crystals and Things
P.O. Box 956
Mount Ida, AR 71957
Phone: (870) 867-2523
Cell: (501) 276-2439
E-mail: judyscrystals@windstream.net
www.judyscrystals.com

Open: March–December, 9:00 A.M.–5:00 P.M. 6 days/week; closed Monday.

Info: Fisher Mountain, also called the Stanley Mine (one of the oldest and best-known mines in Montgomery County), is located about 4 miles from the shop. You must sign a release and pay the fees before mining, and follow a few simple rules: Dig in designated areas; don't dig under high walls or overhangs; supervise any children; wear suitable shoes (no open-toe shoes permitted), gloves, and clothing; and bring water and sunscreen. Bring your own hand tools for digging, and remember that the red Arkansas clay is nearly impossible to clean from your clothes.

Rates: Adults $15.00, children (7–15) $7.50, children 6 and under free.

Other services available: Rock shop, acid for cleaning crystals.

Directions: Call for directions.

MOUNT IDA / *Native and Enriched*
* *Easy to Moderate*

Dig Your Own Quartz Τ Crystals

The following gems or minerals may be found:

- Quartz crystals, amethyst, garnets, rubies

Twin Creek Crystal Mine
Dixie Crystal Mining Co.
177 Collier Springs Rd.
Mount Ida, Arkansas 71957
Phone: (870) 867-4945
www.dixiecrystalco.com

Open: Year round, 7 days/week, 8:00 A.M.–4:00 P.M.

Rates: Adults $25.00, children (12 and under) $12.00.

Info: Dig your own quartz crystals.

Other Services Available: Rock shop, picnic area.

Directions: The mine is 5 miles east of Mount Ida, on Hwy 270. Turn onto Logan Gap Road at Judy's Crystals and travel 2 miles. When the houses end you will cross a one-lane bridge; turn right onto Collier Springs Road. Go another mile across a low bridge, and pass the first gate. Enter at the second gate, which is open on the left side. Follow the signs. The "Do Not Enter—DANGER" sign on the gate refers to when the gate is closed.

MOUNT IDA / *Native and Enriched*
* *Easy to Moderate*

Dig Your Own Quartz Τ Crystals or Pan for Gemstones

The following gems or minerals may be found:

- Quartz crystals; also rubies, emeralds, and diamonds

Wegner Quartz Crystal Mines
82 Wegner Ranch Road
P.O. Box 205
Mount Ida, AR 71957
Phone: (870) 867-2309
E-mail: wegner@wegnercrystalmines.com
www.wegnercrystalmines.com

Open: March 15–December 1, 8:00 A.M.–4:30 P.M., 7 days/week; December 2–March 14, 8:00 A.M.–4:30 P.M. Monday–Friday.

Info: There are six mining options. All are open from 8:00 A.M.–4:30 P.M. all year; except closed weekends December 2–March 14, and closed some holidays.

1. *Crystal Forest Mine:* This is a forty-acre surface mine—collect tailings or dig your own. Groups leave at 9:30, 11:30, and 1:30; arrive 15 minutes before sign-up for a safety briefing. Transportation and tools provided; refundable deposit required. Cost is $15.00 per person for 2 hours collecting.

2. *Gemstone sluice:* Sluice buckets of enriched gem ore in a shaded

100-foot-long gemstone sluice near the tailings area. Buckets are $10.00 to 15.00, and there are family fees and discounts—check website for more details.

3. *Tailings area:* Dig for crystals in truckloads of mine tailings hauled from the mine. A picnic area is near the tailings area. Adults $10.50, seniors and children (under 12) $6.60. Buckets and tools provided.

4. *Phantom Mine.* Advance reservations required—minimum of 10 people. In this pit and the surrounding area are quartz crystals and clusters with manganese inclusions that look like small dark crystals. $24.00 per person for 4 hours of digging. Transportation and tools provided.

5. *Diamond Adventure.* Search through a bag of diamond ore (not from nearby Crater of Diamonds State Park) on a light table. Each bag is guaranteed to have at least ½ carat of diamonds. Use of tools plus a velvet pouch and magnification display case is included. $29.00/bag.

6. *Gems of the World.* Search through a bag of gemstone ore on a light table. Each bag contains emerald, amethyst, peridot, opals, garnets, and more. $16.00/bag.

Directions: 3 miles south of Mount Ida.

MURFREESBORO / *Native* *
Moderate

Dig Your Own Diamonds and Other Gems

The following gems or minerals may be found:

• Diamonds are the chief attraction; however, amethyst, agate, jasper, quartz, calcite, barite, peridot, and up to 40 other gems or minerals can also be found

Crater of Diamonds State Park
209 State Park Road
Murfreesboro, AR 71958
Phone: (870) 285-3113
E-mail: craterofdiamonds@arkansas.com
www.craterofdiamondsstatepark.com

Open: Year-round except major winter holidays. Memorial Day–Labor Day,

---

Diamond-Hunting Tips

Look for small, well-rounded crystals. A diamond weighing several carats may be no larger than a marble. Look for clean crystals, since diamonds have an oily, slick outer surface that dirt and mud don't stick to. The diamonds come in several colors. The most common found at the crater are clear, white, yellow, and brown.

8:00 A.M.–8:00 P.M. daily, except the last two weeks in August, when the site closes at 5:00 P.M. Sunday–Thursday, but is open until 8:00 P.M. Friday and Saturday. Labor Day–Memorial Day, 8:00 A.M.–5:00 P.M. daily.

Info: Crater of Diamonds State Park offers a one-of-a-kind adventure—the chance to find and keep real diamonds. You can search a 37-acre field of lamproite soil, which is the eroded surface of an ancient gem-bearing volcanic pipe (lava tube). Prospectors enter the field through a visitors center that includes exhibits and an audiovisual program explaining the area's geology and providing tips on recognizing diamonds in the rough.

Since diamonds were first discovered there in 1906, more than 70,000 have been found. Since the crater became a state park in 1972, over 30,000 diamonds have been found by visitors, and on the average, more than 600 diamonds are found each year. Among the diamonds that have been found are the Uncle Sam (40.23 carats), the Star of Murfreesboro (34.2 carats), the Star of Arkansas (15.33 carats), and the Amarillo Starlight (16.37 carats).

On June 24, 2015, an 8.52-carat white diamond was found at the park! The diamond, named Esperanza, was cut and polished at a jewelry store in North Little Rock that September. The public was invited to watch the process.

The park consists of 911 pine-covered acres along the banks of the Little Missouri River. The first diamond was found in 1906; the property has changed hands several times over the years. Previous owners made several attempts to mine diamonds commercially. These attempts are mostly shrouded in mystery, and all ultimately failed; lawsuits, fires, or lack of capital are some of the reasons for failure. In 1972, the State of Arkansas bought the property and established Crater of Diamonds State Park.

Lamproite, a relatively rare rock of magmatic origin, is a source rock for diamonds. The lamproite soil, very different from red Arkansas clay, is dark green to black, gummy when wet, and powdery when dry.

This is the only diamond field open to the public in North America. The field is plowed approximately monthly. The park staff at the park's Diamond Discovery Center will aid you in the identification of any stone you find.

Diamond mining tools, such as army shovels, trowels, gardening tools, and screen boxes, can be rented at the park. Two mineral-washing pavilions contain long troughs filled with water to aid in screening for diamonds.

Organized groups may dig at a discount. Advance notice must be given to obtain the reduced rate.

The state park offers a variety of orientation programs during the summer months: programs cover nature, geology, diamond-hunting methods, and history.

Rates: Adults $8.00, children (6–12) $5.00, children under 5 free.

Other services available: Restaurant (seasonal), gift shop, water park (March–November), restrooms, nature trails, interpretive exhibits, historical structures, fishing.

Pets are allowed in all facilities, with the exception of the gift shop, water park, and cafe, as long as they remain on a leash under the owner's control at all times.

A 1.2-mile-long river trail winds its way through the woods to the scenic Little Missouri River. This provides a relaxing 1-hour hike over level terrain.

Campground: Forty-seven class AAA campsites in a secluded woodsview setting. Water, electric hookups, laundry and sewers are available on these campsites. Five primitive tent sites with water only.

Other services available: Shady sites, modern restrooms, clean hot showers, laundry facilities, dump station, tent sites, nearby fishing.

Directions: The state park is located 2 miles southeast of the Murfreesboro courthouse on Arkansas Route 301.

STORY / *Native · Moderate*

Dig Your Own *T* Quartz Crystals

The following gems or minerals may be found:

- Quartz crystals

Sweet Surrender Crystals
269 Cleo Circle (mailing address only)
Sims, AR 71969

Phone: (870) 867-0104
Cell: (870) 867-7014; (870) 867-7075
E-mail: randyskates@windstream.net
www.sweetsurrendercrystals.com

Open: Hours vary depending on weather. Normal hours are 9:30 A.M.–4:00 P.M., or until it gets too late to dig. Call ahead for appointment.

Info: This is a working mine. Mine personnel will give you a brief lesson on safety and show you where to find crystals. This is a primitive area, with no facilities, services, or phones. Bring your own digging equipment, containers, and food and drinks. Suggested tools for digging: an old screwdriver, hand garden tools, sometimes a rock hammer, old digging bar. Stay away from flagged areas and machinery.

Rates: Adults $20.00, children (10–14) $10.00, children under 10 free with paying adult.

Directions: Take Highway 27 north from Mount Ida through Washita. A half mile north of Washita you will see the Sweet Surrender Mine sign on Horseshoe Bend Road. Turn right, go ½ mile. At the first mailbox on the right will be a sign for the crystal mine entrance. Turn right and go to the top of the hill until you see the picnic tables.

LITTLE ROCK

Geology Learning Center

Vardelle Parham Geology Center
Arkansas Geological Survey
3815 W. Roosevelt Road
Little Rock, AR 72204
Phone: (501) 296-1877
E-mail: ags@arkansas.gov
www.geology.ar.gov

Open: All year, 8:00 A.M.–4:30 P.M. Monday–Friday. The learning center is open by appointment only

Info: Some exhibits can be seen at the survey offices. The learning center is intended to give students of all ages who are interested in earth sciences direct exposure to rocks, minerals, fossils, and fuels. Exhibits include the Arkansas Geological Survey, Arkansas' mineral wealth, fossil fuels in Arkansas, Arkansas gems and minerals, Arkansas fossils, and economic minerals and mining.

Admission: Free.

Directions: The survey offices are located at 3815 W. Roosevelt Road. The learning center is located at 1911 Thayer Street, just south of the intersection of Asher and Wright Avenues.

MOUNT IDA

Museum

Heritage House Museum of
Montgomery County, Arkansas
819 Luzerne Street
P.O. Box 1362
Mount Ida, AR 71957-1362
Phone: (870) 867-4422
E-mail: museum@hhmmc.org
www.hhmmc.org

Open: 11:00 A.M.–4:00 P.M. Monday, Wednesday, Friday; 1:00 P.M.–4:00 P.M. Saturday–Sunday; closed Tuesday and Thursday.

Info: The museum has a display on Quartz crystals and samples of minerals from the area with information about mining in Montgomery County, AR.

Admission: Free; donations appreciated.

Other services available: Gift shop.

Directions: Located at 819 Luzerne Street in Mount Ida (at the intersection of Highway 27 and Luzerne Street).

PIGGOTT

Museum

Matilda and Karl Pfeiffer Museum and
    Study Center
1071 Heritage Park Drive
Piggott, AR 72454
Phone: (870) 598-3228
E-mail: pfeiffernd@centurytel.net
www.pfeifferfoundation.com

Open: 9:00 A.M.–4:00 P.M. Tuesday–
Friday, 11:00 A.M–4:00 P.M. Saturday.
Groups of ten or more by appointment.
Info: The museum has a collection of
more than 1,400 mineral specimens
and geodes, some of which are on per-
manent display, and some of which are
displayed on a rotating basis.
Admission: Free, donations accepted.
Directions: Piggott is in the northeast
corner of Arkansas. From U.S. 62, take
N 12th Street south to Heritage Park
Drive, then turn left to the museum.

STATE UNIVERSITY

Museum

ASU Museum
Arkansas State University
Museum/Library Building
P.O. Box 490
State University, AR 72467
Phone: (870) 972-2074
E-mail: museum@astate.edu
www.astate.edu/museum

Open: All year, closed campus holidays.
9:00 A.M.–7:00 P.M. Tuesday; 9:00 A.M.–
5:00 P.M. Monday and Wednesday–
Saturday. Closed Sunday.

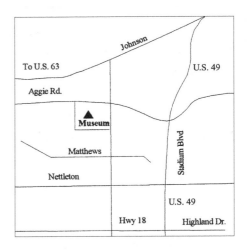

Info: Exhibits include a chart showing
relative lengths of the periods of the
earth's formation, several fossils, and
a variety of minerals, including a large
number found in Arkansas. Arkansas
minerals displayed include fluorite,
bauxite, calcite clusters, halite, granite, gypsum, quartz and drusy quartz,
smithsonite, golden dolomite and dolomite crystals, selenite, nepheline syenite
and septarian concretions.
Admission: Free; donations appreciated.
Directions: ASU is on the eastern out-
skirts of Jonesboro. The museum occu-
pies the west wing of the Dean B. Ellis
Library building.

In Benton, AR, there is a building constructed entirely from bauxite,
which is aluminum ore. It was originally the medical office of Dr. Dewell
Gann, built by his patients who were unable to pay him, and who built
him an office instead. It is the only known building in the world built
from bauxite. It now houses the Gann Museum.

ANNUAL EVENT

Quartz Crystal Festival and World Championship Dig, Mount Ida ✎

In Mount Ida (Quartz Crystal Capital of the World), dig in actual working quartz crystal mines in the heart of the Ouachita Mountains. The contest is held as part of the Annual Quartz, Quiltz, and Craftz Festival. The festival includes a gem and mineral show and is held on the second Friday, Saturday, and Sunday in October.

Dig your own crystals with participating local mines. Contestants keep everything they dig. There is a judging session each afternoon to see who found the best crystals. Win crystal trophies, prizes, and $1,500 in cash. The dig begins on Friday. Diggers have two days to dig. The hours are 9:00 A.M. to 3:00 P.M. Prize money is awarded to the top five winners in each division; crystal trophies go to the first- and second-place winners in each division. Diggers may compete on behalf of their gem or mineral club.

Pre-registration fee: $75.00/person; after August 31, $85.00; after October 1, $100.00. K–6 Kids Dig: Only $1 to enter. Two categories: kindergarten–3rd grade and 4th–6th grades.

Prizes, costs, and deadlines change from year to year, so call for details. Keep all you dig; use hand tools only (provide your own). Ages 10–16 permitted to dig with adult supervision. Primitive toilets are available at dig sites. At the festival, crystals, gems, minerals, jewelry, equipment, supplies, books, dealers, and exhibits are available. For further details and a registration form, write to:

Mount Ida Chamber of Commerce
P.O. Box 6
124 Hwy 270 West
Mount Ida, AR 71957
Phone: (870) 867-2723
E-mail: director@mtidachamber.com
www.mtidachamber.com

The Chamber of Commerce can also provide information on the Ouachita National Forest, the South's oldest and largest national forest, covering 1.6 million acres. Features include Lake Ouachita, which offers fishing, scuba diving, water skiing, sailing, horseback riding, camping, and hiking; 480 miles of hiking trails run throughout the National Forest.

TOURIST INFORMATION

State Tourist Agency 👉

Arkansas Department of Parks
and Tourism
Phone: (501) 682-7777
E-mail: info@arkansas.com
www.arkansas.com

Rockhounding Arkansas
www.rockhoundingar.com

Mount Ida Area Chamber of Commerce
P.O. Box 6
124 Hwy 270 West
Mount Ida, AR 71957
Phone: (870) 867-2723
E-mail: director@mtidachamber.com
www.mtidachamber.com

Hot Springs Convention and
Visitors Bureau
134 Convention Boulevard
Hot Springs, AR 71901
Phone: (501) 321-2835; (800) 722-2489
E-mail: hscvb@hotsprings.org
www.hotsprings.org

FLORIDA

State Gemstone: Moonstone (1970)
State Stone/Rock: Agatized Coral (1979)

Dates refer to when stones and minerals were adopted by the state legislature.

SECTION 1: Fee Dig Sites and Guide Services

OKEECHOBEE / *Native • Easy to Moderate*

Dig Your Own Calcite Crystals 𝑇

The following gems or minerals may be found:

• **Calcite crystals on fossil shells, micropyrite, iridescent marcasite**

Fort Drum Crystal Mine
  (also known as Ruck's Pit)
Eddie and Debbie Ruck
28320 NE 55th Avenue
Okeechobee, FL 34972
E-mail: info@thefortdrumcrystalmine.com
www.thefortdrumcrystalmine.com

Open: 7 days/week, 9:00 A.M.–5:00 P.M. Call a couple of days ahead for arrangements.
Info: Dig through piles of material from the pit. Ruck's Pit was worked primarily for limerock used for road base material. The aggregate from these workings was found to be rich in golden calcite crystals. Changes in mining regulations have closed the active mine to public access, but material from the mine is now hauled to the shop where collectors can dig through it for crystals. This is said to be the only location in the world where calcified marine clam shells can be found. Tools and water hoses are available. Wear old clothes, sturdy shoes, a hat for shade. Bring food, drinking water, chair, your own 5-gallon bucket, newspaper for wrapping your specimens, and cardboard boxes.
Rates: Adults $60.00; children 13–15, $35.00, 8–12, $25.00, 5–7, $15.00, under 5, free. This covers admission and collection of one 5-gallon bucket (bring your own) of specimens. Additional buckets $5.00 each.
Other services available: Large gift shop. Campsites: $25.00/day.
Directions: The Fort Drum Crystal Mine is now located 2 blocks west and across the street from its former location off 304th Street. Take exit 193 off the Florida Turnpike and look for signs. Call for detailed directions.

SECTION 2: Museums and Mine Tours

DELAND

Museum

Gillespie Museum
Stetson University
Physical address:
234 E Michigan Avenue
DeLand, FL 32723
Mailing address:
Stetson University, Unit 8403
421 N Woodland Boulevard
DeLand, FL 32723

Phone: (386) 822-7330
E-mail: gillespie@stetson.edu
www.stetson.edu/other/gillespiemuseum

Open: August–April, 10:00 A.M.–4:00 P.M. Tuesday–Friday. Closed Saturday–Monday, except once a month for Science Saturday, 10:00 A.M.–1:00 P.M. June: 11:00 A.M.–3:00 P.M. Tuesday–Friday. Always check ahead; may be closed for school holidays. Closed May and July.

Info: The Gillespie Museum was created out of a lifelong love of mineral collecting by T. B. and Nellie Gillespie. Learn about their hobby in an exhibit detailing the creation of the museum. The geological collection contains more than 15,000 items. Permanent exhibits include: Minerals A–Z, Meteorites, Petrified Wood, The Ancient Art of Marble Inlay, Gemstones and Birthstones, and Volcanoes.

Admission: Free; donations greatly appreciated.

Directions: Located on the southeast corner of the Stetson University campus in DeLand (intersection of Amelia Avenue and East Michigan Avenue).

GAINESVILLE

Museum 🏛

Geological Museum
Santa Fe College Department of
    Natural Sciences
3000 NW 83rd Street
Gainesville, FL 3260
Phone: (352) 395-5349

www.sfcollege.edu/naturalsciences

Open: When the college is in session; call for hours.

Info: Exhibits include Florida gems and minerals, gemstone carvings, a large collection of fluorescent minerals, prehistoric amber, fossils, and agatized Tampa Bay coral.

Admission: Free

Directions: Take the NW 39th Avenue exit (exit 390) off I-75 in Gainesville. Turn east toward Gainesville, turn right (south) on NW 83rd Street and right on North Road. Parking is free. The museum is in the Department of Natural Science building.

ISLAMORADA

Geological Park 🏛

Windley Key Fossil Reef Geological
    State Park
84900 Overseas Highway
Islamorada, Florida 33036
Phone: (305) 664-2540
www.floridastateparks.org/park/
    Windley-Key

Open: Visitors' center: 8:00 A.M.–5:00 P.M. Thursday–Sunday. Guided tours 10:00 A.M.–2:00 P.M.; self-guided tours are also available when the park is open.

Info: This state park is a former quarry, used to mine Key Largo limestone (fossilized coral). The Florida East Coast Railroad used this stone to build Henry Flagler's Overseas Railroad in the early

1900s. After the railroad was built, the quarry was used until the 1960s to mine decorative stone called Keystone. Visitors can walk within the eight-foot-high quarry walls to see a cross-section of the ancient coral reef formed nearly 125,000 years ago, learn about the quarry and its operation, and see samples of the quarry machinery. There is also a picnic area.

Admission: $2.50; includes self-guided tours. Guided tours are an additional $2.00 per person, 6 and over.

MIAMI

Museum 🏛

Coral Castle Museum
28655 South Dixie Highway
Miami, FL 33033
Phone: (305) 248-6345
www.coralcastle.com

Open: 8:00 A.M.–6:00 P.M. Sunday–Thursday; 8:00 A.M.–8:00 P.M. Friday and Saturday.

Info: Walled sculpture garden with over one thousand tons of coral rock carvings created by one man from in the 1920s through 1950s.

Admission: Adults $15.00, seniors (65+) $12.00, children (7–12) $7.00, under 6 free.

Directions: Check website for detailed directions.

MULBERRY

Museum 🏛

Mulberry Phosphate Museum
101 SE 1st Street
Mulberry, FL 33860
Phone: (863) 425-2823
www.mulberryphosphatemuseum.org

Open: All year, 9:00 A.M.–5:00 P.M. Tuesday–Saturday.

Info: The museum houses educational exhibits on the phosphate industry.

Admission: Free; donations greatly appreciated.

Directions: One block south of State Highway 60 on State Highway 37 in

Phosphate is a key ingredient in fertilizers, and is also used in soda pop, toothpaste, and fine china. The deposits of phosphate in Florida occurred when prehistoric oceans that covered present-day Florida evaporated, leaving beds of sand, clay, and phosphate. Remains of prehistoric marine animals (like sharks) also contributed phosphate material to these beds. The state of Florida is thought to have approximately 80 percent of the total U.S. phosphate reserves. The first discovery of phosphate pebbles in the Peace River led to a phosphate mining rush like the California and Alaskan gold rushes.

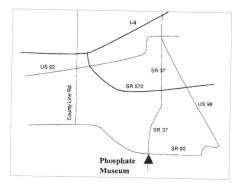

downtown Mulberry.

Note: The phosphate deposits are rich in fossils. You can dig for small phosphate pebbles (containing fossils) next to the museum.

TAMPA

Museum 🏛

Ed and Bernadette Marcin Museum
School of Geosciences
University of South Florida
4207 East Fowler Avenue, NES 109
Tampa, FL 33620
Phone: (813) 974-2236

Open: All year by appointment only, Monday–Friday, except holidays. Special arrangements can be made for groups.

Info: Located in Room 534 of the science center at the University of South Florida's Tampa Campus. This is a small museum created through the donations of Dr. and Mrs. Pious, and it includes minerals and gemstones. They accumulated their collection over a period of about 20 years, largely while traveling through the western U.S. and Florida.

The museum collection is augmented and maintained through gifts to the departmental collection and by collectors throughout Florida. Included in the museum collections are an agatized wood collection and a mineral collection.

Admission: Free.

Directions: The museum is located in the science center at the University of South Florida–Tampa campus.

WEST PALM BEACH

Museum 🏛

South Florida Science Center
    and Aquarium
4081 Dreher Trail N
West Palm Beach, FL 33405
Phone: (561) 832-1988
www.sfsciencecenter.org

Open: 9:00 A.M.–5:00 P.M. Monday–Friday; 10:00 A.M.–6:00 P.M. Saturday and Sunday.

Information: The Out of This World exhibit contains a collection of rare space artifacts and real rocks from space, including a 232-pound meteorite and a moon rock brought back on an Apollo mission.

Admission: Adults $16.95, seniors (60+) $14.95, children (3–12) $12.95.

Directions: From the Florida Turnpike, take the Southern Boulevard exit east, past I-95, to the Dreher Park entrance on the right. From I-95, exit at Southern Boulevard. Turn into Dreher Park and follow Dreher Trail to the South Florida Science Center and Aquarium.

Coquina, a variety of limestone, has been mined on Anastasia Island near St. Augustine for more than three thousand years, since St. Augustine was settled around 1565. Coquina, Spanish for "bulletproof seashells," consists of a mass of shells cemented together by calcium carbonate. After being cut into blocks and exposed to air, any moisture evaporates and calcium carbonate in solution deposits out, cementing the mixture into a firm rock. It was found that this stone makes a very good material for forts, particularly in the period of cannon use. Because of the stone's softness, cannonballs would sink into rather than shatter or puncture the walls. (Coquina rock forms the walls of Costello de San Marcos in St. Augustine.) Pieces of coquina are usually sold in the Colonial Quarter as souvenirs of St. Augustine.

Unlike most gemstones, which of mineral origin, coral is organic, formed by living organisms. Florida designated agatized coral as the official state stone in 1976. Agatized coral is the remains of primal coral reefs that grew in the warm waters of ancient oceans. It forms through a process similar to petrified wood: decaying organic materials are replaced with silica from silica-rich solutions, which over millennia, under pressure, grow into chalcedony formations.

SECTION 3: **Special Events and Tourist Information**

TOURIST INFORMATION

State Tourist Agency
www.visitflorida.com

GEORGIA

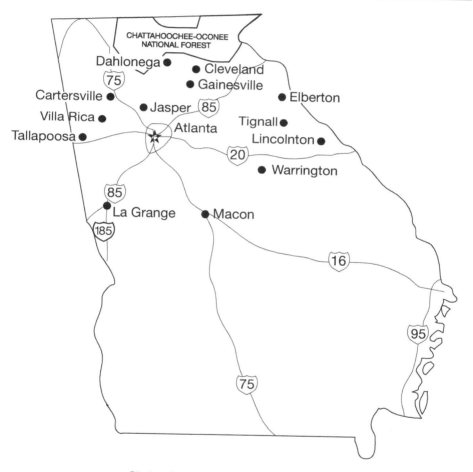

CHATTAHOOCHEE-OCONEE
NATIONAL FOREST

Dahlonega
Cleveland
Gainesville
75
Cartersville
Jasper 85
Elberton
Villa Rica
Tignall
Tallapoosa
Atlanta
Lincolnton
20
Warrington
85
La Grange
Macon
185
16
95
75

State Gemstone: Quartz (1976)
State Mineral: Staurolite (1976)

Dates refer to when stones and minerals were adopted by the state legislature.

CLEVELAND / *Native and Enriched*
- *Easy to Moderate*

Dig Your Own Minerals *T*

The following gems or minerals may be found:

- **Gold, sapphires, rubies, emeralds, amethyst, topaz**

Gold'n Gem Grubbin
75 Gold Nugget Lane
Cleveland, GA 30528
Phone: (706) 865-5454; (800) 942-4436
E-mail: info@goldngem.com
www.goldngem.com

Open: All year, 9:00 A.M.–5:00 P.M. daily.

Info: North Georgia's only commercially operating gold mine. Pan buckets of concentrate taken from the strip mine. Pan for gold in the mine's sluice buckets. The gold ore from the strip mine on the property has been concentrated to increase the likelihood of finding gold. Free panning lessons for first-timers. Buckets of gem ore can be purchased for sluicing. You can also dig your own gold and gems from the stream. Equipment is provided.

Rates: No admission fee; pay by the bucket. Gold buckets: 1 gallon Fine Gold, $30.00; Picker Nugget Bucket, $75.00; Paydirt Bucket, $145.00. Gem buckets: $20.00 for standard 1-gallon bucket; other options range from $30.00–$100.00/bucket and include credits toward having jewelry made. *Mining in the creek:* Ore dug from mining pit is put on the edge of the creek to be mined. Screen and pan right in the creek. Adults $15.00/half day, $25.00/full day; children (7–12) $7.50/half day, $12.50/full day. You can also dredge in the creek. Check website for fees.

Other services available: Gift shop, gem cutting, jewelry, and mining equipment sales. Free parking. Handicap facilities.

Camping: Campground with primitive sites for tents, and full hook ups for RVs. Tent sites are $20.00/night and RV sites are $28.00/night. Weekly rates available.

Directions: Two miles west from Cleveland Square, turn right onto Town Creek Road, then go 2 miles.

DAHLONEGA / *Native* - *Easy*

Pan for Gold *T*

The following gems or minerals may be found:

- **Gold, emeralds, rubies, sapphires, topaz, amethyst, quartz, moonstone, garnets**

Consolidated Gold Mines
185 Consolidated Gold Mine Road
Dahlonega, GA 30533

Dahlonega: Site of America's First Gold Rush

DAH-LON-E-GA is the word in the Cherokee language for the "precious yellow metal" found in these hills. In 1828, the cry "We've found gold" was heard far and near. With the discovery of gold in the foothills of the Blue Ridge Mountains, Dahlonega emerged in 1833 as a full-blown "hustle and bustle" town. Gold was mined into the early 20th century. Now, several attractions highlight the town's historic activities, including a gold museum, gold panning, and gold mine tours. Attend Gold Rush Days, or attend the gold panning championships.

Information on the area may be obtained by contacting the Dahlonega-Lumpkin County Chamber of Commerce, 13 S Park Street, Dahlonega, GA 30533; phone: (706) 864 3711 or (800) 231-5543.

Phone: (706) 864-8473
E-mail: info@consolidatedgoldmine.com
www.consolidatedgoldmine.com

Open: All year, 7 days/week. Winter, 10:00 A.M.–4:00 P.M. Monday–Friday, 10:00 A.M.–5:00 P.M. Saturday–Sunday; summer, 10:00 A.M.–5:00 P.M. daily. Arrive at least one hour before closing.

Info: For further information on the Consolidated Gold Mine tour, see Section 2.

Rates: Rates vary. Gold pans: Regular panning, $6.00/pan; high-grade material, $11.00/pan. Gem buckets range from $15.00 to $1,000.00.

Other services available: Mine tour, shops, gem cutting on site, jewelry making.

Directions: The site is just beside the Walmart shopping center in Dahlonega.

DAHLONEGA / *Native and Enriched* • *Easy*

Pan for Gold or Gemstones

The following gems or minerals may be found:

• Gold, rubies, emeralds, garnets, sapphires, and many more

Crisson Gold Mine
2736 Morrison Moore Parkway East
Dahlonega, GA 30533

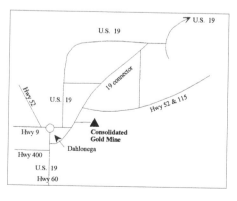

Phone: (706) 864-6363
www.crissongoldmine.com

Open: All year, 7 days/week. March–October, 10:00 A.M.–6:00 P.M.; November–February, 10:00 A.M.–5:00 P.M. Closed Thanksgiving and Christmas.

Info: The mine offers indoor panning in winter; ore is also sold "to go."

Rates: Basic admission: $9.95/person, ages 4 and up. This includes 1 pan gold dirt, 2-gallon bucket of gemstones, self-guided tour of stamp mill. Additional options available: Gold ore, 5-gallon non-concentrated, $15.00; wheelbarrow, $75.00. Tractor scoops, concentrates, and use of highbanker or gold cube among other options, check website. Wagon rides, $3.00.

Other services available: Tour and demonstration of a 125-year-old stamp mill, picnic area, gift shop, restrooms. Trail ride and farm equipment display available during spring, summer, and fall.

Directions: On U.S. 19, 2½ miles north of downtown Dahlonega.

GAINESVILLE / *Native • Easy to Moderate*

Pan for Gold *T*

The following gems or minerals may be found:

- Gold

Forest Supervisor's Office (not actually in the forest)
Chattahoochee-Oconee National Forest
1755 Cleveland Highway
Gainesville, GA 30501
Phone: (770) 297-3000
www.fs.usda.gov (Search "Gold Panning.")

Open: Call ahead for information. Offices are closed weekends and all federal holidays. Office hours are 9:00 A.M.–12:00 P.M., 1:00 P.M.–4:00 P.M. Monday–Friday.

Info: Recreational gold panning and rockhounding are both allowed within the Chattahoochee-Oconee National Forest. In-stream sluicing and dredging are not allowed. Significant surface excavation is not allowed, and no mechanical equipment can be used. In addition, there may be claims that affect where you can pan or collect. Check with the forest ranger's office for information and maps. *Note:* The Appalachian Trail starts in this forest.

LA GRANGE / *Native • Moderate to Difficult*

Hunt for Your Own Crystals *T*

The following gems or minerals may be found:

- **Star rose quartz, aquamarine, beryl, black tourmaline**

Hogg Mine
Chris Painter
LaGrange, GA
Phone: (770) 262-7852
E-mail: rockdgr@yahoo.com
www.hoggmine.com

Open: All year, by reservation. Call or check website for days and times of scheduled digs. Digging times 9:00 A.M.–5:00 P.M.

Info: This is a working mine that allows tailings digging, and sometimes has a machine dig for digging in newly excavated material (spaces limited). Digging in mine tailings occurs once or twice a month. Diggers meet with the miner at a specified meeting place in LaGrange at 9:00 A.M. to sign releases and have a safety briefing, then travel to the mine and dig in the tailings until 5:00 P.M. Bring your own tools, such as pick, shovel, potato rake, rock hammer, sledge hammer, chisel, rock bar, 5-gallon bucket, gloves, and safety glasses. There is a limit of one 5-gallon bucket of material per person and one yard rock per dig. Machine digs are similar, but the mine owner will have an excavator at the mine and will excavate new material from the pit for diggers to search.

Rates: Scheduled tailings digging rates are $35.00/person per day; children 16 and under dig free. Machine digs are an additional $100.00/person per day. Private group digs are $35.00/person plus $100.00 guide fee for under 10 people or $250.00 guide fee for larger groups. Private machine digs are the same as private group digs plus the rental cost of the machine, fuel, and operator. Mobile rockshop on site.

Directions: Meeting place: McDonald's next to the Pilot truck stop at exit 13 off I-85.

LINCOLNTON / *Native • Difficult*

Dig Your Own Minerals *T*

The following gems or minerals may be found:

- Rutile, lazulite, pyrophyllite, kyanite, iridescent hematite, pyrophyllite, pyrite, ilmenite, muscovite, fuchsite, barite, sulfur, blue quartz, quartz crystals, and microcrystals such as woodhouseite, variscite, strengite, phosphosiderite, cacoxenite, crandallite

Graves Mountain
Clarence Norman Jr., caretaker
Lincolnton, GA
Phone: (706) 401-3173 (business);
E-mail: gmsmail@gamineral.org
www.gamineral.org/ft/commercial/
    ftgravesmain.html

Open: The collecting area will be open to the public for a 3-day period twice each year. Call or check on the website for dates (usually in April and October). Open to all, no need to make a reservation.

Info: Dig in the soil or rocks, or simply pick up crystals from the tailings. Bring your own digging equipment and containers. Stay away from the high walls and only collect in designated areas. Sign a liability release and leave a donation at the Hospitality Tent. Portable toilets will be provided. In addition, food and beverages will be available for purchase, and tables can be set up for a "Rock Swap."

Rates: Donations accepted for expenses in opening the mountain to the public and providing portable toilets.

Other information: The mountain will be open to collecting at other times only to colleges, universities, and gem and mineral societies. Fee: donation. Contact the caretaker, Clarence Norman Jr., for reservations.

Directions: From I-285 in Atlanta, take I-20 east to the exit for Washington, which is Georgia Route 78 (SR 10/SR 17). Turn left and travel north to Washington, and take Georgia Route 378 for 11 miles to the Graves Mountain area. The entrance to Graves Mountain is on your right about .8 miles past the Lincoln County line. The entrance is a paved road that goes through a gate and up a hill. Please park along the access road and then proceed to the Welcome Tent at the end of the pavement to obtain a liability release form and to make a donation. (Alternate directions are listed on website.)

TIGNALL / *Native • Moderate to Difficult*

Hunt for Your Own Amethyst Crystals

The following gems or minerals may be found:

- **Amethyst crystals, druse quartz**

Jackson's Crossroads Amethyst Mine (JxR)
Ledford Minerals
Christopher Ryan and Rachel Ledford
Phone: (303) 319-9199
E-mail: ledfordminerals@gmail.com
www.ledfordminerals.com

Open: All year, by prior reservation at least one week in advance. Must be at least 12 years old to dig at the Jackson Crossroads mine, and must sign a release before entering. All visitors must arrive at the mine promptly at 9:00 A.M. on the day they go to the mine.

Info: This is a working mine that allows digging in mine tailings; do not enter the roped off areas. Surface hunt for crystals, dig in clay lumps, break open promising-looking rocks, and keep all you find. Bring your own tools; suggested tools include a pick, shovel, rock hammer, sledge hammer, chisels, rock bars, 5-gallon buckets, gloves, and safety glasses.

Rates: Contact owners.

Directions: From Tignall, turn off Highway 17 onto Independence Road (Country Road 184). Go west about 7.8 miles and turn right at the church onto Hollis Norman Road. The mine is the second entrance on the right.

WARRENTON / *Native · Moderate to Difficult*

Hunt for Your Own Amethyst Crystals 𝑇

The following gems or minerals may be found:

- Amethyst crystals

Dixie Euhedrals
Rodney Moore
1320 Chappell Road
Jackson, GA 30233
E-mail: rodney@digforcrystals.com
www.digforcrystals.com

Open: Collecting occurs on specific dates; check the website for the schedule. Reservations required.

Info: Go through tailings piles as machines bring them up. Some pit digs may be scheduled. Rock hammer, pick or small mattock, and safety glasses and closed-toe shoes are required. Quarter-inch screens are helpful if you have them.

Admission: $50.00/person. Requires release form (on website).

Directions: Meet at a local meeting point on the morning of the dig.

Section 2: Museums and Mine Tours

ATLANTA

Museum 🏛

Fernbank Museum of Natural History
767 Clifton Road NE
Atlanta, GA 30307
Phone: (404) 929-6300
www.fernbankmuseum.org

Open: 10:00 A.M.–5:00 P.M. Monday–Saturday, noon–5:00 P.M. Sunday. Closed Thanksgiving and Christmas.

Info: Some gemstones from the museum's Joachim Gem Collection are included within the Reflections of Culture exhibit, and a children's exhibition, Fernbank NatureQuest, includes a mineral cave feature. Gems from the collection can also be featured in temporary displays; check the website for current exhibitions.

Admission: Adults $18.00, seniors (65+) and students $17.00, children (3–12) $16.00, children 2 and under and museum members free. Accessible to people with disabilities.

Other services available: Museum store.

Directions: Call for directions, or see website.

ATLANTA

Museum 🏛

DeKalb County School Districts
Fernbank Science Center
156 Heaton Park Drive NE
Atlanta, GA 30307
Phone: (678) 874-7102
Fax: (678) 874-7110
www.fernbank.edu

Open: School year hours: Noon–5:00 P.M. Monday–Wednesday; noon–9:00 P.M. Thursday–Friday; 10:00 A.M.–5:00 P.M. Saturday; closed Sunday. (Check website for days science center is closed, based on the school schedule.) Summer hours: 10:00 A.M.–5:00 P.M. Monday–Wednesday and Saturday; 10:00 A.M.–9:00 P.M. Thursday and Friday.

Info: The science center has a meteorite collection and periodically holds programs on rocks and minerals.

Admission: Free.

Directions: Call or check website for directions.

CARTERSVILLE

Museum

Tellus Science Museum (formerly Weinman Mineral Museum)
100 Tellus Drive
Cartersville, GA 30120
Phone: (770) 606-5700
www.tellusmuseum.org

Open: 7 days/week, 10:00 A.M.–5:00 P.M. Closed New Year's Day, July 4, Thanksgiving Day, and Christmas Day.

Info: The Weinman Mineral Gallery, one of four galleries at the Tellus Science Museum, showcases one of the largest and most comprehensive collections in the southeast.

Admission: Adults $14.00, children (3–17) and students (with ID) $10.00 (tax added to admission price).

Other services available: Search for precious gems in the Vulcan Materials Company Gem Panning area. Free with the cost of admission. Check website for info on mineral symposium in April and Rockfest in June.

Directions: From Atlanta: Take I-75 North to Exit 293 (Highway 411), and turn left at the end of the exit ramp. Travel less than ½ mile and turn left at the traffic light on to Tellus Drive, which terminates in the museum parking lot.

DAHLONEGA

Mine Tour

Consolidated Gold Mines
185 Consolidated Gold Mine Road
Dahlonega, GA 30533
Phone: (706) 864-8473
E-mail: info@consolidatedgoldmine.com
www.consolidatedgoldmine.com

Open: All year, 7 days/week. Winter, 10:00 A.M.–4:00 P.M. Monday–Friday, 10:00 A.M.–5:00 P.M. Saturday–Sunday; summer, 10:00 A.M.–5:00 P.M. daily. Arrive at least one hour before closing.

Info: Tour an actual underground gold mine as it appeared at the turn of the century. See displays of the actual equipment used, and discuss the excavating and mining techniques used. Learn the geology of the quartz and pyrite formations with which the early miners worked. Walk through the tunnel network complete with the original

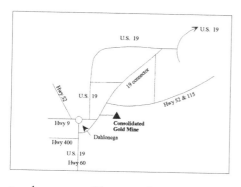

track system. The tour lasts 40 to 45 minutes. The mine is 60°F all year, so dress appropriately.

Admission: Adults $16.00, children (4–14) $11.00. All paid admissions receive gold panning instructions and a sample of material.

Other services available: Souvenir shop (offers a variety of rocks and minerals), restrooms.

Directions: The site is just beside the Walmart shopping center in Dahlonega.

DAHLONEGA

Museum, State Historic Site 🏛

Dahlonega Gold Museum
State Historic Site
1 Public Square
Dahlonega, GA 30533
Phone: (706) 864-2257
www.gastateparks.org/info/dahlonega

Open: 9:00 A.M.–5:00 P.M. Monday–Saturday, 10:00 A.M.–5:00 P.M. Sunday. Closed Thanksgiving, Christmas, and New Year's Day.

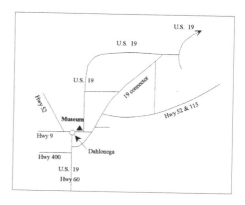

Info: The museum tells the story of the nation's first major gold rush. In 1828, 20 years before the discovery of gold in California, thousands of gold seekers flocked to the area inhabited by the Cherokee Nation in north Georgia. For more than 20 years prospectors continued to arrive, and the gold towns of Auraria and Dahlonega prospered. Between 1838 and 1861, more than $6 million in gold was coined by the U.S. Branch Mint in Dahlonega.

Note: Some exhibits are on the second floor and are not wheelchair-accessible.

Admission: Adults $7.00, seniors (62+) $6.50, children (6–17) $4.50, under 6 $2.00.

Directions: Inside the city limits of Dahlonega, on the Public Square.

Elberton Granite

Elberton is hailed as the Granite Capital of the World. While most granite quarries are less than 150 feet deep, geologists estimate the Elberton deposit to be 2 to 3 miles in depth. The physical properties and characteristics are perfect for the over 200,000 granite monuments, markers, and mausoleums made in Elberton each year.

ELBERTON

Museum 🏛

Elberton Granite Museum & Exhibit
Elberton Granite Association, Inc.
P.O. Box 640
1 Granite Plaza
Elberton, GA 30635
Phone: (706) 283-2551
www.egaonline.com/learn/elberton-
  granite-museum

Open: 2:00 P.M.–5:00 P.M. Monday–Saturday. Closed major holidays.

Info: The museum contains historical exhibits and artifacts, educational displays, and materials about the granite industry. Exhibit space on three levels graphically displays the unique granite products of the past, antique granite-working tools, and yesteryear's methods of quarrying, sawing, polishing, cutting, and sandblasting granite cemetery memorials. Exhibits also show how current quarrying methods and fabricating processes are carried out in Elberton's 35 different quarries and more than 100 manufacturing plants.

Admission: Free. Visitors may obtain a small specimen of granite for their collections.

Directions: Elberton is located in northeast Georgia, midway between I-85 and I-20. From the north, take State Highway 17 south from the Lavonia Exit on I-85 until you come to the granite museum. From the south, take State Highway 77 from the Union Point exit on I-20, to Elberton, then turn left on Highway 17 to the museum, or from the Washington exit on I-20, take State Highway 17/U.S. 78 north and follow State Highway 17 to Elberton, and the museum.

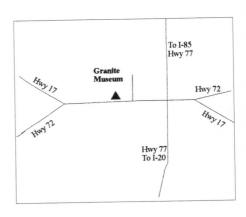

MACON

Museum

Museum of Arts and Sciences
4182 Forsyth Road
Macon, GA 31210
Phone: (478) 477-3232
E-mail: info@masmacon.org
www.masmacon.org

Open: 10:00 A.M.–5:00 P.M. Tuesday–
Saturday; 1:00 P.M.–5:00 P.M. Sunday.
Closed some national holidays.

Info: The museum has a collection of
gems and minerals.

Admission: Adults $10.00, seniors (62+)
and military $8.00, students (with ID)
$7.00, children (3–17) $7.00, under 3 free.

Directions: The museum is located on
U.S. 4/SR 19 just north of downtown
Macon.

TALLAPOOSA

Museum

West Georgia Museum of Tallapoosa
185 Mann Street
P.O. Box 725
Tallapoosa, GA 30176
Phone: (770) 574-3125
E-mail: westgeorgiamuseum@gmail.com
www.tallapoosaga.gov/museum
www.westgeorgiamuseum.com

Open: 9:00 A.M.–4:00 P.M. Monday–
Friday, 11:00 A.M.–3:00 P.M. Saturday.

Info: The museum has a small
collection of minerals from Haralson
County.

Admission: Adults $2.00, children
(4–12) $1.00, children under 4 free.

Directions: From Interstate 20, take
exit 5 (Highway 100), and go north
on Highway 100 to Tallapoosa. In Tallapoosa, stay on Highway 100 to Mann
Street; turn left to the museum.

VILLA RICA

Museum

Pine Mountain Gold Museum at
   Stockmar Park
1881 Stockmar Road
Villa Rica, GA 30180
Phone: (770) 459-8455
www.pinemountaingoldmuseum.com

Open: 10:00 A.M.–4:00 P.M. Monday–
Saturday; 1:00 P.M.–4:00 P.M. Sunday.
Panning and tram close at 3:30 P.M.
Closed major holidays.

Info: Exhibits and a documentary tell
the story of gold mining in the Villa Rica
area. The 27-acre park has over 3 miles
of self-guided walking trails with interpretive signage through the intact ruins
of the gold mines. An authentic 19th-
century gold-stamp mill is on display.

Admission: Adults $5.00 donation,
seniors and children (3–12) $4.00
donation, children under 3 free. Group
rates available.

Other services available: Gold and
gemstone panning; picnic area.

Directions: From Atlanta: Take I-20 West to Exit 26, Liberty Road. Turn right and go 1.3 miles until the road ends at Hwy 61. Turn right and go 0.2 miles to Stockmar Road. Turn right and go 1.2 miles and the park is on your left.

From Alabama: Take I-20 East to Exit 26, Liberty Road. Turn left and go 1.8 miles until the road ends at Hwy 61. Turn right and go 0.2 miles to Stockmar Road. Turn right and go 1.2 miles and the park is on your left.

SECTION 3: Special Events and Tourist Information

ANNUAL EVENT

Pickens County Marble Festival, Jasper, GA 👉

First full weekend of October

For more information:
Pickens County Chamber of Commerce
500 Stegall Drive
Jasper, GA 30143
Phone: (706) 692-5600
Fax: (706) 692-9453
E-mail: info@pickenschamber.com
www.pickenschamber.com
www.georgiamarblefestival.com

Open: 9:00 A.M.–5:00 P.M. Monday–Friday.
Info: Originally the Cherokee Indians' homeland, this part of north Georgia received its first white settlers in the 18th century. In 1834, Sam Tate purchased a large tract of land and opened a tavern. An enormous vein of marble, 2,000 feet wide, 4 miles long, and up to ½ mile deep was soon discovered in the area owned by Sam Tate. Sam's son Stephen began the mining industry, which put Tate on the map. Through his efforts, the railroad was built through Pickens County, and Georgia marble was shipped throughout the country as construction material for many important buildings and monuments.

The Georgia Marble Company currently operates the world's largest open-pit marble quarry. It is open to the public by special tour only during

World's Largest Open-Pit Marble Quarry

What is reported to be the world's largest open-pit marble quarry is located in Tate. A tract of land purchased in 1834 by Sam Tate was found to have a large deposit of marble. Mining began a few years later, and marble from this quarry has been used in building construction around the country. The Marble Festival is held in nearby Jasper, Georgia, every October; this is the only time when the quarry can be toured.

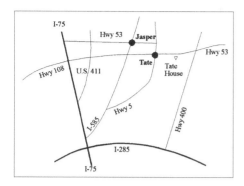

the Marble Festival. Tours leave every half hour from 10:00 A.M. to 2:00 P.M. except noon. Limited handicapped tour available, which can be reserved online or by calling.

No pets are allowed at the festival.

Festival admission: Adults $5.00, students $3.00, children under 5 free.

Quarry tour: Adults $15.00, children (6–12) $13.00, 5 and under free. Tour price includes festival admission.

Directions: Take I-575 to U.S. 515, which goes to the festival grounds.

ANNUAL EVENT

Gold Rush Days, Dahlonega, GA

Third full weekend of October

For more information:
Dahlonega Jaycees
P.O. Box 774
Dahlonega, GA 30533
Phone: (706) 864-7247
E-mail: festival@dahlonegajaycees.com
http://dahlonegajaycees.com/gold-rush

Info: This festival commemorates the first major gold rush in America, which occurred in 1828. Among the various arts and crafts activities is a gold panning contest.

Directions: Most of the activities are located in and around the Town Square.

ANNUAL EVENT

World Open Gold Panning Championship, Dahlonega, GA

Held annually at the same time as Gold Rush Days in October.

Info: Eight gold nuggets are placed in a gold pan filled with sand. The miner who pans the nuggets the fastest wins. The same pan and nuggets are used each year, ensuring consistency of the contest. As a result, this is the only contest of its kind to be recognized by the *Guinness Book of World Records.*

For more information, contact:
Consolidated Gold Mines
185 Consolidated Gold Mine Road
Dahlonega, GA 30533
Phone: (706) 864-8473
E-mail: consolidatedgoldmine@gmail.com
Contest website: www.worldopenpanning.
    homestead.com

TOURIST INFORMATION

State Tourist Agency

Georgia Department of Tourism
Phone: (800) 847-4842
www.exploregeorgia.org

KENTUCKY

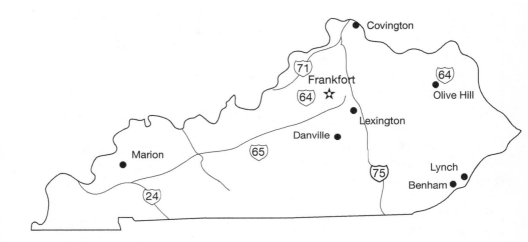

State Gemstone: Freshwater Pearl (1986)
State Mineral: Coal (1998)
State Rock: Kentucky Agate (2000)

Dates refer to when stones and minerals were adopted by the state legislature.

MARION / *Native* ▪ *Easy to Moderate*

Collect Fluorite at an *T* Old Open-Pit Mine

The following gems or minerals may be found:

▪ Fluorite and related minerals, fluorescent minerals

The Ben E. Clement Mineral Museum
205 N. Walker Street
Marion, KY 42064
Phone: (270) 965-4263
E-mail: beclement@att.net
www.clementmineralmuseum.org

Open: Day and night digs are scheduled once a month from April to October. Check the museum website for specific dates.

Info: Two digs are scheduled on the mine dumps once each month—one during the day, and a second that night. During the day, dig for fluorite and related minerals. The night digs are for UV fluorescent minerals. Each person must bring his or her own equipment; suggested equipment includes rock hammers, small pick, small sledge hammer, pry bar, insect repellent, a 5-gallon bucket, and a UV light. You may want to bring food, water, and extra clothing as needed.

Rates: The fee for the day dig is $25.00, and the night dig is $40.00. This allows you to collect one 5-gallon bucket of specimens; additional buckets are $20.00 for day digs and $30.00 for night digs. You must make a reservation; attendance is limited to 30 during the day digs, and 20 for the night digs. Registration forms are available on the website. Private digs may be arranged for groups.

Other services available: Mineral digs and annual gem, mineral, and jewelry show the first weekend in June.

Directions: Contact the mineral museum for directions.

BENHAM

Museum

Kentucky Coal Mine Museum
231 Main Street
Benham, KY 40807
Phone: (606) 848-1530
www.benhamky.org

Open: Year round; closed some holidays. 10:00 A.M.–5:00 P.M. Tuesday–Saturday, closed Sundays and Mondays.

Info: Benham was originally a company town owned by International Harvester; the museum is located in the former company commissary. Photographs, memorabilia, videos, and scale models are used to present the story of coal mining in Kentucky. See the floor plan of a typical underground coal mine, and view displays on the formation of coal. (A personal collection of country music legend Loretta Lynn is displayed on the third floor of the museum.) A mine tour is available in Lynch, 2 miles away. There is an opportunity for visitors to obtain a piece of coal for their personal collections.

Admission: Museum: Adults $8.00, seniors (62+) $6.00, college and high school students $5.00, children (3–12) $3.00, children under 3 free. Combination tickets available for museum and Portal 31 Mine Tour. (See entry on next page under Lynch.)

Directions: The museum is located in Benham, which is on State Highway 160, just off of U.S. 119, 25 miles east of Harlan and approximately 55 miles from 25 E.

COVINGTON

Museum

Behringer-Crawford Museum
Devou Park
1600 Montague Road
Covington, KY 41011
Phone: (859) 491-4003
E-mail: info@bcmuseum.org
www.bcmuseum.org

Open: 10:00 A.M.–5:00 P.M. Tuesday–Saturday, 1:00 P.M.–5:00 P.M. Sunday. Closed Mondays and national holidays.

Info: The museum has periodic displays of gems and minerals from their collection, which includes quartz, barite roses, gold, pyrite, and a large geode.

Admission: Adults $9.00, seniors $8.00, children $5.00. Accessible to visitors with mobility impairment. Free parking.

Other services available: Museum store.

Directions: See website for detailed directions.

LEXINGTON

Museum

Headley-Whitney Museum
4435 Old Frankfort Pike
Lexington, KY 40510
Phone: (859) 255-6653
www.headley-whitney.org

Open: 10:00 A.M.–5:00 P.M. Tuesday–Friday, noon–5:00 P.M. Saturday–Sunday. Closed December 20–March 10. Call or check website for Thanksgiving and other holiday hours.

Info: The museum's Jewel Room exhibits George Headley's collection of jewelry, bibelots (decorative art objects), and mounted semi-precious stones. Pieces date from the early 1930s to the late 1970s.

Admission: Adults $10.00, seniors (62+) and students $8.00, children under 8 free. Group rates available.

Other services available: Gift shop.

Directions: Located 6 miles from downtown Lexington. Take New Circle Road (Route 4) to Exit 6, Old Frankfort Pike. At the end of the ramp, follow signs to Frankfort. The museum is located 4 miles from the exit at 4435 Old Frankfort Pike.

LYNCH

Mine Tour

Portal No. 31 Mine Tour
c/o Kentucky Coal Mine Museum
231 Main Street
Benham, KY 40807
Phone: (606) 848-1530
E-mail: kycoalmuseumportal31@
 kctcs.edu
www.portal31.org

Open: 10:00 A.M.–5:00 P.M. Tuesday–Saturday. Mine closes for the winter; check website for dates.

Info: The mine tour is presented in association with the Kentucky Coal Mine Museum in Benham (see previous listing). Mine tours are available by reservation only; make reservations through the museum. Lynch, located 2 miles from Benham, was originally a company town owned by U.S. Steel. The mine tour features a ride into the mine by rail car. Visitors will be outfitted with the traditional protective gear of coal miners. The tour also includes an exhibit on the pony mine days, and displays of mining technology at various time periods are along the tour. The Louisville and Nashville RR station is open to the public with an exhibit on the UMWA. Portal 31 RV park is located directly across from the Portal.

Admission: Portal 31: Adults $15.00, seniors (62+) $12.00, high school and college students $9.00, students (3–12) $6.00, children under 3 free with parents. Combo Portal and Museum:

Adults $20.00, seniors (62+) $16.00, high school and college students $12.00, students (3–12) $9.00, children under 3 free with parents.

Directions: Follow U.S. 119 to Cumberland and follow 160 on to Lynch.

MARION

Museum

The Ben E. Clement Mineral Museum
205 N. Walker Street
P.O. Box 391
Marion, KY 42064
Phone: (270) 965-4263
E-mail: beclement@att.net
www.clementmineralmuseum.org

Open: June–September, 10:00 A.M.–3:00 P.M. Monday–Saturday. January–May and October–December, 10:00 A.M.–3:00 P.M. Wednesday–Saturday. Closed all major holidays and from December 24 to January 1.

Info: Ben E. Clement operated a succession of fluorspar mines in Kentucky during the period of economic growth of the fluorspar industry. Beginning in the 1920s, the mines supplied fluorspar ore to the steel industry for use as flux (a cleaning or flowing agent). In the 1960s, faced with competition from cheaper foreign fluorspar, Clement turned to supplying fluorite and accessory minerals to a growing collector market. During his career he undertook an effort to preserve the mining past. The resulting museum houses thousands of fluorite specimens, accessory minerals, photographs, and other memorabilia.

Admission: Adults $5.00, seniors $4.50, children (6–11) $3.00. Children under 5 free with a paid adult. Group rates and educational classes are available.

Other services available: Gift shop. Mineral digs and annual gem, mineral, and jewelry show the first weekend in June.

Directions: Call for directions. Map available on website. Parking is off the College Street entrance.

OLIVE HILL

Museum

Northeastern Kentucky Museum
1385 Carter Caves Road
Olive Hill, KY 41164
Phone: (606) 286-6012
E-mail: jimplummer@gmail.com
www.kymuseum.org
www.kentuckytourism.com

Open: Spring and fall, 9:00 A.M.–5:00 P.M.; summer, 9:00 A.M.–dark; winter, by appointment only.

Info: The museum has displays of rocks, minerals, jewelry, and fossils.

Admission: Free.

Other services available: Gift shop.

Directions: The museum is located just outside of Olive Hills, KY, near Carter Caves State Resort Park.

TOURIST INFORMATION

State Tourist Agency

Kentucky Department of Travel
  and Tourism
Capital Plaza Tower, 22nd floor
500 Mero Street
Frankfort, KY 40601
Phone: (800) 225-8747; (502) 564-4930
www.kentuckytourism.com

In 1986, freshwater pearls were designated Kentucky's official state gemstone. Pearls are formed by organisms such as oysters, clams, mussels, and even snails. Freshwater pearls can be found in the Tennessee River Valley and the Mississippi River Valley of Kentucky. While most gemstones come from minerals, which are inorganic, pearls belong to a group of gemstones that come from organic sources, created by or formed from living organisms.

LOUISIANA

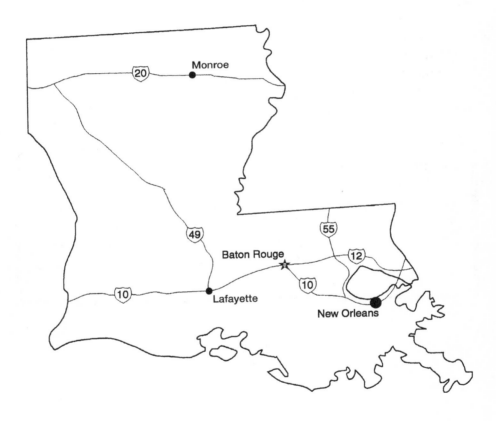

State Gemstone: Cabochon-Cut Oyster Shell (2011)
State Mineral: Agate (1976)

Dates refer to when stones and minerals were adopted by the state legislature.

No information available.

LAFAYETTE

Museum 🏛

Lafayette Science Museum
433 Jefferson Street
Lafayette, LA 70506
Phone: (337) 291-5544
www.lafayettesciencemuseum.org

Open: 9:00 A.M.–5:00 P.M. Tuesday–Friday, 10:00 A.M.–6:00 P.M. Saturday, 1:00 P.M.–6:00 P.M. Sunday.

Info: Meteorite exhibit containing meteorites and tektites from around the world.

Admission: Adults $5.00, seniors (62+) $3.00, children (4–17) $2.00, under 4 free.

Directions: Located in downtown Lafayette. See website for street map.

MONROE

Museum 🏛

Museum of Natural History
University of Louisiana at Monroe
Hanna Hall 1st Floor
Monroe, LA 71209
Phone: (318) 342-1868
www.ulm.edu/mnh

Open: During university semesters, 10:00 A.M.–2:00 P.M. Monday–Thursday; 10:00 A.M.–12:00 P.M. Friday; 10:00 A.M.–2:00 P.M. first Saturday of the month. Closed major holidays and university vacations.

Info: Exhibits of rocks, gems, and minerals, with an emphasis on the natural history of North Louisiana.

Admission: Donations greatly appreciated.

Directions: Located on the first floor of Hanna Hall on University Avenue on the ULM campus.

TOURIST INFORMATION

State Tourist Agency

Louisiana Office of Tourism
Phone: (800) 677-4082
www.louisianatravel.com

Louisiana House Bill 246, signed in 2011, created a new Louisiana state gemstone. The new oyster-shell gemstone is fashioned from a species of mollusk that is bountiful off the Louisiana coast. It is hoped that the new gemstone will be a boost to tourism and the state's struggling seafood industry. As a result of this bill, the former official state gemstone, the agate, found in Louisiana gravel, has been renamed the official state mineral.

MISSISSIPPI

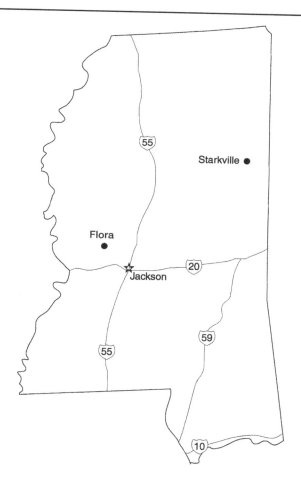

State Stone/Rock: Petrified Wood (1976)

Dates refer to when stones and minerals were adopted by the state legislature.

No information available.

FLORA

Geological Site 🏛

Mississippi Petrified Forest National
   Natural Landmark
124 Forest Park Road
Flora, MS 39071
Phone: (601) 879-8189
E-mail: info@mspetrifiedforest.com
www.mspetrifiedforest.com

Open: 7 days/week. April 1–Labor
Day, 9:00 A.M.–6:00 P.M. Labor Day–
April 1, 9:00 A.M.–5:00 P.M. Closed
Thanksgiving and Christmas.

Info: Huge stone logs along the nature
trail give a glimpse into prehistoric
times. The earth science museum contains a large map with examples of petrified wood found in every state and
other countries. The museum also displays minerals from around the world
and a black–light display of fluorescent
minerals.

Admission: Adults $7.00, seniors $6.00,
students (grades 1–12) $6.00. Admis-
sion price includes use of the picnic
area, museum and displays, and petrified forest nature trail. Gem sluicing is
available at an additional $4.00 per per-
son (+ tax). Pieces of petrified wood can
be purchased at the gift shop.

Other services available: A campground is available: $22.00 (+tax) for
full hookups and $12.00 (+tax) for
primitive camping. Leashed pets are
welcome when accompanied by a
responsible owner.

Directions: Detailed directions can be
obtained on the website.

STARKVILLE

Museum 🏛

Dunn-Seiler Museum
Department of Geosciences
108 Hilburn Hall
P.O. Box 5448
Mississippi State, MS 39762-5448
Phone: (662) 325-3915
www.geosciences.msstate.edu/
   museum.htm

Open: By appointment during the school year.

Info: Mineral and rock collections, including meteorites. Displays on mineral families and properties, the three classes of rocks, plate tectonics, and Mississippi geology.

Admission: Free.

Directions: Call for directions.

SECTION 3: Special Events and Tourist Information

TOURIST INFORMATION

State Tourist Agency

Visit Mississippi
P.O. Box 849
Jackson, MS 39205
Phone: (601) 359-3297
www.visitmississippi.org

While most gemstones are mineral materials, there are organic materials and organic materials that have been mineralized which are considered gemstones. Petrified wood is one such gemstone in which the organic materials in the wood have been replaced by minerals. Petrified wood is not organic, but it does preserve an organic structure. Some other organic materials considered gemstones are pearl, amber, and coral. Mineralized organisms include petrified wood, fossil coral, dinosaur bone, and other fossilized organisms.

MISSOURI

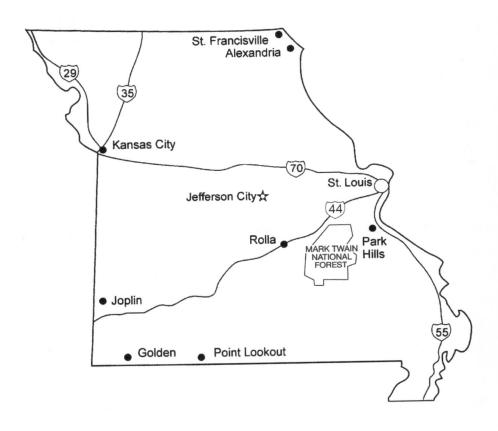

State Mineral: Galena (1967)
State Rock: Mozarkite (1967)

Dates refer to when stones and minerals were adopted by the state legislature.

Recreational Mineral and Rock Collecting in the Mark Twain National Forest

The occasional surficial removal of small amounts of rocks or minerals for personal use only is permitted in the Mark Twain National Forest. No new ground disturbance is permitted. For information on the forest, see www.fs.usda.gov/mtnf. The rockhounding area is in the Potosi/Fredericktown Ranger District. National forest office: Mark Twain National Forest, 401 Fairgrounds Road, Rolla, MO 65401, (573) 364-4621. Potosi/Fredericktown Ranger District office: 10019 West State Highway 8, Potosi, MO 63664, (573) 438-5427.

SECTION 1: Fee Dig Sites and Guide Services

ALEXANDRIA / *Native • Easy to Moderate*

Dig Your Own Geodes 𝑇

The following gems or minerals may be found:

- **Crystal-lined geodes**

Sheffler's Rock Shop and Geode Mine
Tim Sheffler
R.R.1, Box 171
Alexandria, MO 63430
Phone: (660) 754-1134
E-mail: shefflerrockshop@hotmail.com

Open: April 1–December 1, 9:00 A.M.–5:00 P.M., 6 days/week (closed Sundays). Call ahead for conditions at the mine, since weather affects digging at the mine.
Info: Geode mine digging; easily accessible strip mine. You can find geodes lined with minerals such as calcites, pyrites, barites, selenite needles, dolomite, sphalerite, kaolinite, aragonite, and goethite. You must provide your own equipment; you will need a bucket, pry bar, pick, chisel, or rock hammer. A shovel may be useful. Bring plenty of drinking water.
Rates: $25.00 per person for 50 pounds of geodes; $0.75/pound for over 50 pounds. Call to make reservations.

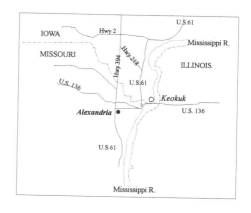

Geodes

Geodes are round stones that have a crystal-filled hollow in the middle. They began as gas-filled bubbles in lava, or as soft areas in rock, which were eroded. Over time, water containing minerals seeped into the hollow and evaporated, leaving the minerals behind as crystals.

Geodes

The geodes from eastern Missouri are lined with a layer of chalcedony, a form of quartz, which holds the geode together. These geodes have clear and smoky quartz crystals inside, with different mineral buildups in them. The buildups could be clear or white calcite, iron pyrite, goethite, or pink dogtooth calcite with brown calcite crystals; some have fluorescent crystals.

Other services available: Rock shop includes a display of opened geodes, mineral specimens, and fossils.

Directions: On U.S. 61, 6 miles west of Alexandria; 3 miles south of Wayland; ⅛ mile north of the intersection of Route 27 and U.S. 61. See Facebook for maps and detailed directions.

ST. FRANCISVILLE / *Native • Easy to Moderate*

Dig Your Own Geodes *T*

The following gems or minerals may be found:

▪ **Geodes**

Hill Top Mud Bogg
St. Francisville, MO 63465
Phone: (660) 754-6361
E-mail: r_k_alvis@hotmail.com
www.randkfireandice.com

Open: Contact in advance for dig dates.
Info: Dig for geodes.
Rates: Call for rates.
Directions: ½ mile south of the Iowa state line on Hwy 27.

SECTION 2: Museums and Mine Tours

GOLDEN

Museum 🏛

Golden Pioneer Museum
Highway 86 and "J"
P.O. Box 216
Golden, MO 65658
Phone: (417) 271-3300

Open: Mid-April–mid-November, 10:30 A.M.–4:30 P.M. Tuesday–Saturday.

Info: The museum displays minerals from around the world, including what is reported to be the world's largest turquoise carving, made from a 68-pound nugget. The museum also contains what is reported to be the largest double terminated single quartz crystal (1,250 pounds), a single cluster of quartz crystals weighing over 4,000 pounds, and a large display of amethyst, fluorite crystals, and selenite clusters. Recent donations of gem and mineral collections have increased the museum exhibits.

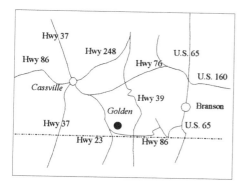

Admission: Free. Donations appreciated.

Directions: Located in Golden at the intersection of Highway 86 and "J," on Table Rock Lake, between Branson, MO, and Eureka Springs, AR.

JOPLIN

Museum 🏛

Everett J. Ritchie Tri-State
    Mineral Museum
Schifferdecker Park
P.O. Box 555
Joplin, MO 64802
Phone: (417) 623-1180
www.joplinmuseum.org

Open: 10:00 A.M.–7:00 P.M. Tuesday, 10:00 A.M.–5:00 P.M. Wednesday–Saturday. Closed Sunday and Monday.

Info: The museum has exhibits of ore specimens and mining artifacts depicting the story of lead and zinc mining in the Tri-State (Kansas, Missouri, and Oklahoma) area.

Admission: Adults $2.00, family rate $5.00/family, free Tuesdays. Group rates available.

Other services available: Schifferdecker Park also contains a swimming pool, playgrounds, picnic tables and shelters, tennis and basketball courts, and a golf course.

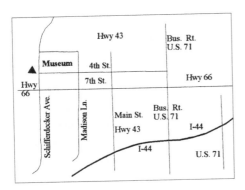

Directions: Located in the Joplin Museum Complex. From I-44, take exit 4 for Coyote Drive north (MO 43) to Schifferdecker Avenue to Schifferdecker Park.

KANSAS CITY

Museum 🏛

University of Missouri–Kansas City
Richard L. Sutton, Jr., MD
Museum of Geoscience
Rm. 271 Robert H. Flarsheim Hall
5110 Rockhill Road
Kansas City, MO 64110
Phone: (816) 235-1334
E-mail: geosciences@umkc.edu
www.cas.umkc.edu/geosciences/
geomuseum.asp

Open: 8:30 A.M.–4:30 P.M. Monday–Friday, when school is in session.

Info: The museum has the following displays: a large collection of petrified wood; agates, including several dozen specimens from the basalt lavas of Lake Superior; thirty crystals containing liquid inclusions; more than 500 matched cabochons of semiprecious stones and unusual stones; selenite crystals, minerals from the Joplin mining district; specimens from the Kansas City area; and a spectacular fulgurite, several feet long, formed when lightning struck the ground and fused the soil and shale.

Admission: Free.

Directions: See website.

PARK HILLS

Museum 🏛

Missouri Mines State Historic Site
P.O. Box 492
Highway 32
Park Hills, MO 63601
Phone: (573) 431-6226; (800) 334-6446
www.mostateparks.com/momines.htm

Open: April–November, 10:00 A.M.–4:00 P.M. Monday–Saturday, noon–6:00 P.M. Sunday; December–March, 10:00 A.M.–4:00 P.M. Friday–Saturday, noon–5:00 P.M. Sunday. Closed major holidays.

Info: The museum has 1,100 specimens of minerals, ores, and rocks on display. The collection is based on an original collection by Missouri's first great mineral collector, Fayette P. Graves. The mineral gallery has 27 cases, some of which are antique display cases built in the 1920s. Eleven of the cases contain a collection demonstrating the systematic classification of minerals. The museum

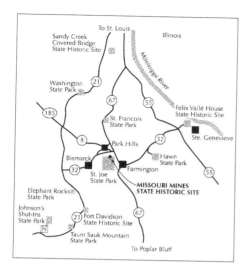

also has a fluorescent mineral room, dominated by minerals from Franklin, N.J., zinc mines. There is also a display featuring Missouri minerals as well as specimens of other minerals easily collected in the state.

The museum has a gallery featuring some of the underground mining machinery used in area mines. In addition, some of the mining buildings at the museum complex are being restored, and historical interpretations and walking tour trails will be installed.

The area is known as the "Old Lead Belt." Major corporation lead mining occurred between 1864 and 1972, and the area was the nation's leading producer of lead for 60 of those years.

The museum is handicapped accessible.

Special note: The mine mill area designated as Missouri Mines State Historic Site is part of the St. Joe State Park, where there is a lead advisory for off-

road vehicle riding in effect.

Admission: Adults $4.00, students (6–12) $2.50, children under 6 free.

Directions: On the south side of Highway 32, 1½ miles west of the junction with U.S. 67 in Park Hills.

POINT LOOKOUT

Museum 🏛

Ralph Foster Museum
College of the Ozarks
1 Cultural Court
Point Lookout, MO 65726
Phone: (417) 690-3407
E-mail: museum@cofo.edu
www.rfostermuseum.com

Open: February–mid-December, 9:00 A.M.–4:30 P.M. Monday–Saturday. Closed Thanksgiving week.

Info: The museum has several displays of minerals and rocks. These include a display of minerals in the Ozarks, which has varied types of quartz, jasper, graphite, mica, pyrite, copper, and others. There are also displays of many types of geodes, quartz crystals, and over 150 different minerals. There is a display of mineral spheres and of fluorescent minerals.

Admission: Adults $6.00, seniors (62+) $5.00, high school age and under free.

Directions: On the college campus in Point Lookout two miles south of Branson.

ROLLA

Museum

Mineral Museum–Missouri University
of Science and Technology
Department of Geology and Geophysics
129 McNutt Hall
1400 N Bishop Avenue
Rolla, MO 65409
Phone: (573) 341-4616

Open: 8:00 A.M.–4:30 P.M. Monday–
Friday, when school is in session.
Info: The museum has about 3,500
specimens of minerals, ores, and rocks
from 92 countries and 47 states on display. The collection is based on an original collection from the state of Missouri exhibit displayed at the 1904 Louisiana Purchase Exposition, along with minerals donated by Mexico and the Missouri geology collection from the 1893 Chicago World Fair. Displays of gemstones and gold specimens from Peru are among the museum highlights.
Admission: Free.
Directions: On the university campus in Rolla.

SECTION 3: Special Events and Tourist Information

TOURIST INFORMATION

State Tourist Agency

Missouri Division of Tourism
P.O. Box 1055
Jefferson City, MO 65102
Phone: (800) 519-2100; (573) 751-4133
www.visitmo.com

NORTH CAROLINA

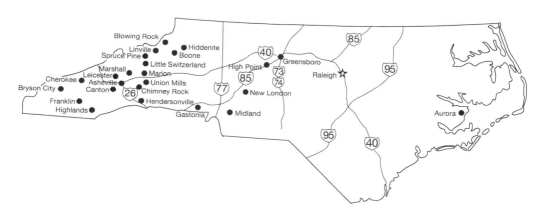

State Gemstone: Emerald (1973)
State Stone/Rock: Unakite/Granite (1979)

Dates refer to when stones and minerals were adopted by the state legislature.

Introduction to Gem Mining in
North Carolina: Cowee Valley Mines

The list of gems and minerals native to this valley in Franklin is said to include the following:

Rubies	Quartz crystal
Sapphires	Rutile
Rhodolite, almandite,	Kyanite
and pyrope garnet	Mica
Periodot	Feldspar
Sillimanite	Moonstone

Although Native Americans probably collected gemstones in the Cowee Creek Valley long before 1800, gemstones found in the valley in the gravel of the Caler Fork of Cowee Creek, a tributary of the Tennessee River, soon after the Civil War resulted in a systematic search of the area. Rubies and sapphires were found in the gravel of the Caler Fork for a distance of 3 miles. These finds led to commercial exploration by two developers in particular, the American Mining and Prospecting Co. and the United States Ruby Mining Co. These developers searched for the source of the gems found in the creek gravel; however, to this day, this source has never been discovered. One theory is that the gem-bearing matrix has completely washed out of the ancient Appalachian Mountains, and consequently there is no mother lode in the range. All that remains are the crystals that settled into the relatively protected beds of the valley.

There are only two places in the world where sandy gravel yields blood-red rubies. One is in the Mogok Valley in Burma, India, and the other is in the Cowee Valley of North Carolina. The blood-red rubies are considered to be more valuable than diamonds of equal quality.

The commercial ventures, meeting failure, pulled out of the area in the early 1900s, and the land was divided into small farms. The sands of the valley were never subjected to intensive commercial mining, thus leaving a wealth of material for the collector. In response, several mines opened to offer mining of gems from the Cowee Valley gravel.

Actually, calling them *mines* is somewhat misleading. There are no tunnels or shafts or any of the equipment associated with underground mining. The gem-bearing ore is located along the Caler Fork of Cowee Creek in a layer of mud, clay, and gravel, which varies from 2 to 10 feet in depth.

Most mine owners excavate the ore in a shallow surface mine and supply the excavated ore to collectors in buckets or bags; the collector washes the same dirt he or she would have dug, but without the work of digging and transporting the ore to the flume. At the time of this writing, the authors have located only one mine in the Franklin area where a collector can still dig his or her own gem ore from the source. There are also mines where prospectors can screen natural gravel, which the mine owners/operators say has not been salted or enriched.

SECTION 1: Fee Dig Sites and Guide Services

BLOWING ROCK / *Native and Enriched • Easy*

Sluice for Gems ⟁

The following gems or minerals may be found:

• Ruby, emerald, sapphire, garnet, topaz, amethyst, citrine, peridot, moonstone, rhodolite, aquamarine, turquoise, ametrine, rose quartz, smoky quartz

Doc's Rocks Gem Mine
111 Mystery Hill Lane
Blowing Rock, NC 228605
Phone: (828) 264-4499
E-mail: goldsmith@docsrocks.net; or
    doc@docsrocks.net
www.docsrocks.net

Open: Year round, 7 days/week, 9:30 A.M.–5:00 P.M. Closed Christmas day.
Info: Gemstone and fossil ore from several different mines in the Appalachian Mountain range (North Carolina, Georgia, Tennessee, Virginia) are mixed, then put in buckets. If you don't find anything of value in your first bucket, the mine will provide second bucket free. There is seeded ore available in the gift shop.
Rates: Gem ore buckets $12.00–$55.00.
Other services available: Rockhound tours; gemstone cutting.
Directions: On U.S. 321, approximately one mile north of the Blue Ridge Parkway.

BOONE / *Enriched • Easy*

Screen Your Own Gems and Minerals ⟁

The following gems or minerals can be found:

• Topaz, garnet, aquamarine, peridot, ruby, star sapphire, amethyst, citrine, smoky quartz, tourmaline, emerald

Foggy Mountain Gem Mine
Nik Vames
4416 NC Highway 105 S
Boone, NC 28607
Phone: (828) 963-GEMS (4367)
www.foggymountaingems.com

> The Old Pressley Sapphire Mine is the source of the Star of the Carolinas, a 1,445-carat sapphire, and the Southern Star, a 1,035-carat sapphire.

Open: All year, 10:00 A.M.–5:00 P.M.; closed major holidays.

Info: Screen your own gems and minerals. Foggy Mountain provides buckets of gem ore that you screen in their flume. Indoor flume for use during bad weather. All equipment is provided.

Rates: Buckets containing both local and non-local ore range in price from $30.00–$325.00.

Other services: Gift shop, gem cutting.

Directions: Located on Highway 105, just south of Boone, NC.

BRYSON CITY / *Native and Enriched • Easy*

Sluice for Gems 𝝉

The following gems and minerals can be found:

- Rubies, emeralds, sapphires, garnets, topaz, amethyst, citrine, peridot, moonstone, rhodolite, aquamarine, turquoise, ametrine, rose quartz, smoky quartz

Nantahala River Gem Mine
Carolina Outfitters, Inc.
12121 Highway 19 West
Bryson City, NC 28713
Phone: (800) 468-7238; (828) 488-6345
E-mail: raft@carolinaoutfitters.com
www.nantahalarafts.com

Open: Memorial Day–Labor Day, 10:00 A.M.–5:00 P.M. daily; rest of the year by reservation.

Info: Sluice a bucket of gem dirt in a covered, lighted gem sluice.

Rates: Gem ore bucket: $45.00. Can be shared by 2 miners.

Other services available: River rafting, cabin rentals, horseback riding,

Directions: On Highway 19 West. Detailed directions are available on website.

CANTON / *Native Material • Easy*

Sluice for Gems 𝝉

The following gems or minerals may be found:

- Sapphires (pink, blue, gray, white, bronze), zircon, garnet, mica

Old Pressley Sapphire Mine
George and Brenda McCannon
240 Pressley Mines Road
Canton, NC 28716
Phone: (828) 648-6320
www.oldpressleymine.com

Open: 7 days/week. Summer, 9:00 A.M.–5:00 P.M. Winter, 9:00 A.M.–4:00 P.M.

Info: Buy buckets of ore from the mine (native stones only) or prospect in mine tailings.

Rates: Buckets of ore range from $10.00–$100.00. Prospecting: April–October $25.00, November–March $20.00. Group rates available.

Other services available: Refreshments, restrooms, picnic area, mountain scenery, rock shop, souvenirs.

Directions: From I-40, take exit 33 and travel north on New Found Road for ½ mile, turn left, and follow the signs to the mine.

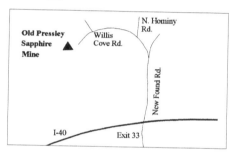

Info: Enriched native ore is sold by the bag or the bucket.

Rates: Bag of gold ore: $5.00, bag of gem ore: $4.00–$10.00.

Other services available: Gem, jewelry, and rock shop. Jeweler and lapidary on site.

Directions: Located on Highway 441 North by the river, about ½ mile south of the Great Smoky Mountains National Park on the Cherokee Indian Reservation.

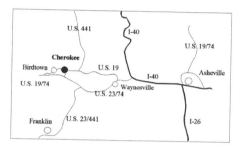

CHEROKEE / *Enriched Native Ore* ▪ *Easy*

Pan for Gold or Gems T

The following gems or minerals may be found:

- Rubies, sapphire, emerald, amethyst, topaz, garnet, citrine, smoky quartz, gold

Smoky Mountain Gold and Ruby Mine
Highway 441 North
Cherokee, NC 28719
Phone: (828) 497-6574
E-mail: info@smgrm.com
www.smgrm.com

Open: 7 days/week, March–November, 10:00 A.M.–6:00 P.M.

CHIMNEY ROCK / *Enriched* ▪ *Easy*

Screen Your Own Gems T
and Minerals

The following gems or minerals can be found:

▪ Aquamarine, emerald, ruby, peridot, garnet, quartz, agate, hematite, amethyst, sodalite, and more

Chimney Rock Gemstone Mine
397 Main Street
Chimney Rock, NC 28720
Phone: (828) 625-5524
E-mail: info@chimneyrockgemmine.com
www.chimneyrockgemmine.com

Mining in North Carolina

Essential equipment is provided by the mine: the flume, a trough with running water, and the sluice box, a wooden tray with a wire mesh screen for a bottom.

Mining at North Carolina mines basically involves putting a small amount of the gem ore (soil) in the sluice box, and then holding and gently shaking the box in the flume so that the dirt is washed away and the stones are left. The stones are then examined, and gems or minerals or stones that the miner wants are removed and placed in a container or small bag. The remaining material is dumped out, and more ore placed in the box and sluiced.

When mining in the natural soil, you may not always find a large quantity of stones, and those found may not be of gem quality or worth cutting. But for the true rockhound, the thrill is in knowing there is always the possibility that one may find that special gem or mineral at a mine, and searching until it is found. Many mines in the area have begun "enriching" or "salting" their native soil to provide additional material to find. Gems and minerals of pretty colors from around the world are mixed in with the ore in the bucket or bag. Children especially enjoy finding and identifying these added materials. When looking for a mine, ask if the gem-bearing soil is native or enriched. (See page 21 for a definition of enriched or salted material.)

Open: 10:00 A.M.–6:00 P.M. Saturday and Sunday, 10:00 A.M.–8:00 P.M. Monday–Friday.

Info: Screen your own gems and minerals. Chimney Rock Gemstone Mine provides buckets of gem ore that you screen in their flume. Some dirt comes from local mines. All equipment is provided.

Rates: Buckets range in price from $8.00–$500.00.

Other services: Gift shop.

Directions: Located in the village of Chimney Rock, NC, east of Asheville on 64 and Highway 74A.

FRANKLIN / *Native • Easy to Moderate*

Sluice for Gems *T*

The following gems or minerals may be found:

• Rubies, sapphires, sillimanite, rutile, moonstone, rhodolite garnet, quartz, kyanite, and pyrope garnet

Cherokee Ruby and Sapphire Mine
41 Cherokee Mine Road
Franklin, NC 28734
Phone: (828) 349-2941
www.cherokeerubymine.com

Open: May 1–late October, 9:00 A.M.–4:00 P.M. Monday–Saturday; noon–5:00 P.M. Sunday, weather permitting. Mid-September–end of the season closed Wednesdays. Check website for other closings. *Note:* Last "dig your own" customer accepted at 2:00 P.M. No admission to mine after 4:00 P.M.

Info: Native gem-bearing soil dug from the mine is provided in buckets for sluicing. The mine also offers a "dig your own." Be aware that this is a strenuous physical activity. Well-behaved pets permitted.

Rates: Cash only. Adults $25.00 (includes 2 starter buckets), children 5 and under free (no separate mining screen). Additional buckets $5.00 each.

Other services available: Dig your own: $30.00 to fill six buckets; $10.00 to fill an additional four buckets.

Directions: Approximately 12 miles from Franklin. Take Highway 28 north from Franklin to Cowee Baptist Church. Just past the church, turn right on Cowee Creek Road. Stay on Cowee Creek Road to the fork of Ruby Mine Road and Leatherman Gap Road. Turn right and follow Ruby Mine Road to the Cherokee Ruby Mine.

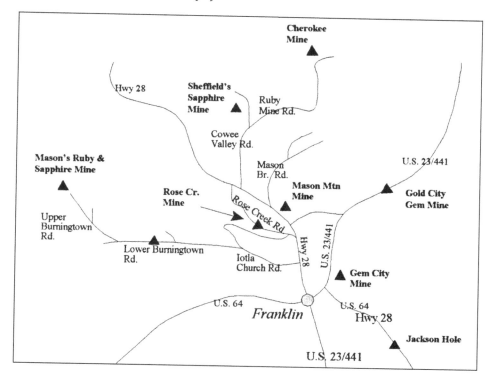

Sluice for Gems *T*

*The following gems or minerals
may be found:*

▪ Rubies, sapphires, garnets, tourmaline, smoky quartz, amethyst, citrine,
moonstone and topaz

Cowee Mountain Ruby Mine
6771 Sylva Road (441 North)
Franklin, NC 28734
Phone: (828) 369-5271
E-mail: cowee@yahoo.com
www.coweemtnrubymine.com

Open: March 1–December 1, 10:00
A.M.–5:00 P.M. 7 days/week. Closed
Thanksgiving Day.

Info: Soil containing gems native to the
region and enriched material from elsewhere can be purchased and sluiced.
Help is provided to beginners, and
there is a covered, lighted flume for
sluicing. Pets are welcome on a leash.

Rates: Bags and buckets of gem ore
range from $5.00 to $500.

Other services available: Gem cutting,
rock and mineral shop, clean restrooms.

Directions: North of Franklin on Highway 441.

Sluice for Gems *T*

*The following gems or minerals
may be found:*

▪ Rubies, sapphires, garnets, emeralds,
tourmaline, smoky quartz, amethyst, citrine,
moonstone, topaz, aquamarine, gold

Gold City Gem Mine
Curtis and Susan Rhoades
9410 Sylva Road, Highway 441 North
Franklin, NC 28734
Phone: (800) 713-7767
E-mail: goldcity1@windstream.net
www.goldcityamusement.com

Open: May–November, 9:00 A.M.–5:00
P.M. 7 days/week; winter: 9:00 A.M.–5:00
P.M. Wednesday–Sunday.

Info: Soil containing gems native to the
region can be purchased and sluiced.
Gold panning is offered. Help is provided, and there is a covered flume for
sluicing, which has been specially constructed for handicapped needs. There
is a heated flume in the winter.

Rates: Gem dirt buckets: $15.00 and
up. Gold dirt buckets: $25.00. Call or
check website for details. Group and
students rates are available.

In 1996, a woman found a 1½-pound sapphire in a 5-gallon bucket at
the Mason Mountain Rhodolite and Ruby Mine. That same year, Gem
City Gold Mine yielded a 1,061-carat sapphire and a 1,104-carat ruby.

Other services available: Clean restrooms, snacks and cold drinks, and picnic tables.

The jewelry and gift shop offers gifts and souvenirs, custom jewelry made on the premises, and jewelry repair. The rock shop sells natural rocks and minerals.

Directions: Six miles north of Franklin on Highway 441.

FRANKLIN / *Native and Enriched Ore • Easy*

Sluice for Gems 𝄆

The following gems or minerals may be found:

• Rhodolite garnets, rubies, sapphires, kyanite, crystal quartz, smoky quartz, moonstones

Cowee Gift Shop and Mason
   Mountain Mine, aka TJRocks
Tom and Ginger Johnson
5315 Bryson City Road
Franklin, NC 28734
Phone: (828) 524-4570
E-mail: tjrocks@tjrocks.org
www.tjrocks.org

Open: March–November: 9:00 A.M.–5:00 P.M. Monday–Saturday; 1:00 P.M.–5:00 P.M. Sunday.

Info: Offers native dig only and gem buckets with added gems from other locations.

Rates: Gem buckets: $30.00–$1,000.00. Dig your own pile: whole day $30.00, half day $20.00.

Other services available: Gift shop, gem cutting (cabbing and faceting), crafts and jewelry, restrooms.

Directions: From Franklin, take Highway 28 north approximately 5½ miles and look for the mine.

FRANKLIN / *Native and Enriched •
Easy to Moderate*

Dig and Sluice for Gems 𝄆

The following gems or minerals may be found:

• Sapphires (all colors) and pink and red rubies, garnets, rutile, kyanite, silimanite, mica, and quartz

Mason's Ruby and Sapphire Mine
The Klatt Family
6961 Upper Burningtown Road
Franklin, NC 28734
Phone: (828) 369-9742
E-mail: miner.al@masonsmine.com
www.masonsmine.com

Open: March–October, 9:00 A.M.–5:00 P.M. 7 days/week. November–February, call for availability.

Info: Only mine in the area where you can dig and sluice your own native gem-bearing dirt. All equipment is furnished at no charge, and help is provided for all. It is strongly recommend that you do not wear open-toe shoes in the mine. Dig from a pile of enriched gem ore, then screen your diggings in the flume, or buy a pre-dug bucket of gem dirt, then screen it in the flume. A night ultraviolet mine tour is also offered. Sapphires glow bright red under long-wave UV light and can be seen on the ground; no digging required. This tour lasts 45 minutes to one hour, and begins one hour after sunset; guaranteed to find a minimum of 50 carats of sapphires for the group. Available all year, weather permitting. Must be scheduled in advance.

Rates: Native mine: Adults $30.00, children (6–11) $15.00. Enriched mining: Dig your own: $25.00 for 5 buckets. Pre-dug buckets $25.00–$100.00. Emerald buckets $40.00 each. Night ultraviolet tour $120.00 for up to four miners; $15.00 each additional miner, to a maximum of 6. No children under 8. Equipment provided. $60.00 to mine using your own light.

Other services available: Picnic tables, portable toilets, free parking, primitive camping. Pets welcome.

Directions: Take Highway 28 north from Franklin to Airport Road. Turn left, and follow signs 8½ miles to the mine.

FRANKLIN / *Native and Enriched Ore • Easy to Moderate*

Dig and Sluice for Gems *T*

The following gems or minerals may be found:

- Rubies, sapphires, garnets, moonstones, amethysts, smoky quartz, citrine, rose quartz, topaz, quartz crystals

Rose Creek Mine and Rock Shop
The Sterrett Family
115 Terrace Ridge Drive
Franklin, NC 28734

Phone (828) 349-3774
E-mail: rocks@rosecreekmine.com
www.rosecreekmine.com

Open: April 1–October 31, 9:00 A.M.–5:00 P.M., 6 days/week. Closed Sunday. Last new miners admitted at 4:00 P.M.

Info: Dig your own gems in the gem tunnel.* Help is provided for beginners, and there is a covered flume for panning rain or shine. Enriched buckets can also be purchased.

* Gem tunnel: dirt from the mine is placed in a covered shed for digging.

Rates: Super buckets and concentrates $50.00–$300.00. Group rates available. Gem tunnel: $10.00 to fill two buckets; refills $5.00 each.

Other services available: Lapidary supplies and equipment, gem rough for cutting and specimens available. Clean restroom, snacks, picnic tables.

Directions: Take Highway 28 north from Franklin. Turn left on Bennett Road at the Little Tennessee River.

FRANKLIN / *Native and Enriched as Indicated • Easy*

Sluice for Gems *T*

The following gems or minerals may be found:

- Native rubies and sapphires, or enriched material from around the world

Sheffield Mine
385 Sheffield Farm Road
Franklin, NC 28734

Gems from the Cowee Valley and Around the World

The Cowee Valley remains a location where natural precious gemstones can be found, but is also a location where you can learn identification of gem specimens from around the world.

The lure of gems has brought people to the Cowee Valley for over 400 years, beginning with Spanish explorers in the 1500s. In recent times, the area has seen the growth of the tourism industry and many "salted" mines have sprung up. These "salted" locations may be actual mine sites or just a flume line set up alongside the road. At these "mines" you can sluice for gemstones from around the world. Besides the educational value of identifying these finds, some of the material can be cabbed or faceted. In addition, they provide practice for sluicing native materials.

On a trip to the Cowee Valley, after only two hours of sluicing, the author's daughter, Annie, found a 12-carat sapphire which could be cabbed to a 7½-carat gem. The authors also found several smaller facetable sapphires — proving to them, at least, that there are natural gems to be found at the mines. While mining, the authors saw another gentleman who had just found a beautiful pigeon-blood-red ruby.

Phone: (828) 369-8383
E-mail: sheffieldmine@yahoo.com
www.sheffieldmine.com

Open: April 1–October 31, 10:00 A.M.– 5:00 P.M. It is advisable to arrive at least 2½ hours before closing for native mining.

Info: The only native Star Ruby mine in all of the Americas; the mine has been in continuous operation for over 100 years.

Rates: Adults (15–60) $20.00, all others $15.00. Each admission includes three starter buckets of dirt. Additional buckets: native dirt $3.00 or 2/$5.00, enriched rainbow dirt $5.00 or 2/$8.00. Many types of specialty buckets, such as emerald buckets, available. Group discounts available; call for more information. Cash only. Check website for updates on credit card availability.

Other services available: Stone cutting is available, along with snacks and cold drinks.

Directions: Take Highway 28 north from Franklin. Turn right on Cowee Creek Road, then, after a mile and a quarter, turn left on Leatherman Gap Road. The sign to the mine is on the left after you cross the little bridge.

HENDERSONVILLE / *Enriched · Easy*

Sluice for Gems *T*

The following gems or minerals may be found:

- Rubies, sapphires, emeralds, quartz crystals, citrine, amethyst, garnets, aventurine, sodalite, opal, fluorite, aquamarine, and more

Elijah Mountain Gem Mine
2120 Brevard Road
Hendersonville, NC 28739
Phone: (828) 692-6560
www.elijahmountain.com

Open: 10:00 A.M.–5:00 P.M. daily. Closed some holidays.

Info: Pan for gems; indoor flume available for rainy or winter weather.

Rates: Buckets range from $10.00–$140.00; specialty buckets are available.

Other services available: Picnic tables; gift shop.

Directions: Located just 2½ miles west of Hendersonville on Hwy 64 West. From Asheville, take I-26 East to Exit 49 B and go 5 miles on Hwy 64 West. The mine is on the left. From Brevard, take Hwy 64 East for about 12 miles. The mine is on the right.

HIDDENITE / *Native or Enriched · Easy to Moderate*

Dig and Sluice for Gems *T*

The following gems or minerals may be found:

- Sapphires, garnets, emeralds, hiddenite, smoky quartz, rutile, tourmaline, clear quartz, aquamarine, sillimanite, and others

Emerald Hollow Mine—Hiddenite Gems, Inc.
Dottie Watkins
P.O. Box 276
484 Emerald Hollow Mine Drive
Hiddenite, NC 28636
Phone: (828) 625-1125;
(828) 632-3394 (sluiceway)
E-mail: info@hiddenitegems.com
www.hiddenitegems.com

Open: All year, 8:30 A.M.–sunset, 7 days/week; closed Thanksgiving, Christmas Eve, and Christmas Day.

Info: Sluice for gems in buckets of pre-dug dirt, dig your own, or search for

---

What Is Hiddenite?

Hiddenite is a transparent, emerald-green variation of the mineral spodumene. Spodumene is a member of a group of rocks known as pyroxenes and occurs in granite pegmatites, together with minerals such as tourmaline and beryl. Hiddenite is found *only* in Alexander County and is rarer and more valuable than emerald.

gems in the creek. Help is provided, and there is a covered flume for sluicing.

Rates: Sluicing at the flume: $5.00/person admission, includes one bucket of mine dirt. Sluicing/creeking: $10.00/person, includes one bucket of ore. Combination (includes digging or prospecting at the mine, as well as sluicing and creeking) $20.00/person. Set of digging tools can be rented for $5.00 with a $10.00 refundable deposit. Additional buckets at the sluice range up to $100.00/bucket. For serious diggers at the mine with serious equipment (more than buckets, shovels, and small rock hammers), the digging permit is $45.00/person per day, and the equipment must be approved by mine personnel before being used.

Other services available: Beverages, picnic tables, lapidary shop, gift shop, and restrooms.

The mine also offers special educational programs for students. The trip includes surface collection, searching creeks for gems, and sluicing a bucket of ore.

Directions: The mine is approximately 20 minutes from I-40 in Statesville. From I-40, take US-64/NC-90 (exit 148) off I-40. Go west on US-64 towards Taylorsville for approximately 11.2 miles. Turn right on Old Mountain Rd. (There will be a small "Hiddenite Next Right" sign at the turnoff.) Proceed through downtown Hiddenite to a stop sign where the road ends. Turn left

and look for a sign and Emerald Hollow Mine Drive immediately on the right. Turn right onto the gravel drive. Observe caution signs when approaching the mine.

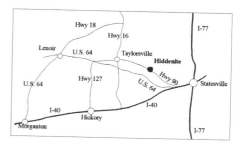

HIGHLANDS / *Native or Enriched Ore · Easy*

Sluice for Gems

The following gems or minerals may be found:

- **Rubies, sapphires, garnets, tourmaline, smoky quartz, amethyst, citrine, moonstone, topaz**

Jackson Hole Trading Post and
   Gem Mine
9770 Highlands Road
Highlands, NC 28741
Phone: (828) 524-5850
E-mail: jacksonholenc@gmail.com
www.jacksonholegemmine.com

Open: 7 days/week, May 1–November 1, 10:00 A.M.–4:00 P.M.

Info: Purchase soil containing gems native to the region and buckets of enriched material, and sluice for gems. Help is provided, and there is a covered flume for sluicing.

Rates: Buckets of ore: Small: $10.00 each. Ultimate: $30.00 each, or 2 for $50.00. Bucket Club: $100.00 each, comes with a $45.00 free cut of a gemstone from your bucket.

Other services available: Clean restrooms, gem shop, gem cutting.

Directions: East of Franklin on US 64 and Highway 28, halfway between Franklin and Highlands.

LEICESTER / *Native and Enriched •* *Easy to Moderate*

Pan for Gold and Sluice for Gems *T*

The following gems or minerals may be found:

- Rubies, sapphires, emeralds, rose quartz, citrine, amethyst, garnets, fluorite, moonstone, smoky topaz, calcite, blue kyanite, gold

Randall Glen Gem Mine
96 Randall Cove Road
Leicester, NC 28748
Phone: (828) 683-5758
E-mail: info@RandallGlen.com
www.randallglen.com

Open: 10:00 A.M.–4:30 P.M. Tuesday–Sunday; last bucket at 4:00 P.M. From December 1 through April 1, call beforehand to be sure the mine is open.

Info: Dig a bucket of gem dirt at the mine shaft and sluice it at the mine's flume. Keep all that you find. Pan for gold in the creek. All equipment is provided.

Rates: Gem mining: Buckets range from $10.00–$150.00. There is even a wooden chest for $1,000.00. Gold panning: $12.50 or $25.00 per person per day.

Other services provided: Picnicking, hiking, horseback riding, gem dirt or gold dirt shipped by mail, luxury vacation cabin rentals.

Directions: The mine is 15 miles northwest of Asheville. Randall Glen is part of the Pisgah National Forest.

MARION / *Native • Moderate*

Mine Your Own Gold and Gems *T*

The following gems or minerals may be found:

- Gold, emeralds, aquamarine, moonstone, feldspar crystals, garnets, smoky quartz, rose quartz, blue quartz, quartz crystals, and tourmaline

Carolina Emerald Mine and Vein
   Mountain Gold Camp
Donald Davidson
1694 Polly Spout Road
Marion, NC 28752
Phone: (828) 738-9544

Open: All year, 7 days/week. Water flume opens at 8:30 A.M.

Info: Pan for gold at this mine, and you may also discover gems. Gold recovery equipment can be rented, including highbankers or a dredge. Gold can be found in the river gravel; gems can also be found there, or can be dug from the pegmatite.

Rates: Gem sluicing: adults $25.00, children under 11 $15.00. Gold panning and gem hunting in the creek (hand panning and digging only) $5.00.

Other services available: Gift shop.

Campground: Campsites are available for $15.00/night; $2.50 per each person more than three.

Directions: From Interstate 40, take exit 85, and drive south on Route 221 for 6½ miles. Turn left onto Polly Spout Road and drive 1¾ miles to the mine.

MARION / *Enriched Ore ▪ Easy*

Sluice for Gems or Pan for Gold 𝑇

The following gems or minerals may be found:

▪ **Gold and gemstones**

The Lucky Strike
Liz McCormick
251 Lucky Strike Drive
Marion, NC 28752
Phone: (828) 738-4893
www.luckystrikegoldandgem.com

Open: All year, 8:00 A.M.–7:00 P.M., except Christmas Day.

Info: All equipment is supplied, and help is available. Instructions on panning are provided. Highbankers and sluice boxes are available for rent.

Rates: Gem buckets range from $10.00–$100.00. Gold nugget bags $25.00–$500.00. Gold buckets $10.00 and $15.00. Crevising for gold in the river: $5.00/day. Highbanking equipment for rent. Dredging: $12.00–$25.00/day, based on nozzle size.

Other services available at the mine: Restaurant; campground. BBQ and Music Jamboree one or two times a year. Call for dates and cost.

Directions: 5.3 miles south of I-40 on Route 221, then turn left on Polly Spout Road.

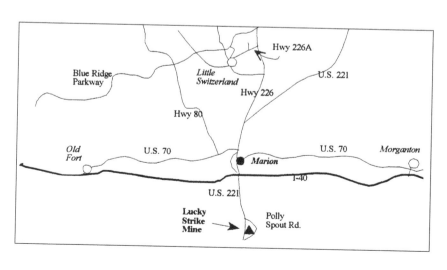

MARSHALL / *Native • Difficult*

Take a Horseback Ride to an Old Garnet Mine or Dig Your Own *T*

The following gems or minerals may be found:

▪ Garnets

Little Pine Garnet Mine
Sandy Bottom Trail Rides
1459 Caney Fork Road
Marshall, NC 28753
Phone: (800) 959-3513, or (828) 649-3464; (828) 649-3788 (evenings)
E-mail: info@sandybottomtrailrides.net
www.sandybottomtrailrides.net

Open: All year; closed Thanksgiving and Christmas. Rides normally leave at 10:00 A.M., noon, and 2:00 P.M., but other times can be arranged. Digging at the mine is from 8:00 A.M.–4:00 P.M.

Info: Rides of three or more hours go to the Little Pine Garnet Mine, where you can dig for gem quality garnets, and keep all that you find. Those who prefer can go directly to the mine for garnets. Horse and wagon rides to the mine can be arranged. For fee-digging only, you must first call to obtain permission and fill out a waiver before you will be allowed to collect at the mine. When you pay, you will be issued a ticket.

Rates: 3-hour trail ride, $85.00; 4-hour ride, $125.00. Fee-digging only $25.00/day. Fee allows collection of 1 gallon of garnet.

Directions: From Asheville, NC, take Highway 19-23 north, then take Highway 25-70 west at Exit 19A. Travel 12.6 miles, then turn left on Little Pine Road, and travel 3.8 miles to Caney Fork Road. Signs are provided.

MIDLAND / *Native • Easy*

Pan for Gold *T*

The following gems or minerals may be found:

▪ Gold

Reed Gold Mine State Historic Site
9621 Reed Mine Road
Midland, NC 28107
Phone: (704) 721-4653
E-mail: reed@ncdcr.gov
www.nchistoricsites.org/reed

Open: Year round, 9:00 A.M.–5:00 P.M. Tuesday–Saturday. Closed Sundays, Mondays, and most major holidays.

Info: Gold panning is available only during the summer months (April 1–October 31) and closes at 4:00 P.M. See full entry in Section 2 for details on the Reed Gold Mine State Historic Site.

Panning fees: $3.00 + tax/pan of ore. Instruction included. Group rate available.

Directions: From I-85 or I-77 in Charlotte, take I-485 to the NC 24/27 (Albemarle) exit #41. Turn left at the top of the ramp to take NC 24/27 east. Go 11 miles east through the community of Midland and across the Rocky River. Watch for the large brown Reed Gold

Mine, NC Historic Site signs. Just across the Rocky River, turn left onto Reed Mine Road. Follow this road for 2½ miles. Entrance is on the right.

NEW LONDON / *Native • Easy to Moderate*

Pan for Gold *T*

The following gems or minerals may be found:

- Gold

Mountain Creek Gold Mine
Bill Tucker
41787A Gurley Road
New London, NC 28127
Phone: (704) 463-7749;
(704) 985-8374 (cell)
www.mtcreekgold.com

Open: All year, 7 days/week, 8:00 A.M.–5:00 P.M.

Info: Originally part of the Crowell Mine, you can pan washed or unwashed dirt, or use a highbanker or dredge to look for gold.

Rates: Call for current prices.

Other services available: Camping: $10.00/night for camp site; $15.00/ night for small camper; $20.00/night for camper sites with sewer, water, and dump station. Cabins and campers available for rental—call for info.

Directions: From I-85 take the Southmont exit, and go south on Highway 8 for 28 miles, to Highway 49. Go south on Highways 8/49 4 miles, then follow Highway 8 when it splits from Highway

49. Drive 2 miles to Baldwin Road, turn left on Baldwin Road, and follow it to the end at Highway 740. Turn left on Highway 740 and travel 1½ miles to Gurley Road (first right). Turn right on Gurley Road, travel 2 miles to the sign for the mine, and follow the signs to the creek.

SPRUCE PINE / *Native and Enriched Ore • Easy to Difficult*

Sluice for Gems *T*

The following gems or minerals may be found:

- Over 100 different rocks, minerals, and gems, including rubies, sapphires, aquamarine, emeralds, garnets, smoky quartz, beryl, uranium, and fluorescent minerals

Emerald Village
Mailing address:
P.O. Box 98
McKinney Mine Road
Little Switzerland, NC 28749
Physical address:
331 McKinney Mine Road
Spruce Pine, NC 28777
Phone: (828) 765-6463
E-mail: info@emeraldvillage.com
www.emeraldvillage.com

Open: 7 days/week. April, 10:00 A.M.–4:00 P.M., May, 9:00 A.M.–5:00 P.M.; summer (Memorial Day Weekend–Labor Day Weekend), 9:00 A.M.–6:00 P.M., September and October, 9:00 A.M.–5:00 P.M. Closed November–March.

Info: Emerald Village is located at two gem mines: Big McKinney and Bon Ami Mines. See Section 2 on Mine Tours for more information.

Sluice enriched gem-bearing soil at a shaded flume. All equipment is supplied, and help is available. Emerald Village gives you the opportunity to prospect and dig for emeralds in the dumps at the Crabtree Emerald Mine. Dig for $20.00/day by permit only—purchase permit at Emerald Village. Only hand tools are allowed, and you can keep anything you find. Must sign a waiver of liability at Emerald Village. The mine is remote and primitive, and there are no facilities of any kind. Requires digging rocks and breaking boulders.

In addition to gem mining, Emerald Village now offers gold panning, using ore from a North Carolina gold mine that has produced gold for over 100 years. The mine staff will show you how to pan and how to collect any gold in your pan.

Rates: Gem buckets range in price from $10.00 to $500.00. Gold buckets range from $10.00–$500.00. Group rates available by reservation only. Mineral collecting on the McKinney Mine Dumps: Adult $20.00, children (12 and under) $10.00.

Other services available: North Carolina Mining Museum; mine tour; picnic area; snacks and drinks; restrooms; cab shop; gemstone identification; gem cutters at work; rock and gift shop offering mining material, cut gems, finished jewelry, rocks and minerals, souvenirs, lapidary equipment; Discovery Mill exhibits and blacklight tours.

Directions: Take exit 334 (Little

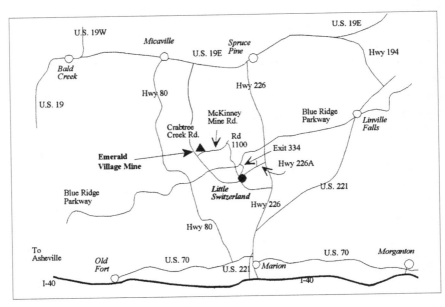

Switzerland) off the Blue Ridge Parkway. At the bottom of the exit ramp, loop around and go under the parkway. Drive approximately 1 mile, then turn left onto McKinney Mine Road (the first paved left). The gemstone mine is at Emerald Village, 2 miles down the road, on the right.

Note: Most mapping systems do not recognize Little Switzerland. To find Emerald Village on MapQuest or GPS, use the street address: 331 McKinney Mine Road, Spruce Pine, NC 28777.

SPRUCE PINE / *Enriched Native Ore* • *Easy*

Sluice for Gems 𝑇

The following gems or minerals may be found:

• Sapphire, crabtree emeralds, Wiseman and Brushy Creek aquamarine, rubies, tourmaline, topaz, garnets, amethyst, citrine, moonstone

Gem Mountain Gemstone Mine
13780 Highway 226 South
Spruce Pine, NC 28777
Phone: (888) 817-5829
E-mail: info@gemmountain.com
www.gemmountain.com

Open: All year except January and February, 6 days/week. 9:00 A.M.–5:00 P.M. until Memorial Day, 9:00 A.M.–6:00 P.M. until Labor Day. Closed Sundays.

Info: Sluice-enriched gem-bearing soil provided in buckets. All equipment is furnished.

Gem Mountain also offers trips to 2 area mines where you can dig your own gems. Equipment, transportation and a guide are furnished. Whatever you find, you get to keep. The Brushy Creek Aquamarine Mine is a relatively new mine that has been producing aquamarine, garnet, golden beryl, tourmaline, and some smoky quartz. The Hoot Owl Mine is a historic mine that has been dormant for many years. Material from other mines will be brought to this location and mixed with material from the Hoot Owl Mine. Years ago the Hoot Owl Mine was worked mainly for feldspar, but aquamarine specimens as large as 150 pounds have been reported along with some small emeralds.

Rates: No admission fee. Buckets are sold at the flume line. Prices range from $20.00 each for a 2-gallon bucket to $125.00 for a 5-gallon bucket. Reservations are not normally required at the flume line unless you have a large group. Prices are subject to change.

Trip fee: Brushy Creek Aquamarine Mine: Adults $75.00, children (11 and under) $35.00. Check with Hoot Owl Mine for fees. At least 6 people required for mine tours. Mine tours are by reservation only; call 888-817-5829. Trips run April–October, Monday–Saturday, weather permitting. Leave from Gem Mountain around 10:00 A.M. and return around 2:00 P.M. Taking small children is discouraged; if you do bring them, keep your eyes on children at all times. A waiver must be signed before anyone goes on the trip.

Other services available: Displays of local minerals and specimens from all over the U.S. and the world, gem cutting, jewelry making, gift shop, sandwich and ice cream shop, picnic area.

Gem Mountain General Store featuring quilts, crafts, candies, gifts, and more. Open 6 days/week from March through December. Groups welcome.

Directions: Located between Spruce Pine and the Blue Ridge Parkway, 1 mile north of the North Carolina Mineral Museum.

SPRUCE PINE / *Enriched Native Ore • Easy*

Sluice for Gems *T*

The following gems or minerals may be found:

- Emeralds; rubies; aquamarine; tourmaline; topaz; garnets; amethyst; rose, clear, rutilated, and smoky quartz; citrine; beryl

Rio Doce Gem Mine
14622 Highway 226 South
Spruce Pine, NC 28777
Little Switzerland, NC 28749
E-mail: ejriodoce@att.net
www.riodoce.com

Open: Easter–October 31, 9:00 A.M.– 6:00 P.M., 7 days/week.

Info: Sluice enriched gem-bearing soil. The gem material is from local area mines and from famous mines in Brazil. All equipment is supplied, and help is available.

Rates: Call for prices.

Other services available at the mine: Picnic area, free stone identification, gem and gift shop, mineral specimens, gem cutting school, rough stones, gem cutting, jewelry.

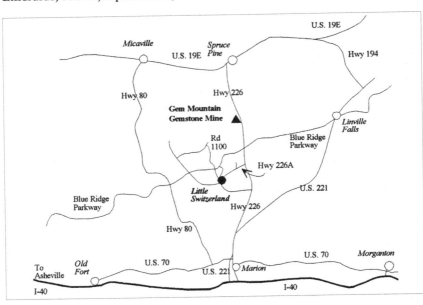

Spruce Pine Area Mines

Another major gem-hunting area in North Carolina is Spruce Pine in Mitchell County. Just as the Cowee Valley is known for rubies and sapphires, the Spruce Pine area is known for emeralds and aquamarine. The only working emerald mine in North America is in Mitchell County. Approximately 250 different kinds of minerals and gems are found there. About 46% of the feldspar used in the production of porcelain, china, and glass in the U.S. comes from Mitchell County. The following gems and minerals are said to be found in mines in the Spruce Pine area:

Beryl (including emerald)	Oligoclase
Hyalite	Moonstone
Autunite	Apatite
Torbernite	Uranium minerals
Tourmaline	Kyanite
Garnet	Quartz, rose and smoky
Columbite	Actinolite
Sphalerite	Spodumene
Thulite	Talc
Epidote	Aquamarine
Amethyst	Citrine
Hiddenite	

Directions: On Highway 226, ½ mile north of the Blue Ridge Parkway.

SPRUCE PINE / *Enriched Native Ore ▪ Easy*

Sluice for Gems *T*

The following gems or minerals may be found:

▪ Many local gems, such as rubies, sapphires, garnets, aquamarine, smoky quartz, moonstone, amethyst, crystal quartz, and emeralds

Spruce Pine Gem Mine
15090 Highway 226 S
Spruce Pine, NC 28777
Phone: (828) 765-7981

E-mail: sprucepinegemmine@gmail.com
www.sprucepinegemmine.com

Open: Hours vary seasonally.

Info: Spruce Pine Gem Mine has been mining the mountains of North Carolina for over 200 years. Use a covered flume to sluice enriched native gem-bearing soil. All equipment is furnished and experienced help is available.

Rates: Gem buckets: $15.00–$125.00.

Other services available: Free gem identification, gem cutting, custom jewelry, local mineral specimens, gift shop.

Directions: Exit 331 off the Blue Ridge Parkway on Highway 226 (next to the North Carolina Museum of Minerals).

UNION MILLS / *Native and Enriched • Easy*

Pan for Gold and Gemstones T

The following gems or minerals may be found:

- **Gold, gemstones**

Thermal City Gold Mine
5240 U.S. 221 N. Highway
Union Mills, NC 28167
Phone: (828) 286-3016
E-mail: info@thermalcitygoldmine.com
www.thermalcitygoldmine.com
www.huntforgold.com

Open: March 15–October 31, 8:30 A.M.–5:00 P.M. 7 days/week.

Info: Site of a family-operated 1830s-era gold mine. Fine gold and an occasional nugget are found; a 7.26-ounce nugget was found in 1993. The site consists of a 1-mile section of the Second Broad River and about 60 acres of placer gravel deposits. Material for gold panning is brought up from the river using a backhoe, and this panning material is not enriched or salted. Gemstone panning material is enriched with native material.

Panning fee: Gold panning: $10.00/day per person. Gem buckets: $5.00–$75.00. Trommel, highbanker, and regular loads $50.00–$60.00, delivered 9:00 A.M. and 1:00 P.M. No loads delivered on Mondays or Tuesdays.

Other services available: Complete line of prospecting equipment, on-site gem flume and rock shop, campground (cabin rentals available), riverside camping, hot showers, most sites have electricity.

Rates: $20.00/night for primitive sites, $25.00/night for full hookup sites. Long-term rates available.

Directions: Take U.S. 221, exit 85 off I-40 at Marion, and go south toward Rutherfordton for approximately 9 miles. Look for the sign on the left and follow the signs to the mine.

SECTION 2: Museums and Mine Tours

ASHEVILLE

Museum 🏛

Asheville Museum of Science
43 Patton Avenue
Asheville, NC 28801
Phone: (828) 254-7162
info@colburnmuseum.org
www.colburnmuseum.org

Open: All year, 10:00 A.M.–5:00 P.M. Tuesday–Saturday, 1:00 P.M.–5:00 P.M. Sunday.

Info: The museum is home to an extraordinary permanent collection of gems and minerals. Opened in 1960 through a bequest by mineral collector Burnham Standish Colburn, the museum's exhibits feature North Carolina minerals (including the rare gem hiddenite), cut gemstones, spectacular crystals from the Elmwood mine, and minerals and gems from around the world. Other exhibits include geology, meteorology, and plate tectonics.

The museum hosts an annual Gem Fest each June featuring gem and mineral dealers from all over the U.S. The museum hosts an after-school Junior Rockhounds Club and summer camps.

Admission: Adults $6.50; children (6–16), students, and seniors $5.50; under 6 free.

Directions: From Interstate 240, take exit 5A/Merrimon Avenue, and follow the signs for Highway 25 South for four blocks to Patton Avenue and turn right. From Interstate 40, take exit 50 (Highway 25, South Asheville) and continue on Highway 25 north through Biltmore Village for three miles. Parking is available streetside or in the parking garage adjacent to Rankin Avenue. Handicapped accessible.

AURORA

Museum 🏛

Aurora Fossil Museum
P.O. Box 352
400 Main Street
Aurora, NC 27806-0352
Phone: (252) 322-4238
E-mail: aurfosmus@yahoo.com
www.aurorafossilmuseum.org

Open: 9:00 A.M.–4:30 P.M. Monday–Saturday, and open Sundays from 12:30 P.M.–4:30 P.M. March 1–Labor Day. Closed major holidays.

Info: Collections include marine fossils (including teeth from the large shark *C. megalodon*) discovered in the neighboring phosphate mine. Other displays include Native American artifacts, fluorescent mineral room, rocks & minerals, and fossils from around the world. Fossil digging also available in museum's park.

Admission: Free; donations are gladly accepted.

Directions: Call for directions.

Museums and Mine Tours · 115

Museum

Franklin Gem and Mineral Museum
  (The Old Jail Museum)
c/o The Gem and Mineral Society of
  Franklin, NC, Inc.
25 Phillips Street
Franklin, NC 28734
Phone: (828) 369-7831
E-mail: franklingemsociety@gmail.com
www.fgmm.org

Open: May–October, noon–4:00 P.M.
Monday–Saturday; November–April,
noon–4:00 P.M. Saturday only. Run by
volunteers, so hours may change. Call
ahead to be sure.

Info: The museum is located in the
old Macon County Jail behind Rankin
Square. It is operated by the Gem and
Mineral Society of Franklin, N.C., Inc.

Collections include mineral specimens from North Carolina and around
the world, and feature gemstones, rocks,
minerals, Native American artifacts, and
related items.

Admission: Free; donations welcome.

Directions: At the intersection of Main
Street and Phillips Street in Franklin.
Take a left and the museum is behind
Rankin Square or left off of Palmer
Street onto Phillips Street. Park on Phil-
lips Street or in museum parking lot.

Museum

Ruby City Gems & Minerals
130 E. Main Street
Franklin, NC 28734
Phone: (828) 524-3967 or
(800) 821-RUBY
E-mail: gems@rubycity.com
www.rubycity.com

Open: April–December, 10:00 A.M.–5:00
P.M. Tuesday–Saturday. January–March,
check website or call for hours.

Info: The museum is located in the
Ruby City Gem and Mineral Store on
East Main Street, and can be entered
from the shop.

The museum features a collection of
500 spheres, cut, ground, and polished
by the original owner of the Gem Shop.
In addition, there is a collection of fluorescent minerals, local minerals, as well
as worldwide specimens, boasting the
world's largest sapphire and an extensive pre-Columbian artifacts collection.

Admission: Free.

Directions: On East Main Street in
Franklin.

GASTONIA

Museum

Schiele Museum
1500 East Garrison Boulevard
Gastonia, NC 28054
Phone: (704) 866-6908
www.schielemuseum.org

Open: 8:00 A.M.–5:00 P.M. Monday–Saturday, 1:00–5:00 P.M. Sunday; closed major holidays.

Info: The museum has a number of displays, including North Carolina gems and minerals, gold, properties of minerals, examples of gem and mineral classification systems, and faceting.

Admission: Adults $7.00, students and seniors $6.00, children under 3 free. Discounts are available for City of Gastonia residents, and museum members are free. Group rates available; call (704) 854-6676.

Directions: Located just 2 miles off of I-85. Check website for directions.

GREENSBORO

Museum 🏛

Greensboro Science Center
4301 Lawndale Drive
Greensboro, NC 27455
Phone: (336) 288-3769
E-mail: info@natsci.org
www.natsci.org

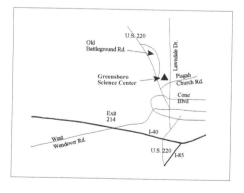

Open: All year, 9:00 A.M.–5:00 P.M. 7 days/week. Closed major holidays.

Info: The collection of minerals is located in the Gem and Mineral Gallery. There are over 50 faceted N.C. mineral specimens on display.

Admission: Adults $12.50, children (3–13) and seniors (65+) $11.00, children under 2 free.

Directions: Off U.S. 220, on the north side of the city.

HENDERSONVILLE

Museum 🏛

Mineral & Lapidary Museum of
    Henderson County, Inc.
400 N. Main Street
Hendersonville, NC 28792
Phone: (828) 698-1977
E-mail: info@mineralmuseum.org
www.mineralmuseum.org

Open: 1:00 P.M.–5:00 P.M. Monday–Friday, 10:00 A.M.–5:00 P.M. Saturday; closed some holidays.

Info: Exhibits cover mineralogy, geology, paleontology, and associated lapidary art. View the Hendersonville meteorite. Geode cracking service available for a moderate fee.

Admission: Free; donations and gift shop purchases appreciated.

Directions: Corner of North Main Street and 4th Avenue, Hendersonville.

LINVILLE

Museum

Grandfather Mountain Nature Museum
P.O. Box 129
2050 Blowing Rock Highway
Linville, NC 28646
Phone: (828) 733-1059 or (800) 468-7325
E-mail: nature@grandfather.com
www.grandfather.com

Open: Spring and fall, 9:00 A.M.–6:00 P.M.; winter, 9:00 A.M.–5:00 P.M.; summer, 8:00 A.M.–7:00 P.M., 7 days/week. Closed Thanksgiving and Christmas.

Info: Grandfather Mountain has been singled out by the United Nations as a biosphere reserve because of its significance to the biodiversity of the planet. It is a privately owned and protected wildlife sanctuary, which is home to 73 rare or endangered species.

The nature museum exhibits represent most of the historically important mines and miners of the last 100 years. Through these exhibits the history of rockhounding in N.C. is traced. Each specimen is identified as to where and by whom it was found.

Displays include most of the gems and minerals found in N.C., organized by common mineral families and location. Families include quartz, garnet, radioactives, kyanite, beryl, and corundum; locations include the Foote Mineral Company in Kings Mountain and the Hiddenite area. The exhibit includes choice N.C. specimens with a focus on emeralds and the largest amount of N.C. gold on display to the public in the state.

Admission: Adults $20.00, seniors (60+) $18.00, children (4–12) $9.00, children under 4 free. Group rates available.

Other services available: Gift shop, family restaurant, hiking and picnicking, highest suspension footbridge in America, hourly nature films.

Directions: Off U.S. 221, one mile south of the Blue Ridge Parkway, and two miles north of Linville.

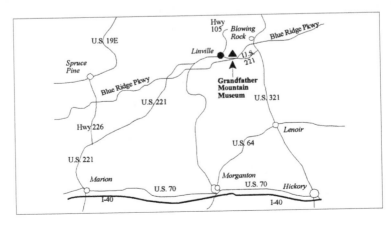

MIDLAND

Mine Tour/State Historic Site

Reed Gold Mine State Historic Site
9621 Reed Mine Road
Midland, NC 28107
Phone: (704) 721-4653
E-mail: reed@ncdcr.gov
www.nchistoricsites.org/reed

Open: Year-round, 9:00 A.M.–5:00 P.M. Tuesday–Saturday. Closed Sundays, Mondays, and most major holidays.
Info: Site of the first documented discovery of gold and the first intensive mining operation in the United States as part of the nation's first gold rush. The mine was in operation from 1803 to 1912. It was noted for the large size and purity of its gold nuggets. Gold discovery spread to nearby counties and into other southern states. North Carolina maintained a leadership in gold production until 1848, when it was eclipsed in importance by the great rush to California. Reed Gold Mine Historic Site is operated by the N.C. Department of Cultural Affairs, Resource Division of Archives and History, Historic Sites Section.

The site's visitors' center features an introductory film and exhibits on historical events, gold mining processes, and equipment. Other features include:

Mine tour: A guided tour is conducted through a restored section of the old underground mine.

Equipment tour: A tour is available of the 19th-century stamp mill used to crush ore (a mechanical engineering landmark).

Walking trails: Trails wind through the historic mining area past several shafts and tunnels and an exhibit interpreting the 1850s Engine House.
Admission: Free.
Directions: From Charlotte, take N.C. Routes 24/27 (Albemarle Road) into Cabarrus County, and travel until you cross Route 601. After crossing 601, look for Reed Mine Road; turn left and travel approximately 3 miles to the site on the right.

SPRUCE PINE

Museum

Museum of North Carolina Minerals
214 Parkway Maintenance Road
Milepost 331 on the Blue Ridge Parkway
Spruce Pine, NC 28777
Phone: (828) 765-2761
www.nps.gov/blri/planyourvisit/
  museum-of-north-carolina-minerals-
  mp-331.htm

Open: 7 days/week, 9:00 A.M.–5:00 P.M. Closed Thanksgiving, Christmas Eve, Christmas Day, and New Year's Day.
Info: The museum is operated by the National Park Service; specimens have been provided by local individuals and commercial enterprises.

The museum provides an introduction to the region's wealth of mineral resources. The primary focus is on minerals mined in the Spruce Pine district.

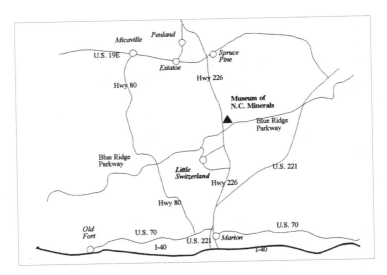

Included are gemstones, fluorescent minerals, and rare radioactive rocks. Featured are quartz, local gold, and several commercial rocks and minerals, including famed feldspar. Various stages of refinement and everyday objects made from end products are displayed. The facing of the museum building itself is made of quartzite from a quarry on nearby Grandfather Mountain.

The Mitchell County Chamber of Commerce, located inside the museum, provides visitors with information about nearby attractions in western N.C.

Park rangers are at the museum during the summer.

Admission: Free.

Directions: Located at milepost 331 on the Blue Ridge Parkway, at the junction with NC Highway 226.

SPRUCE PINE

Museum/Mine Tour

North Carolina Mining Museum and
   Mine Tour
Emerald Village, Inc.
Mailing address:
P.O. Box 98
Little Switzerland, NC 28749
Physical address:
331 McKinney Mine Road
Spruce Pine, NC 28777
Phone: (828) 765-6463
E-mail: info@emeraldvillage.com
www.emeraldvillage.com

Open: 7 days/week. April, 10:00 A.M.–4:00 P.M.; May, 9:00 A.M.–5:00 P.M.; summer (Memorial Day Weekend–Labor Day Weekend), 9:00 A.M.–6:00 P.M.; September and October, 9:00 A.M.–5:00 P.M. Closed November–March.

Info: Take a walking tour of a now-closed feldspar mine. The mine was originally developed by the Bon Ami Company to mine feldspar as an ingredient for its polishing cleaner. Quartz and mica were also found in the mine, along with a complex uranium mineral known as samarskite, specimens of which can be seen in the mine ceiling. Because of the presence of uranium minerals in the mine, many of the rocks contain trace amounts of uranium, making them highly fluorescent when exposed to ultraviolet light. Emerald Village offers special black light tours on selected nights between May and October. Starting time varies with the season, as the tour must begin after dark. Check the website for specific weekends when the tour will be held. Reservations not necessary.

The museum tells the story of the miners, the mining, the ores and minerals found in the mine, the equipment used, and the Bon Ami Mining Company. There are displays of antique equipment, with explanations of how they operated. The displays are in the visitors center, at the entrance to the mine, and inside part of the mine as well. Also included is a replica of a 1920s mining store.

Admission: Bon Ami Mine: Adults $8.00, seniors (60+) $7.00, students $6.00. Black light tour: Adults $15.00, students $10.00.

Directions: Take exit 334 (Little Switzerland) off the Blue Ridge Parkway. At the bottom of the exit ramp, turn right onto Chestnut Grove Road and go under the parkway. Drive approximately 1 mile then turn left onto McKinney Mine Road. The museum is at Emerald Village, 2 miles down the road, on the right.

SECTION 3: Special Events and Tourist Information

ANNUAL EVENTS

Mother's Day Gemboree, Franklin, NC 🐾

Held during Mother's Day weekend in May.

Macon County Gemboree, Franklin, NC 🐾

Second-oldest gem and mineral show in the southeast. Held for 4 days in July.
Admission: Adults $3.00, children 12 and under free. Phone: (888) 337-7529

"Leaf-Looker" Gemboree, Franklin, NC 🐾

Held for 3 days in October.
Admission: Adults $2.00, children (under 12) free.
Info: All three events are sponsored by the Gem and Mineral Society of Franklin, NC, Inc., and by the Franklin Area Chamber of Commerce. They are held at:

Macon County Community Building
U.S. 441 South
Franklin, NC

All three events offer rough and cut gems, minerals, jewelry, equipment, supplies, books, dealers, and exhibits.

For more information:
Franklin Area Chamber of Commerce
425 Porter Street
Franklin, NC 28734
Phone: (828) 524-3161; (866) 372-5546
Fax: (828) 369-7516
E-mail: facc@franklin-chamber.com
www.franklin-chamber.com

ANNUAL EVENT

North Carolina Mineral and Gem Festival, Spruce Pine, NC

Retail shows held for 4 days at the end of July and/or the beginning of August.

Admission: Adults $3.00, children (under 10) free.

Info: The festival is held at 12121 Highway 226 in Spruce Pine, at the Spruce Pine Commons Shopping Center.

For information on the festival and on gem mines in Mitchell County, contact:
Mitchell County Chamber of Commerce
P.O. Box 858
Spruce Pine, NC 28777
Phone: (828) 765-9033
www.mitchellcountychamber.org
www.ncgemfest.com

TOURIST INFORMATION

State Tourist Agency

North Carolina Department of Commerce
Division of Tourism, Film and Sports Development
Phone: (800) VISIT-NC or (800) 847-4862
www.visitnc.com

SOUTH CAROLINA

State Gemstone: Amethyst (1969)
State Stone: Blue Granite (1969)

Dates refer to when stones and minerals were adopted by the state legislature.

SECTION 1: Fee Dig Sites and Guide Services

ANTREVILLE / *Native · Moderate*

Dig Your Own Quartz *T*

The following gems or minerals may be found:

- Milky white quartz crystals, skeletal quartz, amethyst (less common), smoky quartz (less common), pseudomorphs

Diamond Hill
Gina Clary
P.O. Box 158
Belton, SC 29627
Phone: (864) 934-3744
E-mail: dhmine@rocketmail.com
www.diamondhillmine.com

Open: Every day of the year. Sign-in is 9:00 A.M.–2:00 P.M. May dig until dark. If you plan to arrive after 2:00 or wish to camp, make arrangements by calling.

Info: Collect crystals from dump/spoil piles over approximately 5 acres. May also search for veins. Bring gloves, tools (screwdriver, shovel, rake, rock hammer, sledge hammer, pick), boxes, newspaper, drinks, food, snacks, sunscreen, first aid kit. Reservations not required.

Admission: Adults $20.00, seniors (65+) and teens (13–17) $10.00, children (12 and under) $5.00. Camping is free.

Other services available: Outhouse, but no running water. Convenience store about 5 minutes away.

Directions: Take exit 21 off I-85. Go south on US 178 for about a mile and bear right onto SR 28. Stay on SR 28 all the way to Antreville. Drive past Crawford's store till you see Emmanuel Baptist Church and turn right onto SR 284. After 2.3 miles turn right onto Suber Road. Go .7 miles and you will see a gravel road on your right, Diamond Mine Road (be careful not to turn into the gravel driveway just before this road). Turn right. The mine entrance will be on your right after half a mile.

GREENVILLE / *Enriched · Easy*

Sluice for Gems *T*

The following gems or minerals may be found:

- Gems and minerals from around the world

Greenville Gemstone Mine
205 N. Main Street
Greenville, SC 29601
Phone: (864) 283-6300
www.greenvillegemstonemine.com
Note: This is a secondary location of the Chimney Rock Gemstone Mine in Chimney Rock, N.C.

Open: All year, 10:00 A.M.–7:00 P.M. Sunday–Thursday, 10:00 A.M.–9:00 P.M. Fridays and Saturdays.

Rates: Buckets range from $8.00 to $50.00.

Other services available: Store sells jewelry and natural wonders like gems, minerals, and fossils from around the world.

Directions: Inside the storefront across from Atlanta Bread Co. on Main Street in downtown Greenville.

Mineral Collecting and Gold Panning in the Francis Marion and Sumter National Forests

Rockhounding and mineral specimen collecting in the Francis Marion and Sumter National Forests allows for the occasional removal of small amounts of material by hand from surface exposures of rock and quartz veins. Check website for additional information and contacts (www.fs.usda.gov/scnfs).

The Long Cane and Andrew Pickens districts are the two primary areas of interest for recreational gold panning. A letter of authorization is required before you can pan for gold. Prospectors must submit a request for a letter of authorization to the district before arriving. Andrew Pickens Ranger District: 112 Andrew Pickens Circle, Mt. Rest, SC 29664; (864) 638-9568; 8:00 A.M.–12:00 P.M. and 12:30 P.M.–4:30 P.M. Monday–Friday. Long Cane Ranger District: 810 Buncombe Street, Edgefield, SC 29824; (803) 637-5396; 8:00 A.M.–4:30 P.M. Monday–Friday.

SECTION 2: Museums and Mine Tours

CHARLESTON

Museum

The Charleston Museum
360 Meeting Street
Charleston, SC 29403
Phone: (843) 722-2996
E-mail: info@charlestonmuseum.org
www.charlestonmuseum.org

Open: All year, closed major holidays.

12:00 P.M.–5:00 P.M. Monday–Saturday, 1:00 P.M.–5:00 P.M. Sunday.

Info: The museum has a small display of gems and minerals, including some from Russia.

Admission: Adults $12.00, youth (13–17), children (3–12) $5.00, children under 3 free.

Directions: The museum is located in Charleston on Meeting Street at John Street.

CLEMSON

Museum

Bob Campbell Geology Museum
Clemson University
140 Discovery Lane
Clemson, SC 29634
Phone: (864) 656-4600
E-mail: bcgm@clemson.edu
www.clemson.edu/geomuseum

Open: 10:00 A.M.–5:00 P.M. Monday–Saturday, 1:00 P.M.–5:00 P.M. Closed university holidays.

Info: The museum houses over ten thousand rocks, minerals, fossils, lapidary objects (carvings, gemstones), and artifacts, including mining equipment from locations in South Carolina and around the world. A research library and reference collection is available. Staff members are available to identify specimens during the museum's two open houses (Earth Day in April and Museum ID Day in September), or by appointment. The museum is handicapped accessible.

Admission: Free, but donations encouraged and appreciated. Suggested donation $3.00/person.

Directions: The museum is located in the South Carolina Botanical Garden, on the east side of Clemson University's campus. The main entrance is located on Perimeter Road between Highway 76 and Cherry Road. If using GPS, you may need to use 103 Garden Trail as the address.

COLUMBIA

Museum

McKissick Museum
College of Arts and Sciences
University of South Carolina Campus
816 Bull Street
Columbia, SC 29208
Phone: (803) 777-7251
www.cas.sc.edu/mcks

Open: All year, 8:30 A.M.–5:00 P.M. Monday–Friday, 11:00 A.M.–3:00 P.M. Saturday. Closed Sundays and all university and state holidays.

Info: The museum has exhibits on natural history study, geology, and gemstones.

Admission: Free.

Directions: The museum is located at the head of the Horseshoe area on the USC Campus, near Bull and Pendleton Streets.

COLUMBIA

Museum

South Carolina State Museum
301 Gervais Street
Columbia, SC 29201
Phone: (803) 898-4921
www.scmuseum.org

Open: 10:00 A.M.–5:00 P.M. Monday, Wednesday, and Friday; 10:00 A.M.–8:00 P.M. Tuesday; 10:00 A.M.–6:00 P.M. Saturday; noon–5:00 P.M. Sunday. Closed major holidays.

Info: The museum has displays of gems and minerals, mostly as part of other exhibits. Others are found as part of a hands-on natural history exhibit called "NatureSpace." The museum is fully handicapped accessible.

Admission: Adults $8.95, seniors (62+) $7.95, children (3–12) $6.95, infants 2 and under free. Military discount $1.00 off.

Directions: The museum is located at 301 Gervais Street, beside the historic Gervais Street Bridge and just a few blocks west of the state capitol in downtown Columbia.

SECTION 3: Special Events and Tourist Information

TOURIST INFORMATION

State Tourist Agency

South Carolina Department of Parks, Recreation and Tourism
1205 Pendleton Street
Columbia, SC 29201
Phone: (803) 734-1700
www.discoversouthcarolina.com

TENNESSEE

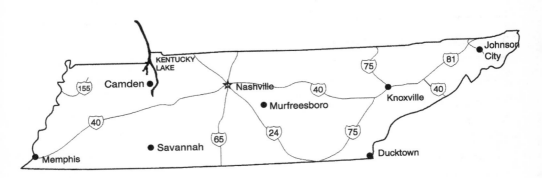

State Gemstone: Tennessee River Pearls (1979)
State Rock: Limestone (1979) and Tennessee Paint Rock Agate (1969)

Dates refer to when stones and minerals were adopted by the state legislature.

DUCKTOWN / *Native • Moderate*

Collect Minerals in Tailings *T*

The following gems or minerals may be found:

- **Garnets, pyrite, chalcopyrite, pyrrhotite, actinolite**

Burra Burra Mine
Ducktown Basin Museum
P.O. Box 458
Ducktown, TN 37326
Phone: (423) 496-5778
www.ducktownbasinmuseum.com

Open: November–December: 9:30 A.M.–4:00 P.M. Monday–Saturday; January–March: 9:30 A.M.–4:00 P.M. Tuesday–Saturday; April–October: 10:00 A.M.–4:30 P.M. Monday–Saturday. Previously open by appointment only, mineral collecting area is now accessible during normal hours of operation.
Info: Burra Burra mine closed in 1958, and the last mine in the Copper Basin closed in 1987. Since their closing, all the mines in the Basin have been allowed to flood. The Basin was mined for copper, iron, sulfur, and zinc from 1850.

Collection area on site (must be reached through the museum). The collection area consists of three dump truck loads of ore, not tailings, that were moved on site from the ore bins at the Tennessee Shaft. This site is in a gated area behind the Shop Building. Bring your own tools, such as a small sledgehammer, chisels, rock hammer, and safety glasses.

Rates: Ore collecting fee: $10.00. (For museum fees, see entry under "Museums.")
Other services available: Gift shop, mine overlook.
Directions: From Atlanta: Take Interstate 575 north from I-75. I-575 will turn into SR 5, then into U.S. 76 (SR 5-SR 515). Stay on SR 5 through McCaysville, and at Copperhill, SR 5 becomes SR 68; stay on SR 68 to Ducktown. The museum is on the right-hand side of the road, about ¾ miles past the intersection with U.S. 64.

CAMDEN KENTUCKY LAKE

Museum, Pearl Farm Tour

Tennessee River Freshwater Pearl
   Farm and Museum
Birdsong Resort and Marina
255 Marina Road
Camden Kentucky Lake, TN 38320
Phone: (731) 584-7880
www.tennesseeriverpearls.com

Open: Year round from 8:00 A.M.–5:00 P.M. Monday–Saturday; 9:00 A.M.–4:00 P.M. Sunday.

Info: North America's only freshwater pearl-culturing facility. See tour information under admission. Museum displays depict the freshwater pearls and mussel industry. The current location in Birdsong Creek was narrowed down from eight pilot locations, all started in 1979. The founders attempted for many years to adapt Japanese culturing techniques to our native waters and species of mussels, and 1984 was the first year they had a productive harvest.

Other services available: Gift shop features Tennessee River pearl designs. Birdsong resort, marina and campground provides accommodations and recreational activities.

Admission: All tours require advance reservations and 15 or more people. Singles and small groups may add on

In the 1800s it was common for people to collect mussels and look for pearls in the Upper Mississippi River. Some historians have compared this treasure hunt to the gold rush in California. People killed millions of mussels in the search, eliminating entire mussel beds in some areas of the river. A much greater "rush" occurred when German button-maker Johann Bopple pioneered the use of freshwater mussel shells for button-making in America in 1889. In 1889, sixty button factories were located in the Mississippi River valley, and the industry supported thousands of workers. But by 1930 the industry began to decline rapidly as mussel beds were wiped out. In the 1950s mussel hunting was again brought to life, as Kokichi Mikimoto of Japan discovered that beads created from the shells of freshwater mussels, placed into marine pearl oysters, served as nuclei for pearl creation. Pearls, valued as gemstones, are organic and formed from living organisms, unlike most other gemstones, which are minerals.

to other existing booked tours. The full tour is $55.00 per person and lasts 3–5 hours. It includes orientation, viewing the facility, visiting with a local diver, meeting the farm manager, lunch, and souvenir shopping. Mini tour $39.50, 1–2 hours, does not include lunch or diver. School and tour bus tours are available.

Directions: 9 miles north of exit 133 on I-40.

DUCKTOWN

Museum 🏛

Ducktown Basin Museum
212 Burra Burra Hill
Ducktown, TN 37326
Phone: (423) 496-5778
E-mail: burrabill@ellijay.com
www.ducktownbasinmuseum.com

Open: November–December: 9:30 A.M.–4:00 P.M. Monday–Saturday; January–March: 9:30 A.M.–4:00 P.M. Tuesday–Saturday; April–October: 10:00 A.M.–4:00 P.M. Monday–Saturday.

Info: They say that when the first astronauts were in orbit around the earth, only two landmarks were clearly visible from space—the Great Wall of China and the denuded mining area of the Copper Basin in Tennessee. The Burra Burra Mine was a major copper-producing mine. Trees for miles around were cut for fuel to smelt the copper, and the fumes of the process devastated all vegetation for miles around. The area has since been re-vegetated, and a small museum exists at the old mine site. The State of Tennessee purchased the museum on March 9, 1988, to be the first state-owned historic industrial site. The 300 acres of denuded land has been set aside as a memorial to the devastation of the Copper Basin.

Admission: Adults $5.00, seniors $4.00, youth (13–17) $2.00, children (6–12) $1.00. For mineral collecting, see prices in entry under "Fee Dig Sites."

Other services available: Gift shop, mine overlook.

Directions: From Atlanta: Take Interstate 575 north from I-75. I-575 will turn into SR 5, then into U.S. 76 (SR 5-SR 515). Stay on SR 5 through McCaysville, and at Copperhill, SR 5 becomes SR 68; stay on SR 68 to Ducktown. The museum is on the right-hand side of the road, about ¾ miles past the intersection with U.S. 64.

JOHNSON CITY

Museum 🏛

Hands On! Regional Museum
315 E. Main Street
Johnson City, TN 37601
Phone: (423) 928–6508
E-mail: main@handsomemuseum.org
www.handsomemuseum.org

Open: March, June–August only. 9:00 A.M.–5:00 P.M. Monday, 9:00 A.M.–5:00 P.M. Tuesday–Friday, 9:00 A.M.–

6:00 P.M. Saturday, 1:00 P.M.–5:00 P.M. Sunday. Closed major holidays.

Info: The museum is aimed at children. As part of its exhibits, it has a simulated coal mine.

Admission: Adults and children 3 and up $8.00, children 2 and under free.

Directions: Take the Market Street exit (exit 23) off I-26. Museum is located one block west, between Main and Market streets.

KNOXVILLE

Museum

The Frank H. McClung Museum
The University of Tennessee
1327 Circle Park Drive
Knoxville, TN 37996-3200
Phone: (865) 974-2144
E-mail: museum@utk.edu
www.mcclungmuseum.utk.edu

Open: 9:00 A.M.–5:00 P.M. Monday–

Saturday, 1:00 P.M.–5:00 P.M. Sunday; closed major holidays.

Info: Exhibits explore Tennessee's geologic history, including the rock cycle, crystals—the building blocks of rocks—and videos explaining geologic processes.

Admission: Free.

Directions: Detailed directions on museum website.

MEMPHIS

Museum

Memphis Pink Palace Museum
c/o Pink Palace Family of Museums
3050 Central Avenue
Memphis, TN 38111
Phone: (901) 636-2362
www.memphismuseums.org

Open: 9:00 A.M.–5:00 P.M. Monday–Saturday, noon–5:00 P.M. Sunday. Closed major holidays.

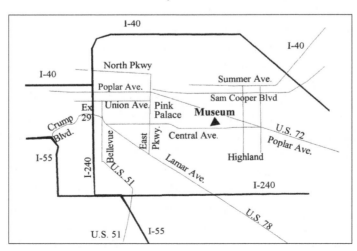

Info: A geology exhibit with two parts: physical geology and historical geology. The physical geology exhibit covers meteorites, including the Canyon Diabolo meteorite, which is as old as the sun and moon; earthquakes; seismology; and mineral exhibits. The mineral exhibit includes minerals from around the world and cases of minerals from famous mid-South localities, and spectacular geodes.

Admission: Adults $12.75, seniors (60+) $12.25, children (3–12) $7.25.

Directions: Take exit 29 off I-240 and drive east on Lamar Avenue. Take the left branch at the Y onto Central Avenue, and follow Central Avenue for several blocks. The museum will be on the left.

MURFREESBORO

Museum

The Earth Experience:
Middle Tennessee Museum of
   Natural History
816 Old Salem Road
Murfreesboro, TN 37129
Phone: (615) 893-6565
www.theearthexperience.org

Open: 11:00 A.M.–4:00 P.M. Thursday–Saturday.

Info: Has a display of minerals from Tennessee, and a large display of fluorite and calcite crystals from the Elmwood Mine in Carthage, TN, gemstones, and artisan jewelry. New location—formerly housed in limited space as the Middle Tennessee State University (MTSU) Mineral, Gem, and Fossil Museum.

Admission: Adults and children 13 and up: $5.00.

Directions: Take I-24 to exit 80 for New Salem Highway. Go left on New Salem, right on Middle Tennessee Boulevard, left on Old Salem Highway. Museum located on the left.

SAVANNAH

Museum 🏛

Tennessee River Museum
495 Main Street
Savannah, TN 38372
Phone: 800-552-FUNN
E-mail: info@tennesseerivermuseum.com
www.tennesseerivermuseum.org

Open: 9:00 A.M.–5:00 P.M. Monday–Saturday; 1:00 P.M.–5:00 P.M. Sunday.

Info: Exhibit on musseling tells the story of the historic pearl button and the modern cultured pearl industries. Included in this exhibit is a section of a mussel boat, along with tools and methods used to harvest them. There are also items from a local 1930s button factory.

Admission: Adults $3.00, students and children free.

Directions: Located on Main Street in Savannah.

SECTION 3: Special Events and Tourist Information

TOURIST INFORMATION

State Tourist Agency

Tennessee Department of Tourism
    Development
Phone: (800) 462-8366
E-mail: tourdev@tn.gov
www.tnvacation.com

VIRGINIA

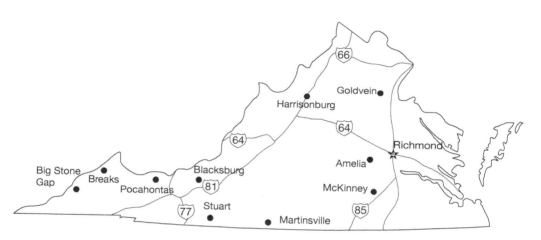

(No State Gemstone, Mineral, or Stone/Rock.)

AMELIA / *Native • Easy to Difficult*

Dig for Gems and Minerals 𝑇

The following gems or minerals may be found:

- Beryl, amazonite, calcite, fluorite, pyrite, quartz, topaz, tourmaline, mica, feldspar, phenakite, minerals in the tantalite-columbite series, microcrystals, and more

Morefield Gem Mine, Inc.
Sam and Sharon Dunaway
13400 Butlers Road
Amelia, VA 23002
Phone: (804) 561-4050 (mine) or
   (804) 561-0344 (home office)
www.morefieldgemmine.com

Open: The mine is seasonal. Call or check website for schedule before visiting.

Info: Mine dump collecting, outcrop digging, and sluicing can all be done at the Morefield Mine. There are at least 80 minerals that can be found here. A collection from the Morefield Mine is on exhibit at the Smithsonian Institute.

   Wear sturdy footwear to the mine and bring a container to carry your treasures home.

Rates: Adults $15.00, children ages 4–18 $8.00–$12.00, age 3 and under free.

Other services available: Gift shop, gem cutting, vending machines, restrooms, picnic area.

Directions: Get on U.S. 360 west into Amelia County. 4.8 miles after crossing the Appomattox River, turn left onto County Road 628, and continue 0.9 miles south to the mine. Map available on website.

MCKENNEY / *Native and Enriched • Easy*

Dig or Sluice for Gems 𝑇 and Minerals

The following gems and minerals may be found:

- **Garnet, citrine, topaz, smoky quartz, tourmaline (rare), plus other gems and minerals from around the world**

Lucky Lake Gem and Mineral Mine
   of Virginia
4125 Harpers Road
McKenney, VA
Phone: (804) 478-5468
E-mail: luckylakegems@yahoo.com
www.luckylakeva.com

Open: Mid-March–August, 10:00 A.M.–5:00 P.M. Monday–Saturday; noon–6:00 P.M. Sunday. September, 10:00 A.M.–3:00 P.M. Monday and Wednesday–Saturday; noon–3:00 P.M. Sunday; closed Tuesday. October–November, 10:00 A.M.–3:00 P.M. Saturday; noon–3:00 P.M. Sunday.

Info: Material excavated from the mine is placed in a pile for digging and sluicing, or sold in buckets enriched with gems and minerals from around the world.

Rates: Admission is free. Dig a bucket and sluice of native gem ore from the pile: $25.00. Buckets of enriched native gem ore range from $15.00–$150.00. A $60.00 bucket includes cutting one stone, a $110.00 bucket includes some rare minerals. The flume is partially covered.

Other services available: Cutting and mounting of gems, picnic area, gift shop, snacks. Handicapped accessible.

Directions: Located on the Nottoway River, just west of McKenney, VA. Take I-85 to exit 4 (Route 40W) toward McKenney. Go 5½ miles, then turn left onto Old Beaver Pond Road (Route 612). Go approximately 1 mile and continue straight on Harpers Road for 2.3 miles. Turn left into Lucky Lake Gem and Mineral Mine (at the yellow sign).

Fairy Stones

Fairy Stone State Park takes its name from the amazing little crystals called fairy stones. Formed and found within the park boundaries, these stone crosses are composed of iron aluminum silicate, which is called staurolite. Single crystals are hexagonal and often intersect at right angles to form Roman or Maltese crosses, or at other angles to form St. Andrew's crosses.

The formation of staurolite crystals involves an exact combination of heat and pressure such as that provided by the folding and crumpling of the earth's crust during the formation of the Appalachian Mountains. Certain types of rock that have been folded and crumpled in this manner are called schists. The staurolite crystals are usually harder than the surrounding schist and less easily weathered. As the staurolite-bearing schist is weathered away, the more resistant crystals are uncovered and come to lie on the surface. Occasionally, staurolites can be found still embedded in their schist matrix.

The crystals are found in various schist bodies from New England, southward through Virginia, and into Alabama and Georgia. Staurolite is also reported to have been found in Montana. Colors range from light brown to dark brownish-black, and sometimes even a deep red. Staurolite has the habit of forming cross-like twinned crystals; 60° twins are most common; and exceptional 90° crosses are the most prized. Also found are staurolite rosettas, unusual specimens found when three crystals grow together to form a common center.

Hunt for Fairy Stones ⊤

*The following gems or minerals
may be found:*

- Staurolite crystals, also called fairy stones

Fairy Stone State Park
967 Fairystone Lake Drive
Stuart, VA 24171
Phone: (276) 930-2424
E-mail: fairystone@dcr.virginia.gov
www.dcr.virginia.gov/state-parks/fairy-
stone

Open: All year, daylight hours.

Info: No digging equipment is permitted. Bring a small container for your finds.

Rates: Free. Can take a small number of crystals for personal use; no commercial digging is permitted.

Other services available: Picnic area; hiking trails; restrooms; boat dock and rentals; swimming Memorial Day to Labor Day (weather permitting).

State Park campground and cabins are available for use; to get more information or make a reservation, call (800) 933-7275.

Directions: Park is located off Highway 57 between Stuart and Bassett. To get to the fairy stone area, leave the park (Route 346) and turn left onto Route 57. Travel approximately 3 miles to the first service station (Haynes 57) on the left. The land on the left of the station is park property, and fairy stones may be hunted in that area.

The Legend of Fairy Stones

It is said that long, long, ago, fairies inhabited a certain quiet and remote region in the foothills of the Blue Ridge Mountains. The fairies roamed freely and enjoyed the beauty and serenity of that enchanted place.

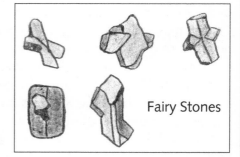

Fairy Stones

One day, they were playing in a sunny glade when an elfin messenger arrived from a city far, far away bearing the sad news of the death of Christ. When the fairies heard the terrible details of the crucifixion, they wept. As their tears fell to the earth, they crystallized into little stone crosses. Though the fairies are no longer to be found there, the fairy stones remain in that enchanted spot as mementos of that day. *(Information courtesy of Fairy Stone State Park)*

SECTION 2: Museums and Mine Tours

BIG STONE GAP

Museum 🏛

Harry W. Meador, Jr., Coal Museum
East Third and Shawnee Avenue
Big Stone Gap, VA 24219
Phone: (276) 523-9209
www.bigstonegap.org/attract/coal.htm

Open: 10:00 A.M.–5:00 P.M. Wednesday–Saturday. 1:00 P.M.–5:00 P.M. Sunday.

Info: Displays in the museum include a collection of photographs, mining equipment and tools, office equipment, and coal company items. The museum is owned and operated by the town of Big Stone Gap, Parks and Recreation Department.

Admission: Free.

Directions: The museum is located in the building that once served as the library and study of John Fox, Jr., author of *The Trail of the Lonesome Dove* and other folk tales, at the intersection of East Third and Shawnee Avenues.

BLACKSBURG

Museum 🏛

Virginia Tech Museum of Geosciences
Department of Geosciences
2062 Derring Hall
Virginia Tech
140 S Perry Street
Blacksburg, VA 24061
Phone: (540) 231-6894
www.outreach.geos.vt.edu/museum

Open: 8:00 A.M.–5:00 P.M. Monday–Friday. Closed university holidays. Check website or call.

Info: The museum features gemstones, a large display of minerals from Virginia, and exhibits highlighting faculty research.

Admission: Free.

Directions: Derring Hall is on the northwest side of the Virginia Tech campus in Blacksburg, VA.

BREAKS

Museum 🏛

Breaks Interstate Park
P.O. Box 100
627 Commission Circle
Breaks, VA 24607
Phone: (276) 865-4413
E-mail: info@breakspark.com
www.breakspark.com

Open: The park is open year-round to visitors but some activities aren't available during the off season. Visitors' Center: March 26–May 27, 10:00 A.M.–6:00 P.M. Saturday and Sunday; May 28–June 30, 10:00 A.M.–6:00 P.M. Friday–Sunday; July 1–31: daily from 10:00 A.M.–6:00 P.M.; August 1–October 30: 10:00 A.M.–6:00 P.M. Thursday–Sunday.

A twenty-four-hour touch-screen kiosk is located outside the Visitor Center which offers park information and trail maps. See website for weekly tours and special events and festivals.

Info: The Russell Fork of the Big Sandy River cut a 5-mile-long gorge as deep as 1,650 feet. Trails provide access to overlooks of the rock formations in the gorge. A museum at the visitor center provides explanations of the park's unusual geological features, and the science behind the local coal industry.

Admission: There is a $2.00/car entrance fee.

Other services provided: Campground and lodges.

Directions: Website gives detailed instructions for coming from multiple directions.

GOLDVEIN

Museum 🏛

The Gold Mining Camp Museum
Monroe Park
14421 Gold Dust Parkway
Goldvein, VA 22720
Phone: (540) 422-8170
E-mail: monroepark@fauquiercounty.gov
www.goldvein.com

Open: 9:30 A.M.–5:00 P.M. Wednesday–Saturday, noon–4:00 P.M. Sunday, closed major holidays. From March–October, gold panning demonstrations are held at 2:00 P.M. Wednesday–Sunday, with an additional demonstration on Saturday at 10:00 A.M. (weather permitting).

Info: At one time, there were 18 gold mines in Fauquier County. The park presents the history of the search for gold in Virginia, shows everyday life in a gold camp, and demonstrates gold panning. Development of the park is ongoing.

Admission: Museum and gold panning demonstration are free.

Other services available: Office sells a variety of basic prospecting equipment, bags of creek sand concentrate with flakes of real gold, and gem specimens. Goldvein Jubilee held annually in September.

Directions: On U.S. 17, approximately 13 miles north from I-95, in Goldvein, VA.

HARRISONBURG

Museum 🏛

The James Madison University
  Mineral Museum
Memorial Hall, Room 6139
James Madison University
Curator: Dr. Lance E. Kearns
Harrisonburg, VA 22807
Phone: (540) 568-6421
E-mail: kearnsle@jmu.edu
www.csm.jmu.edu/minerals

Open: 8:00 A.M.–4:30 P.M. Monday–Friday, when the university is in session.

Info: Has approximately 600 minerals and gems from around the world, including specialty collections of Virginia minerals; Elmwood, TN; and

Franklin Sterling Hill fluorescent display.

Admission: Free.

Directions: Memorial Hall is located at the intersection of Route 42 and W. Grace Street. Enter building at entrance on the south side, on W. Grace Street.

MARTINSVILLE

Museum 🏛

Stone Cross Mountain Museum
Don Hopkins
17529 A.L. Philpot Highway
Martinsville, VA 24112
Phone: (276) 957-4873

Open: By appointment only.

Info: A museum of staurolite crystals, which are natural rock formations in the shape of a cross. The museum has specimens from Virginia, North Carolina, Georgia, New Mexico, Russia, and Australia.

Admission: Adults $4.00, children $2.00.

Directions: On Highway 58, west 2 miles from Highway 220 bypass.

MARTINSVILLE

Museum 🏛

Virginia Museum of Natural History
21 Starling Avenue
Martinsville, VA 24112
Phone: (276) 634-4141
E-mail: information@vmnh.virginia.gov
www.vmnh.net

Open: All year, 9:00 A.M.–5:00 P.M. Monday–Saturday; closed major holidays.

Info: The museum has a collection of rocks and minerals, some of which are displayed. Check website for current exhibits.

Admission: Adults $5.00; seniors, college students, and active military $3.00; children (3–18) $4.00; children under 3 free.

Directions: The museum is located on Business U.S. 58 between E. Church Street and E. Market Street.

POCAHONTAS

Mine Tour 🏛

Pocahontas Exhibition Coal Mine
and Museum
Town of Pocahontas
300 Centre Street
P.O. Box 128
Pocahontas, VA 24635-0128
Phone: (276) 945-9522
E-mail: info@pocahontasva.org
www.pocahontasva.org/museum.html

Open: Mid-April–end of September, 10:00 A.M.–5:00 P.M. Monday–Saturday, 1:00 P.M–5:00 P.M. Sunday.

Info: The mine was originally opened as an exhibition mine in 1938, reportedly the first in the country. The mine is in a 13-foot-high coal seam.

Admission: Mine: Adults $7.00, children (6–12) $4.50, children under 6 free. Museum: Free.

Directions: Call or e-mail for directions.

RADFORD

Museum

Museum of the Earth Sciences
First floor of Curie Hall
Radford University
801 East Main Street
Radford, Virginia 24142
Phone: (540) 831-5257
www.radford.edu/content/csat/home/
    mes.html

Open: The Museum is currently under construction; expected completion date is fall 2016. Check the website or call for information. When construction is complete, the museum will be open when school is in session, or by appointment.

Info: The museum has exhibits of gems, minerals, rocks, and fluorescent minerals. They have a petrified log from Virginia, and a scale model of the Rock of Ages granite quarry; this model was originally displayed in the Smithsonian.

Admission: Free.

Directions: On the Radford University campus. Check the website for detailed directions.

RICHMOND

Museum

University of Richmond Museums
Lora Robins Gallery of Design by Nature
28 Westhampton Way
University of Richmond
Richmond, VA 23173
Phone: (804) 289-8000
E-mail: museums@richmond.edu
www.museums.richmond.edu

Open: 1:00 P.M.–5:00 P.M. Sunday–Friday. Closed Saturdays and university holidays.

Info: Displays include a wide variety of Virginia minerals. Check website for current exhibits.

Admission: Free.

Directions: From I-64, take exit 183/ Glenside Drive south to Three Chopt Road. Turn left onto Three Chopt for one mile, and turn right onto Boatwright Drive, to the main entrance to the University. At the main entrance, turn left onto Campus Drive, and after ¼ mile, turn right onto Gateway Road, then turn right onto Richmond Way. Take Richmond Way down the hill, and the museum is the last building on the left before the lakefront turn, across from Thomas Hall. Limited parking is available on Richmond Way. The museum is located on the ground floor of the Boatwright Memorial Library, with its own entrance of Richmond Way.

TOURIST INFORMATION

State Tourist Agency

Virginia Tourism Corp.
901 East Byrd Street
Richmond, VA 23219
www.virginia.org

WEST VIRGINIA

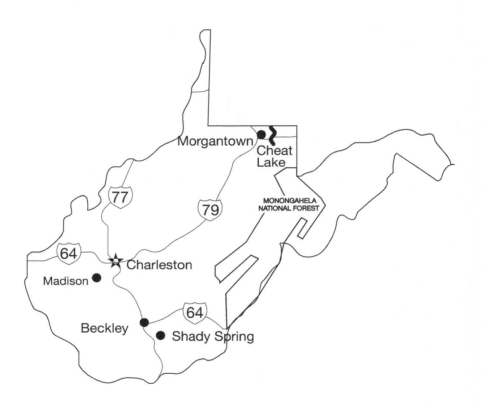

State Gemstone: Silicified Mississippian Fossil Coral (*Lithostrotionella*) (1990)
State Stone/Rock: Bituminous Coal (2009)

Dates refer to when stones and minerals were adopted by the state legislature.

SECTION 1: Fee Dig Sites and Guide Services

SHADY SPRING / *Enriched • Easy*

Find your own Gems, Minerals, and Gold

The following gems or minerals may be found:

- Gems from around the world: Rubies, garnets, emeralds, blue apatite, green/blue kyanite, rose quartz, sodalite, jasper, lepidolite

Someplace Special Gem Mine
323 Rakes Road
Shady Spring, WV 25918
Phone: (304) 575-9732
E-mail: someplacespecialjlt@yahoo.com
www.someplacespecialgemmine.com

Open: Hours vary according to weather. Call or check website for days and times.

Info: Purchase buckets of gem ore, then screen the ore in a sluice with running water. Keep anything you find. There is also an area where you can use your metal detector and keep what you discover.

Rates: Cash only. Bucket of ore (2½ gallons) $10.00, or four buckets for $35.00. Additional discounts for larger quantities.

Other services available: Gem cutting and jewelry making.

Directions: From I-64 take exit 129 (Shady Spring) onto Route 307 East toward Shady Spring. Continue on this road until it intersects with Route 19, then turn left onto 19 and travel 200 yards. Just as you start around the curve, turn right onto Ransom Drive, travel ⅒ mile and turn right on Rakes Road. Do not stop at the first set of buildings that you come to. The mine is located 5 miles up Rakes road at the end.

Note: Do not use a GPS to find the mine. It will not bring you there. There are no signs near the main road, so be sure to bring the directions along.

SECTION 2: Museums and Mine Tours

BECKLEY

Mine Tour

The Beckley Exhibition Coal Mine
513 Ewart Ave.
P.O. Box 2514
Beckley, WV 25801
Phone: (304) 256-1747
E-mail: info@beckleymine.com
www.beckleymine.com

Open: April 1–November 1, 10:00 A.M.–6:00 P.M. Last tour at 5:30 P.M.

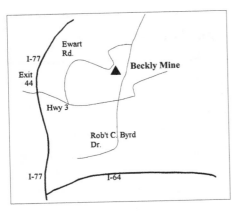

Info: Listed on the National Register of Historical sites, and now part of New River Park, is the restored vintage mine operated by the Phillips family in the late 1800s. Visitors ride a "man trip" car guided through the mine by veteran miners for an authentic view of low seam coal mining from its earliest manual stages to modern mechanized operation. (Bring a jacket—the temperature in the mine is always 58°.)

Visit a company house and a super's (mine superintendent's) house, both of which have been moved to the park and restored. The super's house also has reproductions of the company doctor's offices, the company post office, and the company barbershop. The museum features displays of mining photographs and artifacts from the mining era.

Admission: Adults $20.00, seniors (55+) $15.00, children (4–17) $12.00.

Other services available: Craft and souvenir shop. A 17-site campground at the park provides full hookups.

Directions: From I-77 take exit 44. Turn east on Route 3 (Harper Road). Go 1½ miles, then turn left on Ewart Avenue to Ewart Avenue. Drive 1 mile to the mine entrance.

CHARLESTON

Museum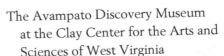

The Avampato Discovery Museum at the Clay Center for the Arts and Sciences of West Virginia
One Clay Square
Charleston, WV 25301
Phone: (304) 561-3570
www.theclaycenter.org

Open: All year, 10:00 A.M.–5:00 P.M. Wednesday–Saturday, noon–5:00 P.M. Sunday. Closed major holidays.

Info: Earth City provides a variety of exhibits that show the story behind West Virginia's geology.

Admission: Museum and galleries: Adults $7.50, seniors and children $6.00.

Other services available: Art museum, performance center, café.

Directions: Take Interstate 64 to exit 100 for Leon Sullivan Way. After exiting, quickly change into the left lane (Leon Sullivan Way). Take the first left onto Washington Street.

MADISON

Museum

Bituminous Coal Heritage
  Foundation Museum
347 Main Street
Madison, WV 25130
Phone: (304) 369-5180; (304) 369-9118
E-mail: boonedevcorp@yahoo.com
www.wvcoalmuseum.org

Open: Noon–4:00 P.M. Wednesday–Friday. Call (304) 369-9118 to schedule a tour during other hours.

Info: Coal in West Virginia was first discovered in Boone County in 1742; the museum showcases the history and culture of the industry and the people in it.

Admission: Free

Directions: Located in downtown Madison. Take the Danville-Madison exit off Route US 119, and drive 2 miles to Madison.

MORGANTOWN

Museum / Visiting
Geologist Program

West Virginia Geological and
  Economic Survey Mini-Museum
Mont Chateau Research Center
1 Mont Chateau Road
Morgantown, WV 26508-8079

Phone: (800) 984-3656 or
  (304) 594-2331
E-mail: info@geostv.wvnet.edu, or
  curator@prehistoricplanet.com
www.wvgs.wvnet.edu/www/museum/
  museum.htm (Click on "Mini-Museum" under "Special Features")

Open: 8:00 A.M.–5:00 P.M. Monday–Friday.

Info: Small display of geologic specimens and geologic processes relating to West Virginia. Repository for specimens, books, maps, manuscripts, and artifacts. The survey also has a geology outreach program in which survey geologists present lectures at different West Virginia state parks in the evening, and then conduct a guided geologic walk in the park the next morning. Check the WVGES website for a schedule.

Admission: Free.

Directions: Located along Cheat Lake, near I-68, east of Morgantown, WV.

Note: The annual gem and mineral show previously held at Cheat Lake is now held in Morgantown and sponsored by Prehistoric Enterprises. Check www.prehistoricstore.com.

TOURIST INFORMATION

State Tourist Agency

West Virginia Travel
Phone: (800) 225-5982
www.wvtourism.com

Index by State

ALABAMA

Fee Dig Mines and Guide Services

Lineville   Alabama Gold Camp—Pan, sluice, dredge, highbank, and metal detect for gold, find garnets and citrine

Trenton   Dixie Euhedrals—Paint rock agate collecting trip

Museums and Mine Tours

Aldrich   Aldrich Coal Mine Museum—Mining history and simulated coal mine

Anniston   Anniston Museum of Natural History—Minerals, artificial indoor cave, earthquake exhibit

Dora   Alabama Mining Museum—Focus on coal mining

McCalla   Tannehill Ironworks Historical State Park, Iron and Steel Museum of Alabama—Geology relevant to the iron industry

ALASKA

Fee Dig Mines and Guide Services

Anchorage   Alaska DNR—Pan, prospect, excavate, limited suction dredging for gold

Chicken   Chicken Gold Camp and Outpost—Pan or dig for gold

Chugach National Forest
    Chugach National Forest—Pan for gold

Copper Center Wrangell-St. Elias National Park and Preserve—Pan for gold, hunt for rocks and minerals (see exceptions in listing)

Fairbanks   Gold Daughters—Pan gold ore from local mines

    Gold Dredge No. 8—Gold panning

Girdwood   Crow Creek Mine—Pan, dredge, or use metal detectors for gold

Nome   AKAU/Alaska Gold and Resort—Recreational gold panning

    Nome Beaches—Pan for gold

Skagway   Klondike Gold Fields—Pan for gold

    Liarsville Gold Rush Trail Camp and Salmon Bake—Pan for gold

Museums and Mine Tours

Anchorage   Alaska Museum of Science and Nature—Displays of rocks and minerals

Central	Circle Historical Museum—Mining equipment and gold display
Chicken	The Chicken Gold Camp & Outpost—Gold dredge tour
Copper Center	George Ashby Memorial Museum/Copper Valley Historical Society—Exhibits on gold and copper mining in the valley
Fairbanks	Gold Dredge No. 8—Gold dredge tour
	University of Alaska Museum of the North—Minerals and gems from Alaska, Arctic Canada, and the Pacific Rim; includes gold and meteorites
Hope	Hope and Sunrise Historical and Mining Museum—Commemorates Turnagain Arm Gold Rush
Juneau	Juneau-Douglas City Museum—History of gold mining
	Last Chance Mining Museum—Hard-rock gold mining museum
Skagway	Klondike Gold Fields—Gold dredge tour
	Liarsville Gold Rush Trail Camp and Salmon Bake—Tour of gold rush camp
	Klondike Gold Rush National Historic Park—History of area gold mining
Wasilla	Independence Mine State Historical Park—Guided mine tour

Annual Event

Anchorage	Chugach Gem & Mineral Society—Field trips

ARIZONA

Fee Dig Mines and Guide Services

Apache Jct.	Apache Trail Tours—Gold panning jeep tours
Prescott	Lynx Creek Gold Pan Day Use Area—Pan for gold
Safford	Black Hills Rockhound Area—Dig for fire agates
	Round Mountain Rockhound Area—Search for fire agates, chalcedony, small geodes

Museums and Mine Tours

Apache Jct.	Superstition Mountain Museum—Geology, minerals, and mining
Bisbee	Bisbee Mining and Historical Museum—Displays on local mining
	Queen Mine Tours—Tour an underground copper mine
Flagstaff	Meteor Crater Enterprises, Inc.—View a meteor crater, museum of astrogeology
	Museum of Northern Arizona—History of Colorado Plateau, geologic models, mineral specimens

Goldfield	Goldfield Ghost Town, Scenic Railroad, and Mine Tours—Gold mine tour, museum, ghost town
Quartzsite	Tyson's Well Stage Station Museum—Displays of mining equipment
Sahuarita	ASARCO Mineral Discovery Center—Geology, mining, minerals, and tour of open-pit mine
Sun City	The Mineral Museum, Sun City Rockhound Club—2,000 rocks and minerals from the U.S. and the world, with emphasis on minerals from Arizona. Over 150 fluorescent rocks and minerals, most from Franklin and Sterling Hill, NJ
Tombstone	Good Enough Mine—Silver mine tour
Tucson	Arizona-Sonora Desert Museum—Mineral collection from Sonora Desert region
	U. A. Science: Flandrau—Arizona minerals, meteorites, fluorescents, borate minerals
Wickenburg	Vulture Gold Mine—Self-guided mine tour

Annual Events

Bisbee	Hunt for Bisbee's Fabulous Blue—Yearly collecting tours of tailings pile from historic No. 7 Mine stockpile
Quartzsite	Gem and Mineral Shows—Mid-January–mid-February
Tucson	Gem and Mineral Shows—End of January through mid-February
	Minerals of Arizona—Symposium three days in March or April

ARKANSAS

Fee Dig Mines and Guide Services

Jessieville	Ron Coleman Mining, Inc.—Dig for quartz crystals
	Jim Coleman's Crystal Mines and Rock Shop—Dig for quartz crystals
Mena	Board Camp Campgrounds & Crystal Mine—Dig for quartz
Mt. Ida	The Crystal Seen Trading Co.—Dig for quartz crystals, wavelite
	Fiddler's Ridge Rock Shop and Bear Mt. Crystal Mine—Dig for quartz crystals
	Judy's Crystals and Things—Dig for quartz crystals
	Ouachita National Forest, Crystal Vista Collecting Site—Collect quartz crystals on the ground, no digging permitted
	Twin Creek Crystal Mine—Dig for crystals
	Wegner Quartz Crystal Mines—Dig, sluice, or pick through tailings for quartz crystals
Murfreesboro	Crater of Diamonds State Park—Dig and screen for diamonds, amethyst, agates, barite, calcite, jasper, quartz, other gems

Story   Sweet Surrender Crystal Mine—Dig for quartz crystals

Museums and Mine Tours
Little Rock   Vardelle Parham Geology Center—Arkansas gems, minerals, fossil fuels

Mt. Ida   Heritage House Museum of Montgomery County—Quartz and mineral exhibits

Piggott   Matilda and Karl Pfeiffer Museum and Study Center—Collection of minerals and geodes

State University ASU Museum—Minerals, many from Arkansas

Annual Event
Mt. Ida   Quartz Crystal Festival and World Championship Dig—Second weekend in October

CALIFORNIA

Fee Dig Mines and Guide Services
Angels Camp   Angels Camp Museum and Carriage House—Pan native gold, quartz, and enriched soil for gems and minerals from around the world

Blythe   BLM, Hauser Geode Beds—Collect geodes, agate, chalcedony roses, jasper, psilomelane, amygdules

Coalinga   California State Gem Mine—Hunt for benitoite and other gems and minerals

Coloma   Marshall Gold Discovery State Historic Park—Gold panning

Columbia   Hidden Treasures Gold Mine—Pan for gold and garnets

Jamestown   Gold Prospecting Adventures, LLC—Sluice, pan, and prospect with metal detectors for gold

Lower Lake   Six Sigma Ranch and Winery—Tour to search for "Lake County Diamonds" (clear quartz) at winery

Lucerne   Lake County Marketing and Economic Development—Rockhounding for Lake County "diamonds" or "moon tears"

Mariposa   Little Valley Inn—Gold panning

Mesa Grande   Himalaya Tourmaline Mine—Look for California tourmaline in mine tailings

Nevada City   Malakoff Diggins State Historical Park—Gold panning

Pala   Oceanview Mine—Hunt for tourmaline (pink, green, bicolor), smoky crystals, garnets, book mica, cleavelandite, kunzite, morganite, gossanite (clear beryl), purple lepidolite, muscovite, aquamarine

	Pala Chief Mine—Dig for tourmaline, kunzite, morganite, aquamarine, quartz, garnets
Palo Verde	Fire Mountain Fire Agate Mine—Dig or screen for fire agate
Pine Grove	Roaring Camp Mining Company—Pan for gold, rockhound for quartz crystals, jade, jasper, and river rubies
Placerville	Hangtown's Gold Bug Park and Mine—Learn gold panning

Museums and Mine Tours

Alleghany	Underground Gold Miners Tours and Museum—Tour an active gold mine
Angels Camp	Angels Camp Museum and Carriage House—Museum features rocks and minerals, gold stamping mill, mining equipment
Avalon	Catalina Island Museum—Exhibits on mining on Catalina Island
Boron	Borax Visitor Center—Story of borax
	Boron Twenty Mule Team Museum—History of area borate mining
Coloma	Marshall Gold Discovery State Historic Park—Gold mining exhibit/museum
Columbia	Museum and State Historic Park—Gold Rush-era artifacts and photographs, tours of gold-mining boom town
Death Valley	Furnace Creek Borax Museum—Rocks and minerals, featuring borate minerals
El Cajon	Heritage of the Americas Museum—Rocks, minerals, and meteorites
Fallbrook	Fallbrook Gem & Mineral Society Museum—Features of minerals from San Diego County
Grass Valley	Empire Mine State Historic Park—Hard-rock gold mine
Independence	Eastern California Museum—Regional gem and mineral collection
Jackson	Kennedy Gold Mine Tours—Surface tour of gold mine
Julian	Eagle and High Peak Gold Mine Tours—Hard-rock gold mine tour
	Julian Pioneer Museum—Rock and mineral display, gold mining tools and equipment displays
Lakeport	Historic Courthouse Museum—Minerals and gems found in Lake County
Los Angeles	Natural History Museum of Los Angeles County—150,000 specimens, minerals of California, native gold, gems, and minerals
Mariposa	California State Mining and Mineral Museum—Gold from California, gems and minerals from around the world
Needles	Needles Regional Museum—Collection of Needles blue agate, Colorado River pebble terrace stones

Nevada City	Malakoff Diggins Park Association—History of hydraulic gold mining
Pacific Grove	Pacific Grove Museum of Natural History—Monterey County rocks, fluorescent minerals
Paso Robles	Paso Robles Area Pioneer Museum—Display of local minerals
Placerville	Hangtown's Gold Bug Park and Mine—Tour hard-rock gold mine
Quincy	Plumas County Museum—Exhibits on gold and copper mining in Plumas County
Rancho Palos Verdes	
	Point Vicente Interpretive Center—Exhibits on area geology
Red Bluff	Gaumer's Jewelry—Minerals from around the world
Redlands	San Bernardino County Museum—45,000 rocks, minerals, and gems
Ridgecrest	Maturango Museum—Small but well-rounded regional gem and mineral collection
Riverside	Jurupa Mountains Discovery Center—Crestmore minerals display, minerals from around the world on display and for sale, family education programs
	World Museum of Natural History—Fluorescent minerals, meteorites, tektites, over 1,300 mineral spheres
San Diego	San Diego Natural History Museum—26,000 mineral specimens, includes minerals found in San Diego County mines
Santa Barbara	Department of Earth Science, UCSB—Gem and mineral collection, minerals and their tectonic settings
Shoshone	Shoshone Museum—Rock collection reflecting the geology of the area
Sierra City	Kentucky Mine and Museum—Exhibits of local gold mining
Sonora	Tuolumne County Museum—Gold from local mines
Yreka	Siskiyou County Museum—Gold exhibit
Yucca Valley	Hi-Desert Nature Museum—Rock and mineral collection, includes fluorescent minerals

Annual Events

Big Sur	Big Sur Jade Festival—Three days in early October
Coloma	Marshall Gold Discovery State Historic Park: Gold Rush Live—Usually second weekend of October
Trona	Gem-O-Rama Searles Lake—Second Saturday in October

COLORADO

Fee Dig Mines and Guide Services

Breckenridge Country Boy Mine—Pan for gold

Idaho Springs Argo Gold Mine and Mill—Pan for gold and gemstones

Phoenix Mine—Pan for gold

Ouray Bachelor-Syracuse Mine Tour—Learn to pan for gold

Silverton Old Hundred Gold Mine Tours, Inc.—Pan for gold

Museums and Mine Tours

Breckenridge Country Boy Mine—Hard-rock gold mine tour

Central City Gilpin History Museum—Displays of local minerals

Hidee Gold Mine—Gold mine tour and gold ore sample

Colorado Springs

Western Museum of Mining and Industry—Displays of mining and demonstrations on gold panning

Creede Creede Underground Mining Museum—Displays of rocks, minerals, and mining equipment

Cripple Creek Cripple Creek District Museum—Mineral displays

Mollie Kathleen Gold Mine—Gold mine tour

Denver Denver Museum of Nature and Science—Over 2,000 specimens; includes gold, topaz, aquamarine, amazonite, and other Colorado minerals

Georgetown Lebanon Silver Mine—Ride a narrow-gauge train, then take a walking tour of the silver mine

Golden Geology Museum, Colorado School of Mines—50,000 specimens, minerals from Colorado and from around the world, gemstones and precious metals

Idaho Springs Argo Gold Mine and Mill—Historic gold mill, mining museum, Double Eagle Mine

Edgar Experimental Mine—Tour an experimental mine (silver, gold, lead, copper)

Phoenix Mine—See a working underground hard-rock mine (gold, silver)

Lake City Hard Tack Mine—Gold mine tour

Leadville Matchless Mine—Tour a symbol of the financial hazards of silver mining

National Mining Hall of Fame and Museum—Story of the American mining industry from coal to gold

Ouray	Bachelor-Syracuse Mine Tour—Underground tour of gold and silver mine
	Ouray County Historical Society—Mineral and mining displays
Salida	Lost Mine Tour—Tour a closed manganese mine
Silverton	Mayflower Gold Mill—Tour a gold mill
	Old Hundred Gold Mine Tour, Inc.—Gold mine tour
	San Juan County Historical Society Museum—Minerals and gems from the Silverton area
Victor	Mine View—View of Colorado's largest open-pit gold mine

CONNECTICUT

Fee Dig Mines and Guide Services
None

Museums and Mine Tours
Portland	Brownstown Quarries—National landmark
East Granby	Old New-Gate Prison and Copper Mine—Tour an old copper mine
Greenwich	Bruce Museum—Exhibits of minerals and rocks
Kent	Connecticut Museum of Mining and Mineral Science—Local minerals
New Haven	Yale Peabody Museum of Natural History—Minerals of New England and the world

Special Event
Connecticut DEP Educational Mineral Collecting—3 sites

DELAWARE

Fee Dig Mines and Guide Services
None

Museums and Mine Tours
Georgetown	Delaware Technical and Community College, Stephen J. Betze Library, Treasures of the Sea Exhibit—Jewels recovered from Spanish galleon Atocha
Newark	Iron Hill Museum—Natural history of Delaware, rock and mineral collections
	University of Delaware, Mineralogical Museum—10,000 specimens (450 on display), crystals, gems, minerals

Special Event
> Delaware Geological Survey—Geo Adventures

DISTRICT OF COLUMBIA

Fee Dig Mines and Guide Services
> None

Museums and Mine Tours
> National Museum of Natural History—Gems and minerals (over 375,000 specimens and a research collection)

FLORIDA

Fee Dig Mines and Guide Services
Okeechobee   Ft. Drum Crystal Mine—Collect calcite encrusted fossil shells, micropyrite, iridescent marcasite

Museums and Mine Tours
Deland   Gillespie Museum, Stetson University—Minerals, gemstones, faceting equipment, replica mine, and a cave
Gainesville   Geological Museum, Santa Fe College Department of Natural Sciences—Florida gems and minerals, gemstone carvings, fluorescent minerals, amber, agatized Tampa Bay coral
Islamorada   Windley Key Fossil Reef Geological State Park—Walk through former fossilized coral quarry
Miami   Coral Castle Museum—Coral rock carvings
Mulberry   Mulberry Phosphate Museum—Exhibits on the phosphate industry, dig for phosphate pebbles
Tampa   Ed and Bernadette Marcin Museum, University of Florida—Minerals and gemstones, mainly from Florida and the western U.S.
West Palm Beach
> South Florida Science Center and Aquarium—Meteorites and moon rock from an Apollo mission

GEORGIA

Fee Dig Mines and Guide Services
Cleveland   Gold'n Gem Grubbin—Dig and pan for gold, sapphires, rubies, emeralds, amethyst, topaz

Dahlonega	Consolidated Gold Mines—Gold panning, gem sluicing
	Crisson Gold Mine—Pan gold ore or enriched gemstone ore
Gainesville	Chattahoochee-Oconee National Forest—Gold panning, rock-hounding (restrictions apply)
LaGrange	Hogg Mine—Collect star rose quartz, aquamarine, beryl, black tourmaline
Lincolnton	Graves Mountain—Search for lazulite, pyrophyllite, kyanite, iridescent hematite, pyrite, ilmenite, muscovite, fuchsite, barite, sulfur, blue quartz, quartz crystals, and microcrystals such as woodhouseite, variscite, strengite, phosphosiderite, cacoxenite, crandallite (collecting allowed on special dates only)
Tignall	Jacksons Crossroads Amethyst Mine—Hunt for amethyst crystals, druse quartz
Warrenton	Dixie Euhedrals—Hunt for amethyst crystals

Museums and Mine Tours

Atlanta	Fernbank Museum of Natural History—Joachim Gem Collection, mineral cave
	Fernbank Science Center—Meteorite collection, outdoor rock and mineral walk
Cartersville	Tellus Science Museum—Weinman Mineral Gallery
Dahlonega	Consolidated Gold Mines—Mine tour
	Dahlonega Gold Museum—Tells the story of the Georgia gold rush
Elberton	Elberton Granite Museum & Exhibit—Granite quarry and products
Macon	Museum of Arts and Sciences—Display of gems and minerals
Tallapoosa	West Georgia Museum of Tallapoosa—Small collection of local minerals
Villa Rica	Pine Mountain Gold Museum at Stockmar Park—Story of gold mining in the Villa Rica area

Annual Events

Jasper	Pickens County Marble Festival—First weekend in October
Dahlonega	Gold Rush Days—Third full weekend in October
	World Open Gold Panning Championship—Third Saturday in October, at the same time as Gold Rush Days

HAWAII

Fee Dig Mines and Guide Services

None

Museums and Mine Tours

Hawaii Volcanoes National Park

Thomas A. Jaggar Museum—Museum on vulcanology and seismology, tour of volcano

Hilo   Lyman Museum—Rocks, minerals, gems

IDAHO

Fee Dig Mines and Guide Services

Rathdrum   Eagle City Park—Mine for gold

Spencer   Spencer Opal Mines—Pick through a stockpile for opal

St. Maries   Emerald Creek Garnet Area—Screen for star garnets

Museums and Mine Tours

Boise   Idaho Museum of Mining and Geology—Exhibits on mining and geology

Challis   Land of the Yankee Fork State Park—Museum exhibits, gold panning station

Cottonwood   The Historical Museum at St. Gertrude—Displays of gems and minerals from Idaho and around the world

Kellogg   Crystal Gold Mine—Mine tour

Shoshone County Mining and Smelting Museum—Rocks, minerals, mining equipment

Pocatello   Idaho Museum of Natural History—Displays of specimens from Idaho and the Intermountain West

Wallace   Sierra Silver Mine Tour—Mine tour

Wallace District Mining Museum—Story of mining in Northern Idaho

ILLINOIS

Fee Dig Mines and Guide Services

Hamilton   Jacobs Geode Shop and Mine—Hunt for geodes containing calcite, barite, quarts, kaolinite

Nick's Geodes (aka Evans Property)—Dig for geodes

Vickers Geodes—Dig for geodes in mine, or hunt for geodes in creek

Woodie's Rock Shop—Guided geode collecting trips

Rosiclare   American Fluorite Museum—Dig for fluorite in mine ore

Harrisburg   Shawnee National Forest—Recreational gold panning and rockhounding

Museums and Mine Tours

Carbondale   University Museum—Over 26,000 geological specimens

Chicago   The Field Museum—Grainger Hall of Gems

Museum of Science and Industry—Simulated coal mine

Elmhurst   Lizzadro Museum of Lapidary Art—1,300 pieces of cut and polished gems, fluorescent rocks, a birthstone display

Rockford   Burpee Museum of Natural History—Displays of rocks, minerals, and gems

Rock Island   Augustana Fryxell Geology Museum—Rock and mineral museum

Rosiclare   The American Fluorite Museum—Story of fluorospar industry

Shirley   The Funk Prairie Home and Gem and Mineral Museum—Gem and mineral collection, petrified wood

Springfield   Illinois State Museum—Illinois specimens, rock collections, copper

Annual Event

Hamilton   Geode Fest—Last weekend in September

INDIANA

Fee Dig Mines and Guide Services

Knightstown   Yogi Bear's Jellystone Park Camping Resort—Midwestern gold prospecting

Museums and Mine Tours

Bedford   Land of Limestone Exhibit, StoneGate Arts and Entertainment Center—History of Indiana limestone industry

Lawrence County Museum of History—Exhibits on limestone, geological specimens from Lawrence County.

Fort Wayne   Indiana Purdue University Fort Wayne—Hallway displays of minerals, meteorites, and rocks

Indianapolis   Indiana State Museum—Indiana and regional minerals

Richmond   Joseph Moore Museum of Natural History, Earlham College—Geology exhibit from local Ordovician limestone

IOWA

Fee Dig Mines and Guide Services

(See annual event—Geode Fest)

Museums and Mine Tours

Cedar Falls   Rod Library—Rock and mineral collection

Centerville   Appanoose County Historical Coal Mining Museum—Coal mine replicas

Cherokee   Sanford Museum and Planetarium—School-age programs and field trips in geology

Danville   Geode State Park—Display of geodes

Decora   Luther College Geology Collection—Geological specimens

Des Moines   State Historical Museum of Iowa—Crystal formations from coal mines and quarry waste piles, geodes, exhibit on how coal is mined

Iowa City   University of Iowa—Displays on state geology

Minburn   Voas Nature Area and Museum—Collection of rocks and minerals

Sioux City   Sioux City Public Museum—Mineralogy exhibit

West Bend   The Shrine of the Grotto of the Redemption—Grotto made of precious stones and gems

Winterset   Madison County Historical Society—Rock and mineral collection

Annual Events

Keokuk   Geode Fest—Three-day weekend at the end of September; field trips for geodes

Keokuk Area Convention and Tourism Office—Display of Brevard Collection of Keokuk geodes found in the tri-state area

KANSAS

Fee Dig Mines and Guide Services

None

Museums and Mine Tours

Emporia   Johnston Geology Museum—Evaporative minerals (salt), fluorescent minerals, selenite, crystalline form of ores from Tri-State Mining District

Galena   Galena Mining and Historical Museum—Focus on local lead mining and smelting industry, including mineral specimens

Greensburg   Brenham Pallasite Meteorite at the Big Well Museum—1,000-pound meteorite on display

Hutchinson   Stratica Kansas Underground Salt Museum—Explains the underground mining of rock salt

La Crosse   Post Rock Museum—History and "post rocks"

McPherson	McPherson Museum—Meteorites, rocks, and minerals
Minneapolis	Ottawa County Historical Museum—Display of rocks and meteorites
Riley	Arts and Memories Museum—Display of gems and minerals
Scott City	El Quartelejo Museum—Geology exhibits featuring the area's famous rock and fossil formations

KENTUCKY

Fee Dig Mines and Guide Services

| Marion | The Ben E. Clement Mineral Museum—Fluorite and fluorescent mineral collecting |

Museums and Mine Tours

Benham	Kentucky Coal Mine Museum—Displays on coal mining and formation of coal
Covington	Behringer-Crawford Museum—Periodic displays of gems and minerals
Lexington	Headley-Whitney Museum—Jewelry and mounted semi-precious stones
Lynch	Lynch Portal No. 31 Mine Tour—Mine tour
Marion	The Ben E. Clement Mineral Museum—Thousands of fluorite specimens and accessory minerals
Olive Hill	Northeastern Kentucky Museum—Displays of rocks, minerals, and jewelry

LOUISIANA

Fee Dig Mines and Guide Services

None

Museums and Mine Tours

| Lafayette | Lafayette Science Museum—Meteorite and tektite exhibit |
| Monroe | Museum of Natural History—Rocks, gems, and minerals with emphasis on North Louisiana |

MAINE

Fee Dig Mines and Guide Services

| Auburn | Mt. Apatite Quarry—Hunt for apatite, tourmaline, and quartz |

Bethel	Mt. Apatite Farm/Hatch Ledge—Hunt for tourmaline, garnet, graphic granite, clevelandite, autenite, mica, beryl, and more
	Maine Mineralogy Expeditions—Collect albite, almandine garnet, beryl, rose and other quartz, black tourmaline, biotite, autunite, zircon, and many others
Poland	Poland Mining Camps—Collect tourmaline and other Maine gems and minerals
Stoneham	Lord Hill Mineral Collecting Area—Search for gems and minerals
Stow	Deer Hill Mineral Collecting Area—Search for gems and minerals
West Paris	Perham's of West Paris—Collect tourmaline and other Maine gems and minerals
Woodstock	Maine Mineral Adventures—Screen mine material or go on a field trip to search for gems and minerals

Museums and Mine Tours

Augusta	Maine State Museum—Gems and minerals of Maine
Bethel	Maine Mineral and Gem Museum—Maine minerals and historical mining materials
Caribou	Nylander Museum of Natural History—Minerals of Maine, lithic artifacts
Presque Isle	The Northern Maine Museum of Science—Rotating displays of Maine minerals, fluorescent minerals, Maine slate

Annual Events

| East Portland | New England Mineral Conference—One weekend in May |
| Poland | Maine Pegmatite Workshop—Week-long program at the end of May or beginning of June |

MARYLAND

Fee Dig Mines and Guide Services

None

Museums and Mine Tours

| Hancock | Hancock Visitor's Center—Exhibit on road cut geology |
| Potomac | C&O Canal National Historical Park—Gold Mine Trail tours scheduled periodically |

MASSACHUSETTS

Fee Dig Mines and Guide Services
None

Museums and Mine Tours
Amherst Beneski Museum of Natural History—Mineral specimens, meteorites

Boston Museum of Science, Boston—Rocks and minerals

Cambridge Harvard Museum of Natural History—Gems, minerals, ores, meteorites

Gloucester Cape Ann Historical Museum—Exhibits of local granite and the granite industry

Pittsfield Berkshire Museum—Specimens from Berkshire County and Massachusetts, polished stones, meteorites, fluorescent display

Quincy Quincy Historical Society Museum—Exhibits on granite industry in Quincy

Saugus Saugus Iron Works National Historic Site—Guided tours

Springfield Springfield Science Museum—Minerals from around the world

MICHIGAN

Fee Dig Mines and Guide Services
Grand Marais Woodland Park Campground—Search beaches for agates

Mohawk Delaware Copper Mine—Search for souvenir copper

Ontonagon The Caledonia Copper Mine—Collect copper specimens, silver, epidote, calcite, datolite, quartz

Petoskey Petoskey State Park—Hunt for Petoskey Stones

Museums and Mine Tours
Ann Arbor University of Michigan Museum of Natural History—Exhibits of rocks and minerals

Battle Creek Kingman Museum—Gem and mineral display

Bloomfield Hills Cranbrook Institute of Science—1,800 on display of more than 11,000 mineral specimens

Calumet Coppertown, U.S.A.—Exhibits on copper mining

Caspian Iron County Museum and Park—Iron mining complex

Chelsea Gerald E. Eddy Discovery Center—Michigan rocks, minerals, crystals, and mining

Copper Harbor Fort Wilkins Historic State Park—History of copper mining in the area

Grand Marais	Gitche Gumee Agate and History Museum—Displays of agates, beach rocks, crystals, fluorescent rocks, historical displays on iron and copper mining
Greenland	Adventure Mine—Tour underground copper mine
Hancock	The Quincy Mine Hoist Association—Tour an underground copper mine
Houghton	The A. E. Seaman Mineral Museum—Crystal collection, minerals from the Lake Superior copper district
Iron Mountain	Iron Mountain Iron Mine—Iron mine tour
	Iron Mining Museum and Gift Shop—Display of underground mining equipment
Ishpeming	Cliffs Shaft Mine Museum—Take guided tour of an iron mine, displays of rocks, gems and minerals
Lake Linden	Houghton County Historical Museum—Copper mining and refining equipment displays
Mohawk	Delaware Copper Mine—Mine tour
Mt. Pleasant	The Museum of Cultural and Natural History, Central Michigan University—Michigan rocks and minerals
Negaunee	Michigan Iron Industry Museum—Story of Michigan iron industry
Republic	Republic Iron Mine—Mine view
South Range	The Copper Range Historical Museum—Exhibits on miners' lives and families

Annual Events

Eastport	Antrim County Petoskey Stone Festival—One day during early summer
Houghton	Keweenaw Mineral Days—End of July, in collaboration with Keweenaw Gem and Gift

MINNESOTA

Fee Dig Mines and Guide Services

Moose Lake	Moose Lake Chamber of Commerce—Hunt for Agates

Museums and Mine Tours

Calumet	Hill Annex Mine State Park—Tour an open-pit iron mine
Chisholm	Minnesota Discovery Center—Tour and mining displays
	Minnesota Museum of Mining, Inc.—Indoor and outdoor exhibits
	Taconite Mine Tours—Iron industry taconite mining tours

Hibbing	Hull-Rust Mahoning Mine—Observe an open-pit iron mine
Moose Lake	Minnesota Agate and Geological Interpretive Center—Showcases Minnesota's gemstone, the Lake Superior Agate
Pipestone	Pipestone National Monument—Tour a Native American pipestone quarry
Soudan	Lake Vermilion–Soudan Underground Mine State Park—Tour an underground iron mine
Virginia	Mine Views/Iron Range Tourism Bureau—Information on mine view sites

Annual Event

Moose Lake	Agate Days—One weekend in July

MISSISSIPPI

Fee Dig Mines and Guide Services

None

Museums and Mine Tours

Flora	Mississippi Petrified Forest National Natural Landmark—Petrified wood, minerals, fluorescent display
Starkville	Dunn-Seiler Museum—Mineral and rock collections

MISSOURI

Fee Dig Mines and Guide Services

Alexandria	Sheffler's Rock Shop and Geode Mine—Dig geodes lined with crystals
St Francisville	Hill Top Mud Bogg—Dig for geodes

Museums and Mine Tours

Golden	Golden Pioneer Museum—Large mineral exhibit
Joplin	Everett J. Richie Tri-State Mineral Museum—Story of area's lead and zinc mining
Kansas City	University of Missouri–Kansas City, Richard L. Sutton, Jr., MD, Museum of Geoscience—Local and regional specimens
Park Hills	Missouri Mines State Historic Site—1,100 specimens of minerals, ores, and rocks
Point Lookout	Ralph Foster Museum, College of the Ozarks—Area minerals, mineral spheres and fluorescent minerals

Rolla	Mineral Museum, Missouri University of Science and Technology—3,500 specimens of minerals, ores, and rocks from 92 countries and 47 states

MONTANA

Fee Dig Mines and Guide Services

Alder	Red Rock Mine and Garnet Gallery—Screen for garnets and corundum (some star)
Dillon	Crystal Park Recreational Mineral Collecting Area—Dig for quartz and amethyst crystal
Hamilton	Sapphire Studio—Purchase and wash bags of ore for sapphires
Helena	Spokane Bar Sapphire Mine and Gold Fever Rock Shop—Dig and screen for sapphires and other gems and minerals
Libby	Libby Creek Recreational Gold Panning Area—Pan for gold
Philipsburg	Gem Mountain—Search for sapphires
	Sapphire Gallery—Wash bags of gravel to look for sapphires

Museums and Mine Tours

Butte	The Berkeley Pit—Observation point for closed open-pit copper mine
	Butte-Silver Bow Visitor and Transportation Center—Presents information on area geology and its mining, including local gold and silver mining
	Mineral Museum, Montana Tech of the University of Montana—Gold, fluorescent minerals, Yogo Gulch sapphires, meteorites, and minerals from Butte and MT
	World Museum of Mining—Tour of underground mine
Ekalaka	Carter County Museum—Fluorescent mineral display
Lewistown	Central Montana Museum—Rocks, minerals, and Yogo sapphires
Philipsburg	Granite County Museum and Cultural Center, Inc.—Tells story of mining community and has a replica of an underground mine

NEBRASKA

Fee Dig Mines and Guide Services

Crawford	High Plains Homestead—Hunt for chalcedony and prairie agate

Museums and Mine Tours

Chadron	Eleanor Barbour Cook Museum of Geology—Displays of rocks and minerals

Crawford	Trailside Museum of Natural History—Displays of western Nebraska geology, photos of Toadstool Geological Park
Hastings	Hastings Museum of Natural and Cultural History—Minerals, rocks, fluorescent minerals, and translucent slabs
Lincoln	University of Nebraska State Museum—Displays of rocks, minerals, and fluorescent minerals

Annual Event

| Crawford | Crawford Rock Swap—Labor Day weekend |

NEVADA

Fee Dig Mines and Guide Services

Black Rock Desert

	High Rock Canyon Emigrant Trails National Conservation Area—Rock collecting
Denio	Bonanza Opal Mines, Inc.—Dig crystal, white and black fire opal
	Rainbow Ridge Opal Mine—Tailings digging for wood opal
	Royal Peacock Opal Mine, Inc.—Dig black and fire opal
Ely	Garnet Fields Rockhound Area—Hunt for almandine garnets
Hawthorne	Bonanza Turquoise Mine—Gem mine collecting tours
Tonopah	Otteson's Turquoise—Dig in mine tailings for turquoise

Museums and Mine Tours

Ely	White Pine Public Museum—Displays of gems, minerals, mining equipment
Las Vegas	Nevada State Museum and Historical Society—Natural history of Nevada
Nelson	Eldorado Canyon Mine Tours, Inc.—Hard-rock gold mine tour
Reno	W. M. Keck Earth Science and Mineral Engineering Museum—Collection of minerals and ores
Virginia City	Chollar Mine—Underground mine tour (gold and silver)

NEW HAMPSHIRE

Fee Dig Mines and Guide Services

| Conway | Moat Mountain Mineral Collecting Area—Search for gems and minerals |
| Grafton | Ruggles Mine—Collect up to 150 different minerals |

Museums and Mine Tours
Dover   Woodman Museum—1,300 specimens including local rocks
Warner   The Little Nature Museum—Rocks, minerals, and ores
Wolfeboro   Libby Museum—Rocks and minerals

NEW JERSEY

Fee Dig Mines and Guide Services
Cape May   Cape May Welcome Center—Hunt for Cape May "diamonds"
Franklin   Franklin Mineral Museum and Nature Center—Tailings diggings for fluorescent minerals and franklinite
Ogdensburg   Sterling Hill Mining Museum—Collect fluorescent minerals

Museums and Mine Tours
Franklin   Franklin Mineral Museum—Minerals and rocks from local and worldwide sources, fluorescent room
Monroe Township
     Displayworld's Stone Museum—Minerals, hands-on exhibits
Morristown   The Morris Museum—Specimens from five continents
New Brunswick Rutgers Univeristy Geology Museum—Minerals and geologic specimens that emphasize the geology of New Jersey and surrounding states
Ogdensburg   Sterling Hill Mining Museum—Underground mine tour
Paterson   The Paterson Museum—Specimens from local basalt flows and basalt flow in the Poona region of India, minerals from NJ and around the world
Rutherford   Meadowlands Museum—Fluorescent minerals, quartz, minerals from NJ
Trenton   New Jersey State Museum—Minerals and rocks, including fluorescents and magnetite ore

NEW MEXICO

Fee Dig Mines and Guide Services
Bingham   Blanchard Rock Shop—Collect over 84 different kinds of minerals in a former lead mine
Deming   Rockhound State Park—Collect a variety of semiprecious stones
Dixon   Harding Mine—Look for over 50 minerals

Gila	Casitas de Gila Guesthouses and Art Gallery—Rockhound on 60 acres when lodging in the Guesthouses. Some of the minerals found are white and pink chalcedony, chalcedony roses, red, brown, and yellow jasper, jasper breccia, picture jasper, banded agate, zeolites, geodes, massive hematite, banded rhyolite, andesite, volcanic bombs, scoria, limonite and hematite-banded welded tuff. Pan for gold in the creek.

Museums and Mine Tours

Albuquerque	Geology Museum, University of New Mexico—Displays of New Mexico minerals and geology
	UNM Meteorite Museum and Geology Museum—Meteorites
	New Mexico Museum of Natural History and Science—Displays with igneous, metamorphic, and sedimentary rock, Harding pegmatite geology
	The Turquoise Museum—Displays of turquoise, focus on New Mexico and Southwest
Grants	New Mexico Mining Museum—Uranium mining
Portales	Miles Mineral Museum—Displays of minerals, gems, and meteorites
Socorro	New Mexico Bureau of Geology and Mineral Resources Mineralogical Museum—Minerals from New Mexico, the southwestern U.S., and the world

Annual Events

Socorro	New Mexico Mineral Symposium—Two days in November

NEW YORK

Fee Dig Mines and Guide Services

Herkimer	Herkimer Diamond Mines Inc.—Dig for "Herkimer diamonds" quartz crystals
Middleville	Ace of Diamonds Mine and Campground—Prospect for Herkimer "diamonds," calcite crystals, and dolomite crystals
North River	Garnet Mine Tours—Tour and hunt for garnets in the Historic Barton Mines
St. Johnsville	Crystal Grove Diamond Mine and Campground—Dig for Herkimer "diamonds"

Museums and Mine Tours

Albany	New York State Museum—Minerals of New York

Hicksville	The Hicksville Gregory Museum—10,000 specimens from the major mineral groups, also NJ zeolites, Herkimer "diamonds," fluorescent minerals
New York City	American Museum of Natural History—Gems, meteorites, emphasis on exceptional specimens from the U.S., ornamental stones, cut and uncut, coral, amber, synthetic stones, decorative objects, and jewelry
Olean	Rock City Park—Museum with fluorescent mineral room
Pawling	The Gunnison Natural History Museum—Minerals

NORTH CAROLINA

Fee Dig Mines and Guide Services

Blowing Rock	Doc's Rocks Gem Mine—Sluice gem ore from natural and enriched mines
Boone	Foggy Mountain Gem Mine—Screen for topaz, garnet, aquamarine, peridot, ruby, star sapphire, amethyst, citrine, smoky quartz, tourmaline, emerald
Bryson City	Nantahala River Gem Mine—Sluice for gems, natural and enriched
Canton	Old Pressley Sapphire Mine—Sluice for sapphires, zircon, garnet, mica
Cherokee	Smoky Mountain Gold & Ruby Mine—Sluice for gold and gems
Chimney Rock	Chimney Rock Gemstone Mine—Screen for aquamarine, emerald, ruby, peridot, garnet, quartz, agate, hematite, amethyst, sodalite, and more
Franklin	Cherokee Ruby and Sapphire mine—Sluice for rubies, sapphires, sillimanite, rutile, moonstone, rhodolite garnet, pyrope garnet
	Cowee Mountain Ruby Mine—Sluice for rubies, sapphires, garnets, tourmaline, smoky quartz, amethyst, citrine, moonstone, topaz
	Gold City Gem Mine—Sluice for rubies, sapphires, garnets, emeralds, tourmaline, smoky quartz, amethyst, citrine, moonstone, topaz, aquamarine, gold
	Cowee Gift Shop and Mason Mountain Mine, aka TJRocks—Sluice for rhodolite garnets, rubies, sapphires, kyanite, crystal quartz, smoky quartz, moonstones
	Mason's Ruby and Sapphire Mine—Dig and sluice for sapphires (all colors), pink and red rubies
	Rose Creek Mine and Rock Shop—Sluice for rubies, sapphires, garnets, moonstones, amethysts, smoky quartz, citrine, rose quartz, topaz, emerald

	Sheffield Mine—Sluice for native rubies and sapphires, or enriched material from around the world
Hendersonville	Elijah Mountain Gem Mine—Pan for a variety of gems and minerals
Hiddenite	Emerald Hollow Mine–Hiddenite Gems, Inc.—Sluice for rutile, sapphires, garnets, hiddenite, smoky quartz, tourmaline, clear quartz, aquamarine, sillimanite, and others
Highlands	Jackson Hole Trading Post and Gem Mine—Sluice for rubies, sapphires, garnets, tourmaline, smoky quartz, amethyst, citrine, moonstone, topaz
High Point	Kersey Valley Gem Dig—Educational family activity
Leicester	Randall Glen Gem Mine—Pan for a variety of gems and gold
Marion	Carolina Emerald Mine and Vein Mountain Gold Camp—Mine for gold, emerald, aquamarine, moonstone, feldspar crystals, garnets, smoky, rose, blue, and clear quartz, tourmaline
	The Lucky Strike—Sluice for gems and pan for gold
Marshall	Little Pine Garnet Mine—Dig for garnets; can take a horseback ride to the mine
Midland	Reed Gold Mine State Historic Site—Gold panning
New London	Mountain Creek Gold Mine—Gold panning
Spruce Pine	Emerald Village—Sluice for 45 different rocks, minerals, and gems
	Gem Mountain Gemstone Mine—Sluice for sapphires, crabtree emeralds, rubies, Brushy Creek and Wiseman aquamarine, and more
	Rio Doce Gem Mine—Sluice for emeralds, rubies, aquamarine, tourmaline, topaz, garnets, amethysts, citrine, beryl, rose, clear, rutilated, and smoky quartz
	Spruce Pine Gem Mine—Sluice for local gems such as sapphires, emeralds, rubies, aquamarine, garnets, amethyst, moonstone, smoky quartz, crystal quartz
Union Mills	Thermal City Gold Mine—Gold and gemstone panning

Museums and Mine Tours

Asheville	Colburn Earth Science Museum—Collection of mineral specimens from NC and the world
Aurora	Aurora Fossil Museum—Geology of the NC Coastal Plain
Franklin	Franklin Gem and Mineral Museum—Specimens from NC and around the world
	Ruby City Gems and Minerals—Specimens from NC and around the world
Gastonia	Schiele Museum—North Carolina gems and minerals
Greensboro	Greensboro Science Center—Mineral specimens from NC

Hendersonville	Mineral and Lapidary Museum of Henderson County, Inc.—Minerals and lapidary arts
Linville	Grandfather Mountain Nature Museum—Specimens from NC
Midland	Reed Gold Mine State Historic Site—Gold mine tour
Spruce Pine	Museum of North Carolina Minerals—Specimens primarily from local mines
	North Carolina Mining Museum and Mine Tour—Tour a closed feldspar mine

Annual Events

Franklin	Mother's Day Gemboree—Mother's Day weekend in May
	Macon County Gemboree—4 days in July
	"Leaf Looker" Gemboree—3 days in October
Spruce Pine	NC Mineral and Gem Festival—Four days at the end of July/beginning of August

NORTH DAKOTA

Fee Dig Mines and Guide Services

None

Museums and Mine Tours

Beulah, Center, Underwood	
	Tours at several area lignite strip mines
Bismarck	State Museum—Story of geology in the state
Medora	Theodore Roosevelt National Park—Petrified forest
Parshall	Paul Broste Rock Museum—Displays of rocks from the area and around the world

OHIO

Fee Dig Mines and Guide Services

| Hopewell | Hidden Springs Ranch—Dig for flint (groups only) |
| | Nethers Flint—Dig for flint |

Museums and Mine Tours

| Cadiz | Harrison County History of Coal Museum—Look at history of coal mining to present |
| Cleveland | The Cleveland Museum of Natural History—The Wade Gallery of Gems and Minerals has over 1,500 gems and minerals |

Columbus	Orton Geological Museum—Rocks and minerals from OH and the world
Dayton	Boonshoft Museum of Discovery—Minerals and crystals
Glenford	Flint Ridge State Memorial—Ancient flint quarrying
Lima	Allen County Museum—Rock and mineral exhibit
Oxford	Karl E. Limper Geology Museum—Geology of Oxford area
Put-in-Bay	Heineman's Crystal Cave—Tour the world's largest geode
Springfield	Hartman Rock Garden—Tour a rock garden filled with folk art and sculptures constructed from rocks
Youngstown	The Clarence R. Smith Mineral Museum—Mineral display

Annual Event

| Glenford | Flint Ridge Knap-In—Learn how prehistoric Native Americans worked flint |

OKLAHOMA

Fee Dig Mines and Guide Services
| Jet | Salt Plains National Wildlife Refuge—Dig for selenite crystals |
| Moyers | K River Campground—Gold panning, events for gold prospecting, treasure hunting |

Museums and Mine Tours
Catoosa	D. W. Correll Museum—Displays of rocks, gems, minerals
Coalgate	Coal County Mining and Historical Museum—Mining museum
Enid	The Midgley Museum—Rock and mineral collection predominantly from Oklahoma and the Texas shoreline
Noble	Timberlake Rose Rock Museum—Displays of barite roses
Tulsa	Elsing Museum, Oral Roberts University—Gems and minerals

OREGON

Fee Dig Mines and Guide Services
Federal lands	Recreational mining on federal lands
Lakeview	Oregon Sunstone Public Collection Area—Dig for sunstones
Madras	Richardson's Rock Ranch—Dig for thundereggs, agate
Mitchell	Lucky Strike Geodes—Dig for thundereggs (picture jasper)
Plush	Dust Devil Mining Co.—Dig for sunstones
	Double Eagle Mining Company—Dig for sunstones
	Spectrum Sunstone Mines—Dig for sunstones

Roseburg	Cow Creek Recreational Gold Panning Area—Pan for gold
Sweet Home	Holleywood Ranch—Collect petrified wood
Tillamook	Oregon Coast Visitors' Association—Information on collecting agates on Oregon Beaches

Museums and Mine Tours

Baker City	Branch of US Bank—Gold display, including Armstrong nugget
Central Point	Crater Rock Museum—Displays of minerals, thundereggs, fossils, geodes, cut and polished gemstones
Corvallis	Oregon State University Dept. of Earth, Ocean and Atmospheric Sciences—Mineral displays
Cottage Grove	Bohemia Gold Mining Museum—Memorial to gold mining era of the Bohemia District
Hillsboro	The Rice Northwest Rock and Mineral Museum—Crystals, northwest minerals, petrified wood, fluorescent minerals, lapidary arts
Redmond	Petersen Rock Garden—Unusual rock garden, fluorescent display
Sumpter	Sumpter Valley Dredge State Heritage Area—View a gold dredge, tour historic gold mine towns

Annual Events

Cottage Grove	Bohemia Mining Days—Held during the third weekend in July, gold panning and exposition
Nyssa	Thunderegg Days—Starts on the 2nd Thursday in July
Prineville	Rockhound Pow-Wow—Third weekend in June

PENNSYLVANIA

Fee Dig Mines and Guide Services

Spring Grove	Jones Geological Services—Guide services for mineral collecting

Museums and Mine Tours

Ashland	Pioneer Tunnel Coal Mine and Steam Train—Tour an anthracite coal mine
Bryn Mawr	Museum, Department of Geology, Bryn Mawr College—Rotating display of 1,500 minerals from a collection of 23,500 specimens, fluorescent minerals from Franklin Mine in NJ
Cornwall	Cornwall Iron Furnace—Displays of iron ore mining and iron production
Elysburg	Knoebels Amusement Resort, Anthracite Mining Museum—Early mining artifacts

Harrisburg	The State Museum of Pennsylvania—Practical applications of geology
Hellertown	The Gilman Museum/Lost River Caverns—Display of minerals and gems, cavern tour
Lancaster	North Museum of Natural History and Science—Extensive geology collection
Lansford	No. 9 Coal Mine and Museum—Coal mine tour
Media	Delaware County Institute of Science—Minerals from around the world
Patton	Seldom Seen Tourist Coal Mine—Tour a bituminous coal mine
Philadelphia	Academy of Natural Sciences—Mineral collection for research only
	Wagner Free Institute of Science—Rocks and minerals
Pittsburgh	Carnegie Museum of Natural History—One of the premier gem and mineral exhibits in the country
Scranton	Anthracite Museum Complex—Several anthracite coal-related attractions, including a mine tour and a museum
	Everhart Museum of Natural History, Science, and Art—Displays of rocks and minerals
State College	Earth and Mineral Sciences Museum and Art Gallery—Displays of minerals, mining equipment, scientific instruments
Tarentum	Tour-Ed Mine—Bituminous coal mine tour
Uniontown	The Coal & Coke Heritage Center—Connellsville Coke Region
Waynesburg	Paul R. Stewart Museum, Waynesburg University—Outstanding mineral collection
West Chester	Geology Museum, West Chester University—Specimens from Chester County, fluorescent specimens
Wilkes-Barre	Luzerne County Historical Society Museum—Display on anthracite coal mining

RHODE ISLAND

Fee Dig Mines and Guide Services
> None

Museums and Mine Tours

Providence	Museum of Natural History and Planetarium—Collections of rocks and minerals

SOUTH CAROLINA

Fee Dig Mines and Guide Services

Antreville   Diamond Hill—Dig your own quartz

Greenville   Greenville Gemstone Mine—Sluice for gems and minerals from around the world

Edgefield   Francis Marion and Sumter National Forests—Rockhounding and mineral specimen collecting, recreational gold panning

Museums and Mine Tours

Charleston   The Charleston Museum—Small display of gems and minerals

Clemson   Bob Campbell Geology Museum—Rocks, minerals, lapidary objects

Columbia   McKissick Museum, University of South Carolina campus—Exhibits on geology and gemstones

South Carolina State Museum—Displays of gems and minerals

SOUTH DAKOTA

Fee Dig Mines and Guide Services

Deadwood   Broken Boot Gold Mine—Pan for gold

Hill City   Wade's Gold Mill—Pan for gold

Keystone   Big Thunder Gold Mine—Pan for gold

Lead   Black Hills Mining Museum—Pan for gold

Wall   Buffalo Gap National Grassland—Hunt for agates

Museums and Mine Tours

Deadwood   Broken Boot Gold Mine—Gold mine tour

Hill City   Wade's Gold Mill—Guided tour and displays of mining equipment

Keystone   Big Thunder Gold Mine—Mine tour

Lead   Black Hills Mining Museum—Simulated underground mine tour

Sanford Lab Homestake Visitor Center—Gold mining displays

Murdo   National Rockhound and Lapidary Hall of Fame—Gems and minerals

Rapid City   Journey Museum—Geology of the Black Hills

South Dakota School of Mines and Technology—Local minerals

TENNESSEE

Fee Dig Mines and Guide Services
Ducktown   Burra Burra Mine—Collection area on site; look for garnets, pyrite, chalcopyrite, pyrrhotite, actinolite

Museums and Mine Tours
Camden Kentucky Lake
                Tennessee River Freshwater Pearl Farm and Museum—Farm, tour
Ducktown   Ducktown Basin Museum—Copper mining heritage
Johnson City Hands On! Regional Museum—Simulated coal mine
Knoxville   The Frank H. McClung Museum—Geology of Tennessee
Memphis   Memphis Pink Palace Museum—Geology and minerals from famous mid-South localities
Murfreesboro The Earth Experience: Middle Tennessee Museum of Natural History—Minerals from Tennessee, fluorite, calcite, gemstones, artisan jewelry
Savannah   Tennessee River Museum—Exhibit of historic pearl button and modern cultured pearl industries

TEXAS

Fee Dig Mines and Guide Services
Alpine   Stillwell Ranch—Hunt for agate and jasper
Mason   Lindsay Ranch Guesthouses—Hunt for topaz and other minerals
                Seaquist Ranch—Hunt for topaz
Three Rivers House's Mother Lode Ranch—Hunt for agate and petrified wood

Museums and Mine Tours
Alpine   Last Frontier Museum and Antelope Lodge—Display of rocks from West Texas
Austin   Texas Memorial Museum—Gems and minerals
Canyon   Panhandle-Plains Historical Museum—Geology of Davis Mountain, mine replica with minerals and ores
Dallas   Lyda Hill Gems and Mineral Hall, Perot Museum of Nature and Science—Learn about colors, shapes, hardness of rocks; how crystals form
Fort Davis Chihuahuan Desert Nature Center—Displays on area mining and minerals

Fort Stockton	Annie Riggs Memorial Museum—Rocks and minerals of Pecos County and the Big Bend area
Fort Worth	Oscar E. Monnig Meteorite Gallery—Meteorites display
Fritch	Alibates Flint Quarries—View ancient flint quarries
Houston	Houston Museum of Natural Science—Displays of gem and mineral specimens
Marble Falls	Granite Mountain—View marble mining operations
Odessa	Odessa Meteor Crater and Museum—Meteorite crater and museum

UTAH

Fee Dig Mines and Guide Services

Delta	Dugway Geodes—The Bug House—Private claim to Dugway Geodes
	Topaz Mountain Adventures—Collecting tours for amber and sherry colored topaz
Dugway Mountains	
	Dugway Geode Beds—Dig for geodes
Kanab	Joe's Rock Shop—Dig for septarian nodules
Moab	Deep Desert Expeditions—Guided collecting tours, dig through mine tailings for azurite, malachite, geodes
Orem	Orem Simple Elegance Rock Shop—Rockhounding excursions
Price	Manti-La Sal National Forest—Hunt for birdseye marble
Salt Lake City	Rockpick Legend Co.—Collecting trips for topaz, red beryl, azurite, malachite and other minerals

Museums and Mine Tours

Bingham Canyon	
	Bingham Canyon Mine Visitors' Center—Overlook for open-pit copper mine
Eureka	Tintic Mining Museum—Mineral display and mining artifacts
Helper	Western Mining and Railroad Museum—Mining exhibits, simulated 1900 coal mine
Lehi	John Hutchings Museum of Natural History—Displays linked to mining districts, display of uncut gems
Moab	Dan O'Laurie Museum of Moab—Displays of rocks and minerals, mining history
Salt Lake City	Natural History Museum of Utah—Utah ores and minerals

VERMONT

Fee Dig Mines and Guide Services
Ludlow   Camp Plymouth State Park—Gold panning

Museums and Mine Tours
Barre   Rock of Ages Visitors' Center—Watch granite being quarried

Vermont Granite Museum and Stone Arts School—Displays on geology, history, art of Vermont's granite heritage. Sculptors from around the world explore stone carving

Proctor   Vermont Marble Museum—Learn how marble is formed, quarried and sculpted

St. Johnsbury Fairbanks Museum and Planetarium—Display of rocks and minerals from Vermont

Annual Event
Barre   Granite Festival—One Saturday in summer or early fall

VIRGINIA

Fee Dig Mines and Guide Services
Amelia   Morefield Gem Mine, Inc.—Dig and sluice for quartz, topaz, and many others

McKenney   Lucky Lake Gem and Mineral Mine of Virginia—Sluice for natural minerals and salted material

Stuart   Fairy Stone State Park—Hunt for staurolite crystals (fairy stones)

Museums and Mine Tours
Big Stone Gap Harry W. Meador, Jr., Coal Museum—Exhibits and mining equipment

Blacksburg   Virginia Tech Geosciences Museum—Large display of Virginia minerals

Breaks   Breaks Interstate Park—Overlook and museum, explains geological features and science behind local coal industry

Goldvein   The Gold Mining Camp Museum, Monroe Park—Tour a mine camp, gold panning demonstrations

Harrisonburg The James Madison University Mineral Museum—Minerals, gems, specimens from Virginia

Martinsville Stone Cross Mountain Museum—A museum of staurolite crystals

Virginia Museum of Natural History—Rocks and minerals

Pocahontas   Pocahontas Exhibition Coal Mine and Museum—Coal mine tour

| Radford | Museum of the Earth Sciences, Radford University—Gems, minerals, rocks, fluorescent minerals |
| Richmond | University of Richmond Museums—Displays Virginia minerals and a 2,400-carat blue topaz |

WASHINGTON

Fee Dig Mines and Guide Services

| Ravensdale | Geology Adventures, Inc.—Field trips; collect quartz, garnets, and others |

Museums and Mine Tours

Castle Rock	Mount St. Helens National Volcanic Monument—Focus on geology
Cle Elum	Coal Mines Trail—Historical walk through mining history
Ellensburg	Kittitas County Historical Museum—Polished rocks
Pullman	Washington State University—Petrified wood, minerals
Seattle	Burke Museum of Natural History and Culture—Rocks, minerals, the geology of Washington, and a walk-through volcano
	Klondike Gold Rush National Historical Park—Commemorates gold rush

WEST VIRGINIA

Fee Dig Mines and Guide Services

| Shady Spring | Someplace Special Gem Mine—Dig, screen, and sluice for various gems, metal detect |

Museums and Mine Tours

Beckley	The Beckley Exhibition Coal Mine—Tour a bituminous coal mine
Charleston	The Avampato Discovery Museum at the Clay Center—Exhibits show the story behind West Virginia's geology
Madison	Bituminous Coal Heritage Foundation Museum—History of coal mining in Boone County
Morgantown	West Virginia Geological and Economic Survey Mini-Museum—Geology of West Virginia

WISCONSIN

Fee Dig Mines and Guide Services

| Rhinelander | Chequamegon-Nicolet National Forest—Pan for gold or collect rocks |

Museums and Mine Tours

Dodgeville The Museum of Minerals and Crystals—Local mineral specimens, specimens from around the world

Hurley Iron County Historical Museum—History of area mining, last remaining mine head frame in Wisconsin (nearby site)

Madison University of Wisconsin Geology Museum—Minerals, fluorescent minerals, meteorites

Menasha Weis Earth Science Museum, University of Wisconsin, Fox Valley—Official state mineralogical museum of Wisconsin

Milwaukee Milwaukee Public Museum—Displays of geological specimens

Platteville The Mining and Rollo Jameson Museum—Lead and zinc mining in the upper Mississippi Valley

Shullsburg Badger Mine and Museum—Displays of lead mining equipment, tour a hand-dug mine

Stevens Point UW–Stevens Point Museum of Natural History—Rock and mineral display

Annual Event

Neenah Quarry Quest—Kid-oriented collecting activities, held in September and sponsored by many businesses in the local community

WYOMING

Fee Dig Mines and Guide Services

None

Museums and Mine Tours

Casper Tate Geological Museum—Rocks and minerals, including Wyoming jade, and fluorescent minerals

Cheyenne Wyoming State Museum—Minerals of Wyoming, coal "swamp"

Kemmerer Fossil County Frontier Museum—Replica of underground coal mine

Laramie Geological Museum, University of Wyoming—Rocks and minerals, fluorescent minerals from Wyoming

Rawlins Rawlins Paint Mines—Geologic feature

Rock Springs Rock Springs Historical Museum—Coal mining exhibits

Saratoga Saratoga Museum—Gem and mineral museum

Worland Washakie Museum and Cultural Center—Geology of Big Horn Basin

Index by Gems and Minerals

This index lists all the gems and minerals that can be found at fee dig mines in the U.S., and shows the city and state where the mine is located. To use the index, look up the gem or mineral you are interested in, and note the states and cities where they are located. Then go to the state and city to find the name of the mine, and information about the mine.

The following notes provide additional information:

(#)   A number in parentheses is the number of mines in that town that have that gem or mineral.

(*)   Gem or mineral is found in the state, but the mine may also add material to the ore. Check with the individual mine for confirmation.

(FT)   Field trip.

(GS)   Guide service (location listed is the location of the guide service, not necessarily the location of the gems or minerals being collected).

(I)   Mineral has been identified at the mine site but may be difficult to find (rare).

(M)   Museum that allows collection of one specimen as a souvenir.

(MM) Micromount (a very small crystal, which, when viewed under a microscope or magnifying glass, is found to be a high-quality crystal).

(O)   Available at mine but comes from other mines (native U.S.).

(S)   Not the main gem or mineral for which the site is known.

(SA)   "Salted" or enriched gem or mineral (not from native U.S. mines).

(U)   Unique to the site.

(Y)   Yearly collecting event.

Actinolite Tennessee: Ducktown

Agate Arkansas: Murfreesboro (S); California: Blythe; Michigan: Grand Marais; Minnesota: Moose Lake; Montana: Helena (S); Nebraska: Crawford; New Mexico: Deming; North Carolina: Chimney Rock (O); Oregon: Madras; South Dakota: Wall; Texas: Three Rivers
> **Banded agate** Texas: Alpine; New Mexico: Gila
> **Fire agate** Arizona: Safford (2); California: Palo Verde
> **Ledge agate** Oregon: Madras
> **Moss agate** Oregon: Madras; Texas: Alpine
> **Paint rock agate** Alabama: Trenton (GS)
> **Polka-dot jasp-agate** Oregon: Madras
> **Prairie agate** Nebraska: Crawford
> **Pom pom agate** Texas: Alpine
> **Rainbow agate** Oregon: Madras

Albite Maine: Bethel, Poland (GS), West Paris; New Hampshire: Grafton (I); New Mexico: Dixon
> **Albite (cleavelandite var.)** Maine: Poland (GS)

Amazonite Virginia: Amelia

Amber Texas: Mason (R); Washington: Ravensdale (GS)

Amethyst Arkansas: Mt. Ida (SA), Murfreesboro (S); Georgia: Cleveland, Dahlonega, Tignall, Warrenton; Maine: Stow, West Paris, Woodstock; Montana: Dillon; New Hampshire: Grafton (I); North Carolina (*): Blowing Rock (O), Boone, Bryson City (SA), Cherokee, Chimney Rock (O), Franklin (4), Hendersonville, Highlands, Leicester, Spruce Pine (3); South Carolina: Antreville

Ametrine North Carolina: Blowing Rock (O), Bryson City (SA)

Amblygonite Maine: West Paris

Amphibolite New Hampshire: Grafton (I)

Amygdule California: Blythe

Andesite New Mexico: Gila

Apatite Maine: Auburn, Poland (GS), West Paris; New Hampshire: Grafton; New Mexico: Dixon
> **Blue apatite** Maine: Auburn; West Virginia: Shady Spring (SA)
> **Fluorapatite** Maine: Poland (GS); New Hampshire: Grafton
> **Hydroxylapatite** Maine: Poland (GS)
> **Purple apatite** Maine: Auburn, West Paris

Aplite New Hampshire: Grafton (I)

Aquamarine California: Pala (2); Georgia: LaGrange; Maine: Bethel, Poland (GS), Woodstock; New Hampshire: Grafton (I); North Carolina (*): Blowing Rock (O), Boone, Bryson City (SA), Chimney Rock (O), Franklin (2), Hendersonville, Hiddenite, Marion, Spruce Pine (2) (FT)

Brushy Creek aquamarine North Carolina: Spruce Pine (I) (FT)
Weisman aquamarine North Carolina: Spruce Pine (I) (FT)

Arsenopyrite Maine: Poland (GS)

Augelite Maine: Poland (GS)

Autunite Maine: Auburn, Bethel, Poland (GS); New Hampshire: Grafton (I)

Azurite Utah: Moab (GS), Salt Lake City

Aventurine North Carolina: Hendersonville

Barite Arkansas: Murfreesboro (S); Georgia: Lincolnton; New Mexico: Bingham; Washington: Ravensdale (GS)

Benitoite California: Coalinga

Beraumite Maine: Poland (GS)

Bermanite Maine: Poland (GS)

Bertrandite Maine: Poland (GS), Stoneham; New Hampshire: Grafton (I)

Beryl Georgia: LaGrange; Maine: Auburn, Bethel, Poland (GS), Stow, West Paris; New Hampshire: Grafton (I); New Mexico: Dixon; North Carolina (*): Spruce Pine (2); Virginia: Amelia
  Aqua beryl New Hampshire: Grafton (I)
  Blue beryl (see also aquamarine) New Hampshire: Grafton (I)
  Golden beryl Maine: Woodstock (I); North Carolina: Spruce Pine (FT); New Hampshire: Grafton (I)
  Red beryl Utah: Salt Lake City

Beryllonite Maine: Poland (GS)

Beta-uranophane New Hampshire: Grafton

Biotite Maine: Bethel; New Hampshire: Grafton (I)

Bornite New Hampshire: Grafton (I)

Brazilianite Maine: Poland (GS)

Brochantite New Mexico: Bingham

Cacoxenite Georgia: Lincolnton

Calcite Arkansas: Murfreesboro (S); Florida: Okeechobee; Michigan: Ontonagon; New Hampshire: Grafton; New Mexico: Bingham; New York: Middleville; North Carolina: Leicester; Texas: Mason; Virginia: Amelia

Cape May "Diamonds" See Quartz

Casserite New Hampshire: Conway

Cassiterite Maine: Poland (GS); West Paris, Woodstock; Texas: Mason

Chalcedony Arizona: Safford; Nebraska: Crawford; New Mexico: Deming
  Pink New Mexico: Gila
  Chalcedony roses California: Blythe; New Mexico: Gila
  White New Mexico: Gila

Chalcopyrite Tennessee: Ducktown

Childrenite Maine: Poland (GS)

Chrysoberyl New Hampshire: Grafton (I)

Citrine Alabama: Lineville (S); North Carolina (*): Blowing Rock (O), Boone, Bryson City (SA), Cherokee, Franklin (4), Hendersonville, Highlands, Leicester, Spruce Pine (2); Virginia: McKenney

Clarkite New Hampshire: Grafton (I)

Cleavelandite California: Pala; Maine: Auburn, West Paris; New Hampshire: Grafton (I); New Mexico: Dixon

Columbite Maine: Poland (GS), Stow, West Paris; New Hampshire: Grafton (I)

Compotite New Hampshire: Grafton (I)

Cookeite Maine: West Paris

Copper, pure Michigan: Mohawk, Ontonagon

Copper minerals Michigan: Mohawk (M)

Corundum Montana: Alder

Crandallite Georgia: Lincolnton

Cryolite New Hampshire: Grafton (I)

Cymatolite New Hampshire: Grafton (I)

Datolite Michigan: Ontonagon

Dendrite New Hampshire: Grafton (I)

Diadochite Maine: Poland (GS)

Diamond Arkansas: Mt. Ida (SA), Murfreesboro

Dickinsonite Maine: Poland (GS)

Djurleite California: Coalinga

Dolomite crystals New York: Middleville

Earlshannonite Maine: Poland (GS)

Elabite See listing under Tourmaline

Emerald Arkansas: Mt. Ida (SA); Georgia: Cleveland (SA), Dahlonega (2); North Carolina (*): Blowing Rock (O), Boone, Bryson City (SA), Cherokee, Chimney Rock (O), Franklin, Hendersonville, Hiddenite, Leicester, Marion, Spruce Pine (3); West Virginia: Shady Spring (SA)
  Crabtree emerald North Carolina: Spruce Pine

Eosphorite Maine: Poland (GS)

Epidote Michigan: Ontonagon; Texas: Mason

Fairfieldite Maine: Poland (GS)

Fairy stones (See Staurolite crystals)

Feldspar Maine: Stoneham, Stow; Michigan: Ontonagon; New Hampshire: Conway, Grafton (I); North Carolina: Marion; Oregon: Plush; Virginia: Amelia
　Albite feldspar Maine: Bethel

Flint Ohio: Hopewell (2)

Fluoroapatite Maine: Stoneham; New Hampshire: Grafton (I)

Fluorescent minerals Kentucky: Marion; New Jersey: Franklin, Ogdensburg; North Carolina: Spruce Pine; Washington: Ravensdale (GS)

Fluorite Illinois: Rosiclare; Kentucky: Marion; New Hampshire: Conway; New Mexico: Bingham; North Carolina: Hendersonville, Leicester; Virginia: Amelia; Washington: Ravensdale (GS)

Franklinite New Jersey: Franklin

Fuchsite Georgia: Lincolnton

Gahnite (spinel) Maine: Poland (GS), Stoneham, West Paris

Gainsite Maine: Poland (GS)

Galena New Mexico: Bingham; Texas: Mason

Garnet Alabama: Lineville (S); Arkansas: Mt. Ida (SA); Arizona: Apache Junction; California: Columbia, Pala (2); Georgia: Dahlonega (2); Idaho: St. Maries; Maine: Auburn, Bethel, Poland (GS), Stoneham, Stow, West Paris; Montana: Alder, Helena (S); Nevada: Ely; New Hampshire: Grafton (I); New Mexico: Dixon; New York: North River; North Carolina (*): Blowing Rock (O), Boone, Bryson City (SA), Canton, Cherokee, Chimney Rock (O), Franklin (5), Hendersonville, Hiddenite, Highlands, Leicester, Marion, Marshall, Spruce Pine (4) (FT); South Dakota: Hill City; Tennessee: Ducktown; Texas: Mason; Utah: Delta; Virginia: McKenney; Washington: Ravensdale (GS); West Virginia: Shady Spring (SA)
　Almandine garnet Maine: Bethel, Poland (GS); Nevada: Ely
　Pyrope garnet North Carolina: Franklin
　Rhodolite garnet North Carolina: Franklin
　Star garnet Idaho: St. Maries

Geodes Arizona: Safford; California: Blythe; Illinois: Hamilton (4); Iowa: Keokuk (FT); Missouri: Alexandria, St. Francisville; New Mexico: Deming, Gila; Utah: Dugway Mountains, Moab (GS)

Lined with:
　Agate, blue New Mexico: Deming
　Aragonite Illinois: Hamilton; Missouri: Alexandria
　Barite Illinois: Hamilton; Missouri: Alexandria
　Calcite Illinois: Hamilton; Missouri: Alexandria
　Chalcedony New Mexico: Deming
　Crystal Missouri: Alexandria; Washington: Ravensdale (GS)
　Dolomite Missouri: Alexandria

Goethite Missouri: Alexandria
Kaoline Missouri: Alexandria
Kaolinite Illinois: Hamilton
Opal, common New Mexico: Deming
Pyrite Missouri: Alexandria
Quartz New Mexico: Deming
Selenite needles Missouri: Alexandria
Sphalerite Missouri: Alexandria

Gold (*) Alabama: Lineville; Alaska: Anchorage, Chicken, Chugach, Copper Center, Fairbanks, Girdwood, Nome, Skagway (2); Arizona: Apache Junction, Prescott; California: Angels Camp, Coloma, Columbia, Jamestown, Mariposa, Nevada City, Pine Grove; Colorado: Breckenridge, Idaho Springs (2), Ouray, Silverton; Georgia: Cleveland, Dahlonega (2), Gainesville; Idaho: Rathdrum; Indiana: Knightstown; Montana: Helena (S), Libby; New Hampshire: Conway; New Mexico: Gila; North Carolina: Cherokee, Franklin (2), Leicester, Marion (2), Midland, New London, Union Mills; Oklahoma: Moyers; Oregon: Roseburg; Pennsylvania: Spring Grove (GS); South Dakota: Deadwood, Hill City, Keystone, Lead; Vermont: Ludlow; Wisconsin: Rhinelander

Gossanite (clear beryl) California: Pala

Goyazite Maine: Poland (GS)

Graftonite Maine: Poland (GS); New Hampshire: Grafton (I)

Granite, graphic Maine: Auburn

Gummite New Hampshire: Grafton (I)

Hematite Montana: Helena (S); North Carolina: Chimney Rock (O)
  Banded welded tuff New Mexico: Gila
  Iridescent Georgia: Lincolnton
  Massive New Mexico: Gila

Herderite hydroxyl Maine: Poland (GS), West Paris

Herkimer "diamonds" See Quartz

Heterosite Maine: Poland (GS)

Hiddenite (spodumene) California: Pala; North Carolina: Hiddenite

Hureaulite Maine: Poland (GS)

Ilmenite Georgia: Lincolnton

Iron ore Michigan: Iron Mountain (M)

Jade California: Pine Grove

Jadite Montana: Helena (S)

Jahnsite Maine: Poland (GS)

Jasper Arkansas: Murfreesboro (S); California: Blythe, Pine Grove; Montana: Helena (S); Oregon: Madras; South Dakota: Hill City; Texas: Alpine; West Virginia: Shady Spring (SA)

Brown jasper New Mexico: Deming, Gila
Chocolate jasper New Mexico: Deming
Jasper breccia New Mexico: Gila
Orange jasper New Mexico: Deming
Picture jasper New Mexico: Gila; Oregon: Mitchell
Pink jasper New Mexico: Deming
Red jasper New Mexico: Gila
Variegated jasper New Mexico: Deming
Yellow jasper New Mexico: Deming, Gila

Joaquinite California: Coalinga

Kaolinite Maine: Poland (GS)

Kasolite New Hampshire: Grafton (I)

Kosnarite Maine: Poland (GS)

Kunzite California: Pala (2)

Kyanite Georgia: Lincolnton; North Carolina (*): Franklin (2), Leicester; West Virginia: Shady Spring (SA)

Labradorite Oregon: Plush (2)

Lake County "diamonds" See Quartz

Landsite Maine: Poland (GS)

Laueite Maine: Poland (GS)

Lazulite Georgia: Lincolnton

Lepidolite Maine: Poland (GS), West Paris, Woodstock; New Mexico: Dixon; North Carolina (*): Spruce Pine; West Virginia: Shady Spring (SA)
Lemon yellow lepidolite New Hampshire: Grafton (I)
Purple lepidolite California: Pala

Lepidomelane New Hampshire: Grafton (I)

Limonite New Mexico: Gila

Linarite New Mexico: Bingham

Lithiophilite Maine: Poland (GS); New Hampshire: Grafton (I)

Lollingite Maine: Poland (GS), Woodstock

Ludlamite Maine: Poland (GS)

Magnesium oxide See Psilomellane

Malachite Utah: Moab (GS), Salt Lake City

Manganapatite New Hampshire: Grafton (I)

Manganese minerals New Mexico: Deming

Manganese oxide minerals New Mexico: Deming

Marble (Birdseye) Utah: Price

Marcasite Florida: Okeechobee; New Hampshire: Grafton (I)

McCrillisite Maine: Poland (GS)

Mica California: Pala; Maine: Auburn, Poland (GS); New Hampshire: Grafton (I), Laconia; North Carolina: Canton, Franklin; Virginia: Amelia
   Biotite mica Maine: Poland (GS)
   Book mica California: Pala
   Lepidolite mica Maine: Poland (GS)
   Muscovite mica Maine: Poland (GS)

Microcline Maine: Poland (GS)

Microlite New Mexico: Dixon

Micropyrite Florida: Okeechobee

Mitridatite Maine: Poland (GS)

Molybdenite New Hampshire: Grafton (I)

Montebrasite Maine: Poland (GS), Woodstock

Montmorillonite Maine: Poland (GS), West Paris; New Hampshire: Grafton (I)

Monzaite Maine: Poland (GS)

Moonstone Georgia: Dahlonega; North Carolina (*): Blowing Rock (O), Bryson City (SA), Franklin (6), Highlands, Leicester, Marion, Spruce Pine (2)

Moraesite Maine: Poland (GS)

Morganite California: Pala (2)

Muscovite California: Pala; Georgia: Lincolnton; Maine: Stow; New Hampshire: Grafton (I); New Mexico: Dixon

Natrolite California: Coalinga

Neptunite California: Coalinga

Opal Nevada: Denio; North Carolina: Hendersonville (SA)
   Black opal Nevada: Denio
   Common opal New Mexico: Deming
   Fire opal Nevada: Denio (2)
   Precious opal Idaho: Spencer
   Wood opal Nevada: Denio

Palm Wood Texas: Alpine, Three Rivers

Perhamite Maine: Poland (GS)

Peacock Ore Washington: Ravensdale (GS)

Petrified Wood Oregon: Sweet Home; Texas: Alpine, Three Rivers

Parsonite New Hampshire: Grafton (I)

Perlite (black to gray) New Mexico: Deming

Peridot Arkansas: Murfreesboro (S); North Carolina (*): Blowing Rock (O), Bryson City (SA), Boone, Chimney Rock (O)

Petalite Maine: Poland (GS), West Paris

Petoskey Stones Michigan: Petoskey

Phenakite Maine: Stoneham; Virginia: Amelia

Phosphosiderite Georgia: Lincolnton; Maine: Poland (GS)

Phosphouranylite Maine: Poland (GS)

Phosphyanylite New Hampshire: Grafton (I)

Pitch Stone (with seams of red and brown) New Mexico: Deming

Pollucite Maine: Poland (GS), West Paris, Woodstock

Psilomelane California: Blythe; New Hampshire: Grafton (I)

Purpurite Maine: Poland (GS); New Hampshire: Grafton (I)

Pseudomorphs South Carolina: Antreville

Pyrite Georgia: Lincolnton; Maine: Bethel, Poland (GS), Stow; New Hampshire: Grafton (I); Tennessee: Ducktown; Virginia: Amelia; Washington: Ravensdale (GS)
   Iron pyrite Arizona: Apache Junction

Pyrophyllite Georgia: Lincolnton

Pyrrhotite New Hampshire: Grafton (I); Tennessee: Ducktown

Quartz Arkansas: Jessieville (2), Mena, Mt. Ida (6) (Y), Murfreesboro (S), Story; California: Angels Camp, Pala, Pine Grove; Delaware: Wilmington; Georgia: Dahlonega, Lincolnton; Maine: Auburn, Bethel, Poland (GS), Stoneham, West Paris, Woodstock; Michigan: Ontonagon; Montana: Dillon, Helena (S); New Mexico: Bingham, Deming, Dixon; North Carolina: Chimney Rock (O), Franklin (3), Hendersonville, Marion, Spruce Pine; South Dakota: Hill City; Texas: Mason; Virginia: Amelia; Washington: Ravensdale (GS)
   Blue Georgia: Lincolnton; North Carolina: Marion
   Clear Arkansas: Jessieville; Maine: Woodstock; North Carolina (*): Hiddenite, Spruce Pine
   Doubly Terminated Scepters Washington: Ravensdale (GS)
   Druse Georgia: Tignall
   Milky South Carolina: Antreville
   Phantoms Washington: Ravensdale (GS)
   Pseudocubic crystals Maine: West Paris
   Rose Maine: Bethel, Woodstock; New Hampshire: Grafton (I); North Carolina (*): Blowing Rock (O), Bryson City (SA), Franklin, Leicester, Marion, Spruce Pine (O); West Virginia: Shady Spring (SA)
   Rutilated North Carolina (*): Spruce Pine
   Skeletal quartz South Carolina: Antreville
   Smoky California: Pala; Maine: Auburn, Bethel, Woodstock; New Hampshire: Conway, Grafton; North Carolina (*): Blowing Rock (O), Boone, Bryson City (SA), Cherokee, Franklin (4), Hiddenite, Highlands, Marion, Spruce Pine (3); South Carolina: Antreville; Virginia: McKenney

Star rose Georgia: LaGrange
White Arkansas: Jessieville; New Hampshire: Grafton
Quartz "diamonds"
    Lake Co. "diamonds" (moon tears) California: Lower Lake, Lucerne
    Cape May "diamonds" New Jersey: Cape May
    Herkimer "diamonds" New York: Herkimer, Middleville, St. Johnsville

Reddingite Maine: Poland (GS); New Hampshire: Grafton

Rhodochrosite Maine: Poland (GS)

Rhodolite (garnet) North Carolina: Blowing Rock (O), Bryson City (SA), Franklin (2)

Rhyolite, banded New Mexico: Gila

Riebeckite New Hampshire: Conway

Rochbridgeite Maine: Poland (GS)

Rose rocks See Barite

Rubalite Maine: Auburn

Ruby Arkansas: Mt. Ida (SA) (2); California: Pine Grove; Georgia: Cleveland, Dahlonega (2); Montana: Helena (S); North Carolina (*): Blowing Rock (O), Boone, Bryson City (SA), Cherokee, Chimney Rock (O), Franklin (7), Hendersonville, Highlands, Leicester, Spruce Pine (4); West Virginia: Shady Spring (SA)

Rutile Georgia: Lincolnton; Maine: Poland (GS); North Carolina: Franklin, Hiddenite

Safflorite New Hampshire: Grafton (I)

Sapphire Georgia: Cleveland (SA), Dahlonega (2); Montana: Hamilton, Helena, Philipsburg (2); North Carolina (*): Blowing Rock (O), Bryson City (SA), Cherokee, Franklin (7), Hendersonville, Hiddenite, Highlands, Leicester, Spruce Pine (2)

    Sapphire, blue North Carolina: Canton
    Sapphire, gray North Carolina: Canton
    Sapphire, white North Carolina: Canton
    Sapphire, bronze North Carolina: Canton
    Sapphire, pink North Carolina: Canton
    Star sapphire North Carolina: Boone (SA)

Scheelite Maine: West Paris

Scoria New Mexico: Gila

Selenite crystals New Mexico: Bingham; Oklahoma: Jet

Septarian nodules Utah: Kanab

Serpentine Montana: Helena (S)

Silica minerals New Mexico: Deming

Sillimanite New Hampshire: Grafton (I); North Carolina (*): Franklin, Hiddenite

Silver Michigan: Ontonagon

Sodalite North Carolina: Chimney Rock (O), Hendersonville (SA); West Virginia: Shady Spring (SA)

Soddylite New Hampshire: Grafton (I)

Spessartine New Mexico: Dixon

Spodumene Maine: Poland (GS), West Paris, Woodstock; New Mexico: Dixon
   Altered spodumene Maine: West Paris

Staurolite New Hampshire: Grafton (I); Virginia: Stuart

Stewartite Maine: Poland (GS)

Strengite Georgia: Lincolnton

Strunzite Maine: Poland (GS)

Sulfur Georgia: Lincolnton

Sunstone Oregon: Lakeview, Plush (3)

Switzerite Maine: Poland (GS)

Tantalite-Columbite Virginia: Amelia

Thundereggs New Mexico: Deming; Oregon: Madras, Mitchell, Nyssa (Y)

Tobernite New Hampshire: Grafton (I)

Topaz Georgia: Cleveland (SA), Dahlonega; Maine: Poland (GS), Stoneham; Montana: Helena (S); New Hampshire: Conway, Grafton (I); North Carolina (*): Blowing Rock (O), Boone, Bryson City (SA), Cherokee, Franklin (4), Highlands, Leicester, Spruce Pine (2); Texas: Mason (2); Utah: Delta, Salt Lake City; Virginia: Amelia, McKenney

Torberite Maine: Poland (GS)

Tourmaline California: Mesa Grande, Pala; Maine: Auburn (2), Poland (GS), West Paris, Woodstock; New Hampshire: Grafton (I); North Carolina (*): Boone, Franklin (3), Hiddenite, Highlands, Marion, Spruce Pine (2); Texas: Mason; Virginia: Amelia, McKenney (I)
   Bi-colored California: Pala
   Black tourmaline Georgia: LaGrange; Maine: Auburn, Bethel, Poland (GS), West Paris; New Hampshire: Grafton (I)
   Green tourmaline California: Pala; Maine: West Paris
   Pink tourmaline California: Pala

Triphyllite Maine: Poland (GS); New Hampshire: Grafton (I)

Triplite Maine: Poland (GS), Stoneham

Turquoise Nevada: Hawthorne, Tonopah; North Carolina: Blowing Rock (O), Bryson City (SA)

Uralolite Maine: Poland (GS)

Uranite Maine: Poland (GS), Stoneham; New Hampshire: Grafton (I) (species with gummite, world-famous)

Uranium minerals New Hampshire: Grafton (I); North Carolina: Spruce Pine

Uranophane New Hampshire: Grafton (I)

Vandendriesscheite New Hampshire: Grafton (I)

Variscite Georgia: Lincolnton

Vesuvianite Maine: West Paris (I)

Vivianite Maine: Poland (GS), Stoneham; New Hampshire: Grafton (I)

Voelerkenite New Hampshire: Grafton (I)

Volcanic Bombs New Mexico: Gila

Wardite Maine: Poland (GS)

Wavelite Arkansas: Mt. Ida

Whitlockite Maine: Poland (GS)

Whitmoreite Maine: Poland (GS)

Woodhouseite Georgia: Lincolnton

Wodginite Maine: Poland (GS)

Zeolite New Mexico: Gila

Zircon Maine: Bethel, Poland (GS), Stoneham, West Paris; New Hampshire: Grafton (I); North Carolina: Canton; Texas: Mason

Annual Events

JANUARY

Quartzite, AZ, Gem and Mineral Shows—Mid-January–mid-February
Tucson, AZ, Gem and Mineral Shows—End of January–mid-February

FEBRUARY

Quartzsite, AZ, Gem and Mineral Shows—Mid-January–mid-February
Tucson, AZ, Gem and Mineral Shows—End of January–mid-February

MARCH

Tucson, AZ, Minerals of Arizona—Symposium one day in March or April

APRIL

Jet, OK, Birding and Crystal Festival—One weekend in late April or early May
Tucson, AZ, Minerals of Arizona—Symposium one day in March or April

MAY

Bisbee, AZ, Bisbee's Fabulous Blue—Friday afternoon or Saturday morning in May
Eastport, MI, Antrim County Petoskey Stone Festival—Held the Saturday of Memorial Day weekend
Franklin, NC, Mother's Day Gemboree—Mother's Day weekend in May
Glenford, OH, Flint Ridge Knap-In—Memorial Day weekend and Labor Day weekend
Jet, OK, Birding and Crystal Festival—One weekend in late April or early May
Newry, ME, New England Mineral Conference—One weekend in May
Poland, ME, Maine Pegmatite Workshop—One week at the end of May or beginning of June

JUNE

Poland, ME, Maine Pegmatite Workshop—One week at the end of May or beginning of June
Prineville, OR, Rockhound Pow-Wow—Third weekend in June

JULY

Cottage Grove, OR, Bohemia Mining Days—Third weekend of July

Franklin, NC, Macon County Gemboree—Four days in July

Houghton, MI, Keweenaw Mineral Days—end of July

Hurley, WI, Iron County Heritage Days—From the last week in July to mid-August

Moose Lake, MN, Agate Days—One weekend in July

Nyssa, OR, Thunderegg Days—Begins on the second Thursday of July

Spruce Pine, NC, North Carolina Mineral and Gem Festival—Four days at the end of July and / or the beginning of August

AUGUST

Hurley, WI, Iron Country Heritage Days—From the last week in July to mid-August

Spruce Pine, NC, North Carolina Mineral and Gem Festival—Four days at the end of July and / or the beginning of August

SEPTEMBER

Crawford, NE, Crawford Rock Swap—Labor Day weekend

Glenford, OH, Flint Ridge Knap-In—Memorial Day weekend and Labor Day weekend

Hamilton, IL, Geode Fest—Last weekend in September

Keokuk, IA, Geode Fest—Held end of September

OCTOBER

Big Sur, CA, Big Sur Jade Festival—Second weekend in October

Coloma, CA, Marshall Gold Discovery State Historic Park: Gold Rush Live—Usually second weekend in October

Dahlonega, GA

Gold Rush Days—Third full weekend in October

World Open Gold Panning Championship, in October, at the same time as Gold Rush Days

Franklin, NC, "Leaf Looker" Gemboree—Three days in October

Jasper, GA, Pickens County Marble Festival—First full weekend in October

Mt. Ida, AR, Quartz Crystal Festival and World Championship Dig—Second weekend in October

Trona, CA, Gem-O-Rama Searles Lake—Second Saturday in October

NOVEMBER

Socorro, NM, New Mexico Mineral Symposium and Mining Artifact Collectors Symposium—Two days in November

DECEMBER

No information available.

OTHER

Barre, VT, Granite Festival—Held one Saturday in summer or early fall

Newry, ME, New England Mineral Conference

State Gem and Mineral Symbols

Dates refer to when stones and minerals were adopted by the state legislature.

STATE	GEMSTONE	MINERAL	STONE/ROCK
Alabama	Star Blue Quartz (1990)	Hematite (1967)	Marble (1969)
Alaska	Jade (1968)	Gold (1968)	
Arizona	Turquoise (1974)	Copper	
Arkansas	Diamond (1967)	Quartz crystal (1967)	Bauxite (1967)
California	Benitoite (1985)	Gold (1965)	Serpentine (1965)
Colorado	Aquamarine (1971)	Rhodochrosite (2002)	Yule Marble (2004)
Connecticut		Almadine Garnet (1977)	
Delaware		Sillimanite (1977)	
Florida	Moonstone (1970)		Agatized Coral (1979)
Georgia	Quartz (1976)	Staurolite (1976)	
Hawaii	Black Coral (1987)		
Idaho	Star Garnet (1967)		
Illinois		Fluorite (1965)	
Indiana			Salem Limestone (1971)
Iowa			Geode (1967)
Kansas			
Kentucky	Freshwater Pearl (1986)	Coal (1998)	Kentucky Agate (2000)
Louisiana	Cabochon-cut Oyster Shell (2011)	Agate (2011)	Petrified Palm
Maine	Tourmaline (1971)		
Maryland	Patuxent River Stone (2004)		
Massachusetts	Rhodonite (1979)	Babingtonite (1971)	Roxbury Pudding Stone (Conglomerate), Granite (Building and Monuments Stone), Plymouth Rock (Historic Rock), Dighton Rock (Explorer Rock) (1983)
Michigan	Isle Royal Greenstone (Chlorostrolite) (1973)		Petoskey Stone (1965)
Minnesota	Lake Superior Agate (1969)		
Mississippi			Petrified Wood (1976)
Missouri		Galena (1967)	Mozarkite (1967)

STATE	GEMSTONE	MINERAL	STONE/ROCK
Montana			Sapphire & Montana Agate (1969)
Nebraska	Blue Chalcedony (Agate) (1967)		Prairie Agate (1967)
Nevada	Virgin Valley Black Fire Opal (1987) (Precious) Nevada Turquoise (1987) (Semiprecious)	Silver (State metal)	Sandstone (1987)
New Hampshire	Smoky Quartz (1985)	Beryl (1985)	Granite (1985)
New Jersey			Stockton Sandstone (Brownstone) (legislation pending)
New Mexico	Turquoise (1967)		
New York	(Barton) Garnet (1969)		
North Carolina	Emerald (1973)		Unakite/Granite (1979)
North Dakota			
Ohio	Flint (1965)		
Oklahoma	Hourglass Selenite Crystals (2005)		Barite Rose (1968)
Oregon	Sunstone (1987)		Thunderegg (1965)
Pennsylvania			
Rhode Island		Bowenite (1966)	Cumberlandite (1966)
South Carolina	Amethyst (1969)		Blue Granite (1969)
South Dakota	Fairburn Agate (1966)	Rose Quartz (1966) (Mineral/Stone)	Black Hills Gold (1988) (official jewelry)
Tennessee	Tennessee River Pearls (1979)		Limestone (1979) and Tennessee Paint Rock Agate (1969)
Texas	Texas Blue Topaz (1969) Lone Star Cut (1977) (Gemstone Cut)	Silver (2007)	Petrified Palm Wood (1969)
Utah	Topaz (1991)	Copper (1994)	Coal (1991)
Vermont	Grossular Garnet (1991)	Talc (1991)	Granite, Marble, Slate (1991)
Virginia			
Washington	Petrified Wood (1975)		
West Virginia	Mississippian Fossil Coral (*Lithostrotionella*) (1990)		Bituminous coal (2009)
Wisconsin		Galena (1971)	Red Granite (1971)
Wyoming	Jade (Nephrite) (1967)		

Finding Your Own Birthstone

Following is a listing of fee dig sites presented in this four-volume guide where you can find your birthstone! Refer to the individual mine listings for more information on individual mines.

Garnet (January Birthstone) Alabama: Lineville (S); Arkansas: Mt. Ida (SA); Arizona: Apache Junction; California: Columbia, Pala (2); Georgia: Dahlonega (2); Idaho: St. Maries; Maine: Auburn, Bethel, Poland (GS), Stoneham, Stow, West Paris; Montana: Alder, Helena (S); Nevada: Ely; New Hampshire: Grafton (I); New Mexico: Dixon; New York: North River; North Carolina (*): Blowing Rock (O), Boone, Bryson City (SA), Canton, Cherokee, Chimney Rock (O), Franklin (5), Hendersonville, Hiddenite, Highlands, Leicester, Marion, Marshall, Spruce Pine (4) (FT); South Dakota: Hill City; Tennessee: Ducktown; Texas: Mason; Utah: Delta; Virginia: McKenney; Washington: Ravensdale (GS); West Virginia: Shady Spring (SA)

> **Almandine garnet** Maine: Bethel, Poland (GS); Nevada: Ely
>
> **Pyrope garnet** North Carolina: Franklin
>
> **Rhodolite garnet** North Carolina: Franklin
>
> **Star garnet** Idaho: St. Maries

Amethyst (February Birthstone) Arkansas: Mt. Ida (SA), Murfreesboro (S); Georgia: Cleveland, Dahlonega, Tignall, Warrenton; Maine: Stow, West Paris, Woodstock; Montana: Dillon; New Hampshire: Grafton (I); North Carolina (*): Blowing Rock (O), Boone, Bryson City (SA), Cherokee, Chimney Rock (O), Franklin (4), Hendersonville, Highlands, Leicester, Spruce Pine (3); South Carolina: Antreville

Aquamarine or Bloodstone (March Birthstone)

> **Aquamarine** California: Pala (2); Georgia: LaGrange; Maine: Bethel, Poland (GS), Woodstock; New Hampshire: Grafton (I); North Carolina (*): Blowing Rock (O), Boone, Bryson City (SA), Chimney Rock (O), Franklin (2), Hendersonville, Hiddenite, Marion, Spruce Pine (2) (FT)
>
> **Brushy Creek aquamarine** North Carolina: Spruce Pine (I) (FT)
>
> **Weisman aquamarine** North Carolina: Spruce Pine (I) (FT)

Bloodstone No listing

Diamond (April Birthstone) Arkansas: Mt. Ida (SA), Murfreesboro

Emerald (May Birthstone) Arkansas: Mt. Ida (SA); Georgia: Cleveland (SA), Dahlonega (2); North Carolina (*): Blowing Rock (O), Boone, Bryson City (SA), Cherokee, Chimney Rock (O), Franklin, Hendersonville, Hiddenite, Leicester, Marion, Spruce Pine (3); West Virginia: Shady Spring (SA)

> **Crabtree emerald** North Carolina: Spruce Pine

Alexandrite, Moonstone, or Pearl (June Birthstone)

Alexandrite No listing

Moonstone Georgia: Dahlonega; North Carolina (*): Blowing Rock (O), Bryson City (SA), Franklin (6), Highlands, Leicester, Marion, Spruce Pine (2)

Pearl Tennessee: Camden Kentucky Lake (M)

Ruby (July Birthstone) Arkansas: Mt. Ida (SA) (2); California: Pine Grove; Georgia: Cleveland, Dahlonega (2); Montana: Helena (S); North Carolina (*): Blowing Rock (O), Boone, Bryson City (SA), Cherokee, Chimney Rock (O), Franklin (7), Hendersonville, Highlands, Leicester, Spruce Pine (4); West Virginia: Shady Spring (SA)

Peridot or Sardonyx (August Birthstone)

Peridot Arkansas: Murfreesboro (S); North Carolina (*): Blowing Rock (O), Boone, Bryson City (SA), Chimney Rock (O)

Sardonyx No listing

Sapphire (September Birthstone) Georgia: Cleveland (SA), Dahlonega (2); Montana: Hamilton, Helena, Philipsburg (2); North Carolina (*): Blowing Rock (O), Bryson City (SA), Cherokee, Franklin (7), Hendersonville, Hiddenite, Highlands, Leicester, Spruce Pine (2)

Sapphire, blue North Carolina: Canton
Sapphire, gray North Carolina: Canton
Sapphire, white North Carolina: Canton
Sapphire, bronze North Carolina: Canton
Sapphire, pink North Carolina: Canton
Star sapphire North Carolina: Boone (SA)

Opal or Tourmaline (October Birthstone)

Opal Nevada: Denio; North Carolina: Hendersonville (SA)
Black opal Nevada: Denio
Common opal New Mexico: Deming
Fire opal Nevada: Denio (2)
Precious opal Idaho: Spencer
Wood opal Nevada: Denio

Tourmaline California: Mesa Grande, Pala; Maine: Auburn (2), Poland (GS), West Paris, Woodstock; New Hampshire: Grafton (I); North Carolina (*): Boone, Franklin (3), Hiddenite, Highlands, Marion, Spruce Pine (2); Texas: Mason; Virginia: Amelia, McKenney (I)
Bi-colored California: Pala
Black tourmaline Georgia: LaGrange; Maine: Auburn, Bethel, Poland (GS), West Paris; New Hampshire: Grafton (I)
Green tourmaline California: Pala; Maine: West Paris
Pink tourmaline California: Pala

Topaz or Citrine (November Birthstone)

Citrine Alabama: Lineville (S); North Carolina (*): Blowing Rock (O), Boone, Bryson City (SA), Cherokee, Franklin (4), Hendersonville, Highlands, Leicester, Spruce Pine (2); Virginia: McKenney

Topaz Georgia: Cleveland (SA), Dahlonega; Maine: Poland (GS), Stoneham; Montana: Helena (S); New Hampshire: Conway, Grafton (I); North Carolina (*): Blowing Rock (O), Boone, Bryson City (SA), Cherokee, Franklin (4), Highlands, Leicester, Spruce Pine (2); Texas: Mason (2); Utah: Delta, Salt Lake City; Virginia: Amelia, McKenney

Turquiose, Tanzanite, or Zircon (December Birthstone)

Turquoise Nevada: Hawthorne, Tonopah; North Carolina: Blowing Rock (O), Bryson City (SA)

Tanzanite No listing

Zircon Maine: Bethel, Poland (GS), Stoneham, West Paris; New Hampshire: Grafton (I); North Carolina: Canton; Texas: Mason

The preceding list of birthstones is taken from a list adopted in 1912 and updated in 2013 by the American National Association of Jewelers ("The Evolution of Birthstones" from *Jewelry & Gems—The Buying Guide* by Antoinette Matlins and A. C. Bonanno, GemStone Press, 2009; and "Birthstones, Modern Myth, and Industry" from *Gems and Gemstones: Timeless Natural Beauty of the Mineral World* by Lance Grande and Allison Augustyn, University of Chicago Press, 2009).

Finding Your Anniversary Stone

The following is a listing of fee dig sites contained in this four-volume guide where you can find the stone that is associated with a particular anniversary.

First: Gold (Jewelry) Alabama: Lineville; Alaska: Anchorage, Chicken, Chugach, Copper Center, Fairbanks, Girdwood, Nome, Skagway (2); Arizona: Apache Junction, Prescott; California: Angels Camp, Coloma, Columbia, Jamestown, Mariposa, Nevada City, Pine Grove; Colorado: Breckenridge, Idaho Springs (2), Ouray, Silverton; Georgia: Cleveland, Dahlonega (2), Gainesville; Idaho: Rathdrum; Indiana: Knightstown; Montana: Helena (S), Libby; New Hampshire: Conway; New Mexico: Gila; North Carolina: Cherokee, Franklin (2), Leicester, Marion (2), Midland, New London, Union Mills; Oklahoma: Moyers; Oregon: Roseburg; Pennsylvania: Spring Grove (GS); South Dakota: Deadwood, Hill City, Keystone, Lead; Vermont: Ludlow; Wisconsin: Rhinelander

Second: Garnet Alabama: Lineville (S); Arkansas: Mt. Ida (SA); Arizona: Apache Junction; California: Columbia, Pala (2); Georgia: Dahlonega (2); Idaho: St. Maries; Maine: Auburn, Bethel, Poland (GS), Stoneham, Stow, West Paris; Montana: Alder, Helena (S); Nevada: Ely; New Hampshire: Grafton (I); New Mexico: Dixon; New York: North River; North Carolina (*): Blowing Rock (O), Boone, Bryson City (SA), Canton, Cherokee, Chimney Rock (O), Franklin (5), Hendersonville, Hiddenite, Highlands, Leicester, Marion, Marshall, Spruce Pine (4) (FT); South Dakota: Hill City; Tennessee: Ducktown; Texas: Mason; Utah: Delta; Virginia: McKenney; Washington: Ravensdale (GS); West Virginia: Shady Spring (SA)

    Almandine garnet Maine: Bethel, Poland (GS); Nevada: Ely

    Pyrope garnet North Carolina: Franklin

    Rhodolite garnet North Carolina: Franklin

    Star garnet Idaho: St. Maries

Third: Pearl Tennessee: Camden Kentucky Lake (M)

Fourth: Blue topaz No listing

Fifth: Sapphire Georgia: Cleveland (2), Dahlonega (2); Montana: Hamilton, Helena, Philipsburg (2); North Carolina (*): Blowing Rock (O), Bryson City (SA), Cherokee, Franklin (7), Hendersonville, Hiddenite, Highlands, Leicester, Spruce Pine (2)

    Sapphire, blue North Carolina: Canton

    Sapphire, gray North Carolina: Canton

    Sapphire, white North Carolina: Canton

    Sapphire, bronze North Carolina: Canton

    Sapphire, pink North Carolina: Canton

    Star sapphire North Carolina: Boone (SA)

Sixth: Amethyst Arkansas: Mt. Ida (SA), Murfreesboro (S); Georgia: Cleveland, Dahlonega, Tignall, Warrenton; Maine: Stow, West Paris, Woodstock; Montana: Dillon; New Hampshire: Grafton (I); North Carolina (*): Blowing Rock (O), Boone, Bryson City (SA), Cherokee, Chimney Rock (O), Franklin (4), Hendersonville, Highlands, Leicester, Spruce Pine (3); South Carolina: Antreville

Seventh: Onyx No listing

Eighth: Tourmaline California: Mesa Grande, Pala; Maine: Auburn (2), Poland (GS), West Paris, Woodstock; New Hampshire: Grafton (I); North Carolina (*): Boone, Franklin (3), Hiddenite, Highlands, Marion, Spruce Pine (2); Texas: Mason; Virginia: Amelia, McKenney (I)
  Bi-colored California: Pala
  Black tourmaline Georgia: LaGrange; Maine: Auburn, Bethel, Poland (GS), West Paris; New Hampshire: Grafton (I)
  Green tourmaline California: Pala; Maine: West Paris
  Pink tourmaline California: Pala

Ninth: Lapis Lazuli No listing

Tenth: Diamond (Jewelry) Arkansas: Mt. Ida (SA), Murfreesboro

Eleventh: Turquoise Nevada: Hawthorne, Tonopah; North Carolina: Blowing Rock (O), Bryson City (SA)

Twelfth: Jade California: Pine Grove

Thirteenth: Citrine Alabama: Lineville (S); North Carolina (*): Blowing Rock (O), Boone, Bryson City (SA), Cherokee, Franklin (4), Hendersonville, Highlands, Leicester, Spruce Pine (2); Virginia: McKenney

Fourteenth: Opal Nevada: Denio; North Carolina: Hendersonville (SA)
  Black opal Nevada: Denio
  Common opal New Mexico: Deming
  Fire opal Nevada: Denio (2)
  Precious opal Idaho: Spencer
  Wood opal Nevada: Denio

Fifteenth: Ruby Arkansas: Mt. Ida (SA) (2); California: Pine Grove; Georgia: Cleveland, Dahlonega (2); Montana: Helena (S); North Carolina (*): Blowing Rock (O), Boone, Bryson City (SA), Cherokee, Chimney Rock (O), Franklin (7), Hendersonville, Highlands, Leicester, Spruce Pine (4); West Virginia: Shady Spring (SA)

Twentieth: Emerald Arkansas: Mt. Ida (SA); Georgia: Cleveland (SA), Dahlonega (2); North Carolina (*): Blowing Rock (O), Boone, Bryson City (SA), Cherokee, Chimney Rock (O), Franklin, Hendersonville, Hiddenite, Leicester, Marion, Spruce Pine (3); West Virginia: Shady Spring (SA)
  Crabtree emerald North Carolina: Spruce Pine

Twenty-fifth: Silver Michigan: Ontonagon

Thirtieth: Pearl Tennessee: Camden Kentucky Lake (M)

Thirty-fifth: Emerald Arkansas: Mt. Ida (SA); Georgia: Cleveland (SA), Dahlonega (2); North Carolina (*): Blowing Rock (O), Boone, Bryson City (SA), Cherokee, Chimney Rock (O), Franklin, Hendersonville, Hiddenite, Leicester, Marion, Spruce Pine (3); West Virginia: Shady Spring (SA)

   Crabtree emerald North Carolina: Spruce Pine

Fortieth: Ruby Arkansas: Mt. Ida (SA) (2); California: Pine Grove; Georgia: Cleveland, Dahlonega (2); Montana: Helena (S); North Carolina (*): Blowing Rock (O), Boone, Bryson City (SA), Cherokee, Chimney Rock (O), Franklin (7), Hendersonville, Highlands, Leicester, Spruce Pine (4)

Forty-fifth: Sapphire Georgia: Cleveland (SA), Dahlonega (2); Montana: Hamilton, Helena, Philipsburg (2); North Carolina (*): Blowing Rock, Bryson City, Cherokee, Franklin (7), Hendersonville, Hiddenite, Highlands, Leicester, Spruce Pine (2)

   Sapphire, blue North Carolina: Canton

   Sapphire, gray North Carolina: Canton

   Sapphire, white North Carolina: Canton

   Sapphire, bronze North Carolina: Canton

   Sapphire, pink North Carolina: Canton

   Star sapphire North Carolina: Boone (SA)

Fiftieth: Gold (*) Alabama: Lineville; Alaska: Anchorage, Chicken, Chugach, Copper Center, Fairbanks, Girdwood, Nome, Skagway (2); Arizona: Apache Junction, Prescott; California: Angels Camp, Coloma, Columbia, Jamestown, Mariposa, Nevada City, Pine Grove; Colorado: Breckenridge, Idaho Springs (2), Ouray, Silverton; Georgia: Cleveland, Dahlonega (2), Gainesville; Idaho: Rathdrum; Indiana: Knightstown; Montana: Helena (S), Libby; New Hampshire: Conway; New Mexico: Gila; North Carolina: Cherokee, Franklin (2), Leicester, Marion (2), Midland, New London, Union Mills; Oklahoma: Moyers; Oregon: Roseburg; Pennsylvania: Spring Grove (GS); South Dakota: Deadwood, Hill City, Keystone, Lead; Vermont: Ludlow; Wisconsin: Rhinelander

Fifty-fifth: Alexandrite No listing

Sixtieth: Diamond Arkansas: Mt. Ida (SA), Murfreesboro

Finding Your Zodiac Stone

The following is a listing of fee dig sites contained in this four-volume guide where you can find the stone that is associated with a particular zodiac sign. Refer to the individual mine listings for more information.

Aquarius (January 21–February 21) Garnet Alabama: Lineville (S); Arkansas: Mt. Ida (SA); Arizona: Apache Junction; California: Columbia, Pala (2); Georgia: Dahlonega (2); Idaho: St. Maries; Maine: Auburn, Bethel, Poland (GS), Stoneham, Stow, West Paris; Montana: Alder, Helena (S); Nevada: Ely; New Hampshire: Grafton (I); New Mexico: Dixon; New York: North River; North Carolina (*): Blowing Rock (O), Boone, Bryson City (SA), Canton, Cherokee, Chimney Rock (O), Franklin (5), Hendersonville, Hiddenite, Highlands, Leicester, Marion, Marshall, Spruce Pine (4) (FT); South Dakota: Hill City; Tennessee: Ducktown; Texas: Mason; Utah: Delta; Virginia: McKenney; Washington: Ravensdale (GS); West Virginia: Shady Spring (SA)
   Almandine garnet Maine: Bethel, Poland (GS); Nevada: Ely
   Pyrope garnet North Carolina: Franklin
   Rhodolite garnet North Carolina: Franklin
   Star garnet Idaho: St. Maries

Pisces (February 22–March 21) Amethyst Arkansas: Mt. Ida (SA), Murfreesboro (S); Georgia: Cleveland, Dahlonega, Tignall, Warrenton; Maine: Stow, West Paris, Woodstock; Montana: Dillon; New Hampshire: Grafton (I); North Carolina (*): Blowing Rock (O), Boone, Bryson City (SA), Cherokee, Chimney Rock (O), Franklin (4), Hendersonville, Highlands, Leicester, Spruce Pine (3); South Carolina: Antreville

Aries (March 22–April 20) Bloodstone (green chalcedony with red spots)
   No listing

Taurus (April 21–May 21) Sapphire Georgia: Cleveland (SA), Dahlonega (2); Montana: Hamilton, Helena, Philipsburg (2); North Carolina (*): Blowing Rock (O), Bryson City (SA), Cherokee, Franklin (7), Hendersonville, Hiddenite, Highlands, Leicester, Spruce Pine (2)
   Sapphire, blue North Carolina: Canton
   Sapphire, gray North Carolina: Canton
   Sapphire, white North Carolina: Canton
   Sapphire, bronze North Carolina: Canton
   Sapphire, pink North Carolina: Canton
   Star sapphire North Carolina: Boone (SA)

Gemini (May 22–June 21) Agate Arkansas: Murfreesboro (S); California: Blythe; Michigan: Grand Marais; Minnesota: Moose Lake; Montana: Helena (S); Nebraska: Crawford; New Mexico: Deming; North Carolina: Chimney Rock (O); Oregon: Madras; South Dakota: Wall; Texas: Three Rivers

Banded agate Texas: Alpine; New Mexico: Gila
Fire agate Arizona: Safford (2); California: Palo Verde
Ledge agate Oregon: Madras
Moss agate Oregon: Madras; Texas: Alpine
Paint rock agate Alabama: Trenton (GS)
Polka-dot jasp-agate Oregon: Madras
Prairie agate Nebraska: Crawford
Rainbow agate Oregon: Madras

Cancer (June 22–July 22) Emerald Arkansas: Mt. Ida (SA); Georgia: Cleveland (SA), Dahlonega (2); North Carolina (*): Blowing Rock (O), Boone, Bryson City (SA), Cherokee, Chimney Rock (O), Franklin, Hendersonville, Hiddenite, Leicester, Marion, Spruce Pine (3); West Virginia: Shady Spring (SA)
Crabtree emerald North Carolina: Spruce Pine

Leo (July 23–August 22) Onyx No listing

Virgo (August 23–September 22) Carnelian No listing

Libra (September 23–October 23) Peridot (Chrysolite)

Peridot Arkansas: Murfreesboro (S); North Carolina (*): Blowing Rock (O), Boone, Chimney Rock (O)

Scorpio (October 24–November 21) Beryl Georgia: LaGrange; Maine: Auburn, Bethel, Poland (GS), Stow, West Paris; New Hampshire: Grafton (I); New Mexico: Dixon; North Carolina (*): Spruce Pine (2); Virginia: Amelia
Aqua beryl New Hampshire: Grafton (I)
Blue beryl (see also aquamarine) New Hampshire: Grafton (I)
Golden beryl Maine: Woodstock (I); North Carolina: Spruce Pine (FT); New Hampshire: Grafton (I)
Red beryl Utah: Salt Lake City

Sagittarius (November 22–December 21) Topaz Georgia: Cleveland (SA), Dahlonega; Maine: Poland (GS), Stoneham; Montana: Helena (S); New Hampshire: Conway, Grafton (I); North Carolina (*): Blowing Rock (O), Boone, Bryson City (SA), Cherokee, Franklin (4), Highlands, Leicester, Spruce Pine (2); Texas: Mason (2); Utah: Delta, Salt Lake City; Virginia: Amelia, McKenney

Capricorn (December 22–January 21) Ruby Arkansas: Mt. Ida (SA) (2); California: Pine Grove; Georgia: Cleveland, Dahlonega (2); Montana: Helena (S); North Carolina (*): Blowing Rock (O), Boone, Bryson City (SA), Cherokee, Chimney Rock (O), Franklin (7), Hendersonville, Highlands, Leicester, Spruce Pine (4); West Virginia: Shady Spring (SA)

The preceding list of zodiacal stones has been passed on from an early Hindu legend (taken from *Jewelry & Gems—The Buying Guide* by Antoinette Matlins and A. C. Bonanno; GemStone Press, 2009).

The following is an old Spanish list, probably representing Arab traditions, which ascribes the following stones to various signs of the zodiac (taken from *Jewelry & Gems—The Buying Guide* by Antoinette Matlins and A. C. Bonanno; GemStone Press, 2009).

Aquarius (January 21–February 21) Amethyst Arkansas: Mt. Ida (SA), Murfreesboro (S); Georgia: Cleveland, Dahlonega, Tignall, Warrenton; Maine: Stow, West Paris, Woodstock; Montana: Dillon; New Hampshire: Grafton (I); North Carolina (*): Blowing Rock (O), Boone, Bryson City (SA), Cherokee, Chimney Rock (O), Franklin (4), Hendersonville, Highlands, Leicester, Spruce Pine (3); South Carolina: Antreville

Pisces (February 22–March 21) Undistinguishable in original list

Aries (March 22–April 20) Quartz Arkansas: Jessieville (2), Mena, Mt. Ida (6) (Y), Murfreesboro (S), Story; California: Angels Camp, Pala, Pine Grove; Delaware: Wilmington; Georgia: Dahlonega, Lincolnton; Maine: Auburn, Bethel, Poland (GS), Stoneham, West Paris, Woodstock; Michigan: Ontonagon; Montana: Dillon, Helena (S); New Mexico: Bingham, Deming, Dixon; North Carolina: Chimney Rock (O), Franklin (3), Hendersonville, Marion, Spruce Pine; South Dakota: Hill City; Texas: Mason; Virginia: Amelia; Washington: Ravensdale (GS)

> **Blue** Georgia: Lincolnton; North Carolina: Marion
> **Clear** Arkansas: Jessieville; Maine: Woodstock; North Carolina (*): Hiddenite, Spruce Pine
> **Doubly Terminated Scepters** Washington: Ravensdale (GS)
> **Druse** Georgia: Tignall
> **Milky** South Carolina: Antreville
> **Phantoms** Washington: Ravensdale (GS)
> **Pseudocubic crystals** Maine: West Paris
> **Rose** Maine: Bethel, Woodstock; New Hampshire: Grafton (I); North Carolina (*): Blowing Rock (O), Bryson City (SA), Franklin, Leicester, Marion, Spruce Pine (O); West Virginia: Shady Spring (SA)
> **Rutilated** North Carolina (*): Spruce Pine
> **Skeletal quartz** South Carolina: Antreville
> **Smoky** California: Pala; Maine: Auburn, Bethel, Woodstock; New Hampshire: Conway, Grafton; North Carolina (*): Blowing Rock (O), Boone, Bryson City (SA), Cherokee, Franklin (4), Hiddenite, Highlands, Marion, Spruce Pine (3); South Carolina: Antreville; Virginia: McKenney
> **Star rose** Georgia: LaGrange
> **White** Arkansas: Jessieville; New Hampshire: Grafton

Quartz "diamonds"
> **Lake Co. "diamonds" (moon tears)** California: Lower Lake, Lucerne
> **Cape May "diamonds"** New Jersey: Cape May
> **Herkimer "diamonds"** New York: Herkimer, Middleville, St. Johnsville

Taurus (April 21–May 21) Ruby and Diamond

Ruby Arkansas: Mt. Ida (SA) (2); California: Pine Grove; Georgia: Cleveland, Dahlonega (2); Montana: Helena (S); North Carolina (*): Blowing Rock (O), Boone, Bryson City (SA), Cherokee, Chimney Rock (O), Franklin (7), Hendersonville, Highlands, Leicester, Spruce Pine (4); West Virginia: Shady Spring (SA)

Diamond Arkansas: Mt. Ida (SA), Murfreesboro

Gemini (May 22–June 21) Sapphire
Georgia: Cleveland (SA), Dahlonega (2); Montana: Hamilton, Helena, Philipsburg (2); North Carolina (*): Blowing Rock (O), Bryson City (SA), Cherokee, Franklin (7), Hendersonville, Hiddenite, Highlands, Leicester, Spruce Pine (2)

Sapphire, blue North Carolina: Canton
Sapphire, gray North Carolina: Canton
Sapphire, white North Carolina: Canton
Sapphire, bronze North Carolina: Canton
Sapphire, pink North Carolina: Canton
Star sapphire North Carolina: Boone (SA)

Cancer (June 22–July 22) Agate and Beryl

Agate Arkansas: Murfreesboro (S); California: Blythe; Michigan: Grand Marais; Minnesota: Moose Lake; Montana: Helena (S); Nebraska: Crawford; New Mexico: Deming; North Carolina: Chimney Rock (O); Oregon: Madras; South Dakota: Wall; Texas: Three Rivers

Banded agate Texas: Alpine; New Mexico: Gila
Fire agate Arizona: Safford (2); California: Palo Verde
Ledge agate Oregon: Madras
Moss agate Oregon: Madras; Texas: Alpine
Paint rock agate Alabama: Trenton (GS)
Polka-dot jasp-agate Oregon: Madras
Prairie agate Nebraska: Crawford
Rainbow agate Oregon: Madras

Beryl Georgia: LaGrange; Maine: Auburn, Bethel, Poland (GS), Stow, West Paris; New Hampshire: Grafton (I); New Mexico: Dixon; North Carolina (*): Spruce Pine (2); Virginia: Amelia

Aqua beryl New Hampshire: Grafton (I)
Blue beryl (see also aquamarine) New Hampshire: Grafton (I)
Golden beryl Maine: Woodstock (I); North Carolina: Spruce Pine (FT); New Hampshire: Grafton (I)
Red beryl Utah: Salt Lake City

Leo (July 23–August 22) Topaz
Georgia: Cleveland (SA), Dahlonega; Maine: Poland (GS), Stoneham; Montana: Helena (S); New Hampshire: Conway, Grafton (I); North Carolina (*): Blowing Rock (O), Boone, Bryson City (SA), Cherokee, Franklin (4), Highlands, Leicester, Spruce Pine (2); Texas: Mason (2); Utah: Delta, Salt Lake City; Virginia: Amelia, McKenney

Virgo (August 23–September 22) Lodestone (Magnet) No listing

Libra (September 23–October 23) Jasper Arkansas: Murfreesboro (S); California: Pine Grove; Montana: Helena (S); Oregon: Madras; South Dakota: Hill City; Texas: Alpine; West Virginia: Shady Spring (SA)

Brown jasper New Mexico: Deming, Gila

Chocolate jasper New Mexico: Deming

Jasper braccia New Mexico: Gila

Orange jasper New Mexico: Deming

Picture jasper New Mexico: Gila; Oregon: Mitchell

Pink jasper New Mexico: Deming

Red jasper New Mexico: Gila

Variegated jasper New Mexico: Deming

Yellow jasper New Mexico: Deming, Gila

Scorpio (October 24–November 21) Garnet Alabama: Lineville (S); Arkansas: Mt. Ida (SA); Arizona: Apache Junction; California: Columbia, Pala (2); Georgia: Dahlonega (2); Idaho: St. Maries; Maine: Auburn, Bethel, Poland (GS), Stoneham, Stow, West Paris; Montana: Alder, Helena (S); Nevada: Ely; New Hampshire: Grafton (I); New Mexico: Dixon; New York: North River; North Carolina (*): Blowing Rock (O), Boone, Bryson City (SA), Canton, Cherokee, Chimney Rock (O), Franklin (5), Hendersonville, Hiddenite, Highlands, Leicester, Marion, Marshall, Spruce Pine (4) (FT); South Dakota: Hill City; Tennessee: Ducktown; Texas: Mason; Utah: Delta; Virginia: McKenney; Washington: Ravensdale (GS); West Virginia: Shady Spring (SA)

Almandine garnet Maine: Bethel, Poland (GS); Nevada: Ely

Pyrope garnet North Carolina: Franklin

Rhodolite garnet North Carolina: Franklin

Star garnet Idaho: St. Maries

Sagittarius (November 22–December 21) Emerald Arkansas: Mt. Ida (SA); Georgia: Cleveland (SA), Dahlonega (2); North Carolina (*): Blowing Rock (O), Boone, Bryson City (SA), Cherokee, Chimney Rock (O), Franklin, Hendersonville, Hiddenite, Leicester, Marion, Spruce Pine (3); West Virginia: Shady Spring (SA)

Crabtree emerald North Carolina: Spruce Pine

Capricorn (December 22–January 21) Chalcedony Arizona: Safford; Nebraska: Crawford; New Mexico: Deming

Pink New Mexico: Gila

Chalcedony roses California: Blythe; New Mexico: Gila

White New Mexico: Gila

Some Publications on Gems and Minerals

Lapidary Journal Jewelry Artist

P.O. Box 433289
Palm Coast, FL 32142
(800) 676-4336, US and Canada
www.jewelryartistmagazine.com
jewelryartist
   @emailcustomerservice.com

Rocks & Minerals

Taylor & Francis Group, LLC
530 Walnut Street, Suite 850
Philadelphia, PA 19106
(800) 354-1420 press 4;
   (215) 625-8900
www.rocksandminerals.org
customerservice
   @taylorandfrancis.com

Rock & Gem

Beckett Media, LLC
4635 McEwen Road
Dallas, TX 75244
(972) 448-4626
www.rockngem.com
editor@rockngem.com

Gold Prospectors Magazine

Gold Prospectors Association of
   America, Inc.
43445 Business Park Drive
Temecula, CA 92590
(800) 551-9707
www.goldprospectors.org
info@goldprospectors.org

The Mineralogical Record

5347 N. Ridge Spring Place
Tucson, AZ 85749
www.mineralogicalrecord.com

ICMJ's Prospecting and Mining Journal

California Mining Journal, Inc.
P.O. Box 2260
Aptos, CA 95001-2260
(831) 479-1500
www.icmj.com

Other sources of information are local and regional rock, gem, and mineral clubs and federations, and rock, gem, and mineral shows. Many times clubs offer field trips and some shows have collecting trips associated with their annual event. Among these are The American Federation of Mineralogical Societies (www.amfed.org), which lists member clubs (many have yearly shows/swaps), and Bob's Rock Shop (www.rockhounds.com), which has a U.S. club directoy (supplied information).

Send Us Your Feedback

Disclaimer

The authors have made every reasonable effort to obtain accurate information for this guide. However, much of the information in the book is based on material provided by the sites and has not been verified independently. The information given here does not represent recommendations, but merely a listing of information. The authors and publisher accept no liability for any accident or loss incurred when readers are patronizing the establishments listed herein. The authors and publisher accept no liability for errors or omissions. Since sites may shut down or change their hours of operations or fees without advance notice, please call the site before your visit for confirmation before planning your trip.

The authors would appreciate being informed of changes, additions, or deletions that should be made to this guide. To that end, a form is attached, which can be filled out and mailed to the authors for use in future editions of the guide.

Have We Missed Your Mine or Museum?

This is a project with a national scope, based on extensive literature search, phone and mail inquiry, and personal investigation. However, we are dealing with a business in which many owners are retiring or closing and selling their sites. In addition, many of the mines, guide services, and smaller museums have limited publicity, known more by word of mouth than by publication. Thus, it is possible that your operation or one you have visited was not included in this guide. Please let us know if you own or operate a mine, guide service, or museum, or have visited a mine, guide service, or museum that is not in the guide. It will be considered for inclusion in the next edition of the guide. Send updates to:

Treasure Hunter's Guides
GemStone Press
Route 4, Sunset Farm Offices
P.O. Box 237
Woodstock, VT 05091

Do You Have a Rockhounding Story to Share?

If you have a special story about a favorite dig site, send it in for consideration for use in the next edition of the guide.

A Request to Mines and Museums:

For sites already included in this guide, we request that you put us on your annual mailing list so that we may have an updated copy of your information.

Notes on Museums

In this guide we have included listings of museums with noteworthy gem, mineral, or rock collections. We particularly tried to find local museums displaying gems or minerals native to the area where they are located. This list is by no means complete, and if you feel we missed an important listing, let us know by completing the following form. Since these guides focus specifically on gems and minerals, only those exhibits have been recognized in the museum listings, and we generally do not mention any collection or exhibits of fossils. See our sequel on fossils for information on fossil collections.

The authors are considering a sequel that will cover authorized fossil collecting sites and educational digs, as well as museums on fossils and dinosaurs. It will include such topics as where to view and even make plaster casts of actual dinosaur tracks. There are even museums where kids of all ages can dig up a full-sized model of a dinosaur. If you represent such a site, or have visited one you would recommend, please consider sending us the site's information for possible inclusion in such a guide.

READER'S CONTRIBUTION

I would like to supply the following information for possible inclusion in the next edition of *The Treasure Hunter's Guide*:

Type of entry: ☐ fee dig   ☐ guide service   ☐ museum   ☐ mine tour
☐ annual event

This is a: ☐ new entry   ☐ entry currently in the guide

Nature of info: ☐ addition   ☐ change   ☐ deletion

Please describe (brochure and additional info may be attached):

_____

_____

_____

_____

Please supply the following in case we need to contact you regarding your information:

Name: _____

Address: _____

_____

Phone: ( ) _____

E-mail: _____

Date: _____

FIELD NOTES

FIELD NOTES